Analyses
of
Contemporary
Education

Analyses
of
Contemporary
Education

EDITED BY

Allan C. Ornstein
LOYOLA UNIVERSITY OF CHICAGO

W. Eugene Hedley
STATE UNIVERSITY OF NEW YORK
AT STONY BROOK

THOMAS Y. CROWELL COMPANY
NEW YORK · ESTABLISHED 1834

Library of Congress Cataloging in Publication Data

ORNSTEIN, ALLAN C., comp.
    Analyses of contemporary education.

    Includes bibliographical references.
    CONTENTS: Doll, R. C. Foreword.—Conant, J. B.
The education of American teachers.—Holt, J. How
children fail.—Dewey, J. Democracy and education.
[etc.]
        1. Education—Philosophy—Addresses, essays,
lectures.   I. Hedley, W. Eugene, joint comp.
II. Title.
LB7.074   370.1   72–11771
ISBN 0–690–08727–6

1 2 3 4 5 6 7 8 9 10

from
GENE
to
CAROLYN AND JOHN

from
ALLAN
to
FRANCINE AND RICKY

PREFACE

This anthology is intended for use in historical, philosophical, and social foundations courses in education. It can also be used as a supplement in almost any other education course in which the instructor wishes to acquaint his students with some of the books pertinent to education in the twentieth century.

The complexity of the material covered is no mere potpourri. The editors attempt to bring the reader into contact with the quality and content of nine major books in contemporary education—books that have had continuing or significant impact in the field. The excerpts provide the reader with an adequate representation of the authors' viewpoints; in fact, the excerpts are extensive enough to enable the reader to study the data in depth and appreciate the authentic flavor of each book. Together, the nine selections constitute an interdisciplinary approach: the practice of teaching (Holt, Goodman, and Silberman), the teaching profession (Conant), philosophy (Dewey and Whitehead), psychology (Erikson and Rogers), and curriculum (Bruner).

The nine authors and their respective books deserve a place on everyone's reading list. All have made an impact in the field of education. Their philosophies and biases range from conservatism to radicalism, but regardless of their specific labels and "isms" they have initiated new trends and ideas upon which education is based or advancing.

Each selection is introduced by the editors, placing the author's viewpoints in perspective, summarizing the content of the book, and helping the reader understand the importance of the book. The selections themselves provide the reader with the principal content of each book and enable him to see old ideas and issues in new perspectives and new ideas and issues in relation to the past. They provide the subject matter of study required by preservice and inservice teachers in order for them to sense and formulate the philosophies, ideologies, theories, and problems which have become increasing concerns for all segments of the educational community. Finally, the selections, by virtue of their importance to education, act as a catalytic agent for discussing and understanding the field.

Because of the nature and scope of the anthology, the editors invite criticism from almost anyone familiar with the field of education. The bases for including each work reflect the editors' biases and knowledge, but this is a problem with all anthologies; they also reflect accessibility for permission to reproduce the material and practical decisions concerning space limitations. The editors chose to limit the size of the book so as not to overwhelm the reader. Rather than present numerous and shorter selections, we decided on fewer, and therefore lengthier, materials. As previously indicated, we made this decision so as to provide the reader with the major points expressed in each book. In some cases, such as with the Bruner and Holt selections, the material seems abbreviated in comparison with the other selections. To some extent, this impression is misleading, for the two books themselves are brief in their entirety; in fact, the Bruner excerpt actually represents 30 percent of the entire book and the Holt excerpt represents more than 20 percent of the entire book.

In the final analysis, the editors hope that the reader will appreciate direct contact with nine major books on education in one volume. It should benefit the student who has limited library facilities at his disposal, wishes to be acquainted with selected important books in contemporary education, and needs a basis for determining which of these books he wants to read in full. Similarly, it should aid the instructor who wants to assign several important books in the field but is handicapped by book prices, varied student interests, and the constraints of time.

A debt of gratitude is owed to the authors and publishers who so graciously permitted their work to be reproduced in this anthology. Thanks are also extended to Jim Bergin, of the College Department of the Thomas Y. Crowell Company, for encouraging this venture, and to Russell C. Doll, Associate Professor of Education at the University of Missouri—Kansas City, for writing the Foreword.

A.C.O.

W.E.H.

FOREWORD

The editors of *Analyses of Contemporary Education* make no small claim. In fact, the claim is rather audacious. They present selections bearing on educational foundations which, in their opinion, are some of the most important in contemporary education. Yet, sensitivity to the vagaries of historical judgment would urge caution in the making of such a claim. Look how literary opinion is now dealing with Ernest Hemingway, Thomas Wolfe, and H. L. Mencken. The stuff of "importance" should indeed be stern stuff else time's grindstone wear it away to nothing.

One would be misled, however, to judge the contribution of this book of readings on the basis of the prophetic powers of the editors. A question could be raised, for example, as to why they chose John Dewey's *Democracy and Education* as the most important of his works rather than *Schools of Tomorrow*. The latter work transformed a loose conglomeration of seemingly unrelated ideas into the social movement we call progressive education. In fact, it is thought by many that *Democracy and Education* cannot be understood fully without a reading of the other book. Similar kinds of questions could be raised in regard to the other selections. Why choose Erik Erikson's *Childhood and Society* over Jean Piaget's *The Origin of Intelligence*? Might not Piaget's work on cognition have a greater impact on education than Erikson's synthesis of child development and psychoanalytic and anthropological theory? Whether or not the editors are able to choose, with accuracy, works to stand the tests of time should not be the issue.

The significance of this book lies in the kinds of questions it raises. Significance lies apart from the particular selections per se. Questions of "says who?" and "why?" might be the most valuable outcomes of such a volume as this one rather than any attempt to argue or claim historical or contributory significance to education. The question, then, should not be centered on whether *Democracy and Education* is more important than *Schools of Tomorrow* but on how the selections are related to contemporary education, how they agree or disagree with other works, and how these works reflect our past and point to our future.

Looking at the book in this way, one finds an excellent rationale for the selections. They each raise questions of a historical, philosophical, and practical nature. They provide insight into major schools of thought which have influenced policy and planning. They offer an interplay of ideas diverse enough to open discussions on almost any facet of education, philosophy, sociology, and psychology and on questions of how and why we are about these things. The selections offer opportunities to explore the forces that have helped shape what we have built and to question the wisdom of the premises and ideas upon which we built. The selections are diverse enough to carry us into questioning our plans for the future of education in a rapidly changing "future shock" society. The selections can be grist for any mill that grinds the thoughts of men. If this kind of dialogue can be started among readers, then the editors of this book have done their job, irrespective of the selections having classical importance.

The editors have not only selected excerpts from important books which can stand alone in starting a flow of ideas and dialogue; they also have provided a structure to help the reader better understand the significance and relationship of the selections to different facets of education and society. Each selection is accompanied by a valuable introduction designed to put the work in perspective. These introductions are of great help to those not familiar with the field of educational foundations, and they assist in the interpretation of the selected works. The editors' comments also put the selections into historical and sociological perspective, thus enabling the reader to understand the readings within a network of ideas and within the social and ideational context which helped spark them.

The book can be used in many different ways and in many different fields. It may serve as an introductory text or supplementary text in foundations courses. Certainly those interested in educational psychology, sociology, philosophy, or history would find it very valuable. The ideas in the book would be invaluable for those interested in curriculum development and its philosophical-psychological foundations. *Analyses of Contemporary Education* should be of value to anyone interested in ideas and willing to engage in dialogue and speculation as to how diverse ideas fit into the wider framework of that which we call "society" and the process we call "education." It is a book the reader should return to many times after the first reading.

Russell C. Doll
UNIVERSITY OF MISSOURI—KANSAS CITY

Contents

Analyses
of
Contemporary
Education

The education of American teachers

JAMES BRYANT CONANT

The Education of American Teachers, by James B. Conant, is the result of a two-year investigation of the problems, and weaknesses of teachers in this country. The study was financed by the Carnegie Corporation and enabled the Conant team to visit seventy-seven institutions of higher learning of various sizes and prestige in twenty-two states.

Although there are many other accounts of the problems and weaknesses of teacher education, this is perhaps the most honest, comprehensive, and thoroughly researched analysis, done with great insight and concern—without emotionalism or polemics but with detached objectivity and supported by hard-hitting facts. While there are many critics of education, the author is perhaps the most influential and prestigious educator of the second half of the twentieth century. His straightforwardness, independence from vested interest groups, and sensible judgments have earned him the respect of both political and educational audiences. He is not considered an outsider, a sensationalist, or an ax-grinder, but a friendly critic, knowledgeable scholar, and enlightened statesman of education. Therefore, his unusually harsh criticism of the education of American teachers cannot easily be dismissed by the educational establishment, the very same people he condemns in his study.

In his book, Conant relinquishes his usual tact; he is appalled by and disgusted with the chaos and rigidity of the *training* and

SOURCE: James Bryant Conant, *The Education of American Teachers* (New York: McGraw-Hill, 1963), pp. 56–72, 74, 76–84, 92–95, 97, 99, 101–103, 105–107, 109–112, 124–129, 131–138, 141–144. Copyright © 1963. Reprinted by permission of Educational Testing Service.

certifying process of teachers and the mediocrity and senselessness of the people involved in this twin process. He is critical of the state department of education personnel, staff members of the National Education Association, college trustees, college administrators, professors, school-board members, school administrators, and teachers. Together, these groups make up the educational establishment and constitute a powerful group.

The author's knowledge of the political, economic, and legal nuances involved in education, along with his familiarity and experiences with schools and colleges, enable him to deal with the complexity of the problems of educating teachers and to come to grips with the real issues—not just to engage in generalities and surface attacks. Conant points out that the teacher-training programs and state certifying requirements do not guarantee that teachers know how to teach or even know their subject matter. Many of the licensed teachers are incompetent; moreover, many of the professors who train these teachers are also incompetent and unqualified as scholars, and their teaching experience is remote from the classroom. With the exception of student teaching, he is ruthless in his description of education courses—labeling them as boring, irrelevant, and "Mickey Mouse" (Conant's term). Even worse, teachers often take an unnecessary number of these courses, beyond the state requirements, as electives and at the expense of their liberal education and field of specialization.

The professors of liberal arts and the quality of their courses do not escape Conant's eye and pen. In all disciplines in all institutions, he finds a tiresome dependence on textbooks, priggish reading lists, and boring lectures by uninspired professors. He questions the academic standards of many colleges and universities. (Today these standards seem to be further lowered as we move toward mass education.) At the prestige colleges and universities staffed with distinguished scholars, he finds many professors unconcerned about teaching and more devoted to their research and writing, where the rewards are more obvious, and relying heavily on graduate students as teaching assistants in freshman classes. Thus there is no guarantee that a student attending a prestige institution of higher learning receives a better education than a student attending a smaller or lesser-known college or university.

Conant points out that teachers certified in one state are unable to teach in another state. He explicitly shows that teachers once certified in one subject are teaching almost any other subject on an emergency basis. This is especially prevalent at the junior high school level in mathematics and science. For example, it was (and still is to some extent) not uncommon for an art or physical education teacher to be teaching mathematics or science—or to be going through the motions of teaching. This is how most school systems "solved" their teacher shortage. He is concerned that teachers are paid salary differentials for taking graduate courses that are unrelated to each other and to the classroom situation. He severely attacks the various groups of the educational establishment, with their rigidity and conservativeness, each protecting its own vested interests and tending to simplify the problem of teacher education while ignoring or rationalizing its own responsibilities for aggravating the problem. Most of these criticisms appear in the selection given here.

Conant sets forth twenty-seven recommendations. The multiplicity of the recommendations reflects the complexity of the field and the author's comprehensive design, not for reforming, but for completely reshaping teacher training and certification. The recommendations appear in two places in the text: in context with the discussion (most of these appear in the excerpt) and in the summary chapter (which is not included in the excerpt). For our purposes, the basic recommendations can be grouped under (1) preservice training, (2) certification, and (3) inservice training.*

Preservice training. According to Conant, the accrediting functions of many agencies would be dissolved and transferred to advisory bodies to teacher training institutions. The colleges should be free to develop their own teacher-training programs and would assume maximum responsibility for their programs. There should be a truce between educators and academicians, and they should all share in the responsibility of training teachers. Candidates for teaching should be selected from the top thirty percent of the high school

* This grouping does not coincide with Conant's. His twenty-seven recommendations are divided into five different categories: state boards of education; state legislators; school-board members; college trustees, administrators, and professors; and voluntary accrediting agencies.

graduating class. The general education of teachers should be strengthened: education courses should be minimized; elective courses should be abolished; and a field of specialization should be required for all teachers who work beyond the third-grade level. Professors who taught courses in philosophy, history, psychology, or sociology of education should be professors of these respective fields and not education professors. Student teaching should be the main source for guaranteeing competence. The professor supervising the student teacher would be called a "clinical professor" and teach the related methods courses; he would have the full salary and title of a professor. Small colleges and weak colleges that lacked adequate facilities and staff should go out of business or combine their facilities and staff to improve their programs.

Certification. Conant would abolish state department of education certification requirements that were expressed in terms of courses and credits. He would outlaw standard tests for certification purposes. The colleges would assume major responsibility for certifying teachers. Once a teacher was certified he would be permitted to teach anywhere in the country—thus introducing a national certification policy. Colleges would maintain their prestige by turning out competent teachers and by convincing schools that their teachers were well trained and qualified. Local schools would be free to hire anyone certified by a college. Teachers would only be hired to teach subjects for which they were specially prepared.

Inservice training. Beginning teachers would be placed in a four-year internship, where they would be supervised on the job by competent teachers in the school. Beginning teachers, and the teachers who trained them, would have a reduced teaching load. The beginning teachers' progress would be evaluated without false sentimentality or patronage. Thus, before the teachers obtained tenure, there would be opportunity to eliminate those who are incompetent. There would be a large salary increase when a teacher moved from intern status to tenure. Increments in teachers' salaries would not be linked to course credits but only to earning a master's degree based on full-time residence during the school year or four consecutive summer sessions. School boards would provide leaves of absence with full salary for a full-time semester and financial assistance for those attending summer school. To ensure continuous growth, teachers would be required to take short inservice seminars during the school year; no credit toward salary increases would be given for these seminars.

Most of the recommendations are conservative and practical and did not irritate the educational establishment. However, a few of them were considered radical and questionable. At this point we will briefly raise a few questions regarding some of the recommendations that were vexing. What we say provides, in part, the reason why Conant's recommendations were never fully accepted.

Conant's recommendations give maximum responsibility to teacher-training institutions to improve the training and certifying of teachers. It is questionable whether many of them, especially the weaker institutions, could be trusted to perform these twin tasks and upgrade teacher education. While Conant maintains that the competitive market would drive out the weaker programs, this is easily said on paper but difficult to accomplish in reality. Indeed, there are many intellectually limited students and incompetent preservice teachers seeking admission to colleges and education departments, thus encouraging the existence and perpetuation of weak programs. Whereas Conant criticizes the fifty different state patterns of certification, his method would lead to more than 1,000 different patterns. Although it may not be wrong to have student teaching serve as the focus of preservice training, we still do not know how to objectively evaluate the classroom performance of preservice teachers and predict their success. Furthermore, some professors who supervise student teachers are incompetent themselves, and it is doubtful that the colleges would just fire them or transfer them into other positions. Similarly, most professors are not interested in working with student teachers, because this is not where the rewards lie. Supervision of student teachers is often performed by junior members of the faculty at prestige colleges and universities, and once they gain in rank they usually abandon this chore.

Conant assumes that the state requirements and accrediting policies are unnecessary restraints on teacher-training institutions and local school boards. The trouble is, one might question the practicality and the quality of many teacher-training programs and the knowledge and political ideologies of many school-board members.

Some kind of outside professional standards are needed at least to maintain minimum standards and hold weak and politically minded groups in line. The stipulations advocated by state education departments and accrediting agencies are usually minimum, and strong teacher-training institutions and school systems go beyond these requirements.

While Conant's book is an excellent analysis of the problems and weaknesses of American teacher education, it has led to little change. The recommendations were subject to countless educational editorials, discussions, papers, and even programs, but the revolution that was supposed to result never materialized. Although the educational establishment could not ignore Conant because of his prestige, or dismiss him as an outsider or unfriendly critic, it was still able to maintain the general status quo. People in power did not rush headlong into implementing his recommendations, as they did with his previous book on the American high schools. At best, those with vested interests at the state level, the colleges, and the accrediting agencies felt some discomfort with the book and were surprised at the tone of the writing.

It is possible that had the Conant report been published in the late 1960's or early 1970's, when public dissonance was at a peak, and demands for teacher accountability were being voiced, the recommendations would have had greater impact. Although the Conant report was originally compared to the 1910 Flexner report (which led to the closing of more than one third of the medical schools within a few months after the report was released and to the reform of American medical schools in general), the Conant report did not have a comparable impact on teacher education in America —or the powerful impact intended by Conant. His criticisms and ideas, however, remain valid and viable. They must still be dealt with by anyone concerned with promoting change and improvement in the education of American teachers.

THE REDIRECTION OF PUBLIC AUTHORITY

The employment of teachers in our public schools is a legal responsibility of a local school board, which should act on the advice of a professional school administrator in whom the board has confidence.

The responsibility to make wise appointments is inescapable and may not safely be neglected. The assumption that prescribed programs of teacher education, or certification procedures, can insure public protection from individual incompetence is largely illusory. The final door to the classroom is guarded, it is hoped responsibly, by the local board.

• • • • •

Given a school system that is attractive to teachers and a board that is answerable to many interest groups, the ultimate responsibility for the appointment of teachers should be clearly laid on the shoulders of the local school board. The existing pattern of excessive dependence on state regulations as well as the not infrequent use of end runs that permit boards to evade this responsibility, whether by reason of indifference or of favoritism, should cease. At the same time the state should not, through certification, make requirements so specific that the local school authorities are denied the opportunity to try teachers with varied patterns of preparation.

What, then, should be the role of the state education authorities? The state as a whole has a legitimate interest in insuring reasonable equality of educational opportunity and in protecting its educational system from local corruption and inadequacy. It is, after all, constitutionally charged with the maintenance and supervision of the public schools. In discharging this responsibility, states have utilized teacher examinations, specific course requirements, and approval of institutional programs.

Certification by examination, whether on subject matter or on professional knowledge, has been attacked on several grounds. It is alleged that if a state were to set up such examinations, the wrong kind of information would be tested; that the ability to write test answers would not insure the ability to function effectively in the classroom; that the testing instruments would lend themselves to preparation by cramming or to corrupt administration; and that the tests would have an unwholesome effect of imposing a strait jacket on the teaching function. It is claimed that tests may discriminate against certain persons who do not perform well when taking a test, or that the tests themselves are culturally biased. Finally, since in many fields there is no way to measure the degree of mastery except in terms of relative scores within a standardized population, the issue of what score should be used as a "passing" grade raises difficult problems. For example, if one designates the average score as "passing," then half the people fail despite the possibility that all may in fact know much or little about the matter being tested.

Because of these objections, I do not favor the use by the states of standardized tests as the basis of certification. I agree with the contention that it is too difficult on a statewide basis to determine the proper cut-off score. And furthermore, I believe that the ultimate test should be *how the teacher actually performs in a classroom,* as judged by experienced teachers. I am convinced that a single test cannot be relied upon for a state judgment that has the force of law.

. . . I am also opposed to certification based on specific required courses. In my judgment, no state has been able to insure a high quality of teacher preparation by simply listing course titles and credit-hour requirements. But there is in this system an even more fundamental fault, which remains to be examined. For better or worse, the college professor actually determines what goes on in his own classroom. He may bow to state authorities concerning the title and syllabus of his course. But ultimately, he will teach what he knows and considers to be important. In brief, both the content and the quality of instruction are in fact determined on the individual campus no matter what the state may do. State regulations consistent with the beliefs of the college are unnecessary. Those inconsistent with the college's beliefs receive at best only lip service; at worst, they hamstring the able professors and faculties who, with greater understanding of their own strengths and the characteristics of their own student body, can design a superior program if given greater freedom.

The approved-program approach goes awry, as we have seen, because too often those who do the approving end by dictating the total teacher-preparation program and the total institutional structure. In these cases it often becomes even more inflexible than the process of certification by courses and credits. For example, even in what I consider to be one of the more enlightened states, I was told by one faculty member that the approval of his program depended on his bowing to a state Department official on the issue of whether to give two or three credits for a particular course in physical education. In another state, an institution's authority to prepare teachers of one language was being challenged because it did not offer enough courses in a second and unrelated language. Yet another institution had asked NCATE [National Council for Accreditation of Teacher Education] rather than a state

Department for approval, and I was told that NCATE demanded as a condition of full accreditation that the institution abandon its present policies of offering two different programs of general education and of subject matter specialization in the sciences and social sciences.

Thus, no one of the three devices—the use of objective examinations, the requirement of specific courses, the approved-program approach—seems to offer a satisfactory basis for state certification. What, then, should the states require of candidates for teaching jobs? It seems to me that we need to find one or two critical points by which to test the quality of teacher preparation, and then focus attention on these points *so far as certification is concerned.* In other words, we need a *restricted* approved-program basis for certification.

Interestingly enough, amid all the conflict over teacher education, I have found only two points on which all are agreed: first, before being entrusted with complete control of a public school classroom, a teacher should have had opportunities under close guidance and supervision actually to teach—whether such opportunities are labeled "practice teaching," "student teaching," "apprenticeship," "internship," or something else; and second, the ultimate question the state should ask is "Can this person teach adequately?" There is also near consensus, with which I am in agreement, that public school teachers cannot be adequately educated in less than the time required to obtain a baccalaureate degree. On the basis of these agreements, I come to my first recommendation concerning state certification [Of the twenty-seven recommendations proposed by Conant, sixteen are discussed in this selection.]:

1. *For certification purposes the state should require only (a) that a candidate hold a baccalaureate degree from a legitimate [1] college or university, (b) that he submit evidence of having successfully performed as a student teacher under the direction of college and public school personnel in whom the state Department has confidence, and in a practice-teaching situation of which the state Department approves, and (c) that he hold a specially endorsed teaching certificate from a college or university which, in issuing the official document, attests that the institution as a whole con-*

[1] I do not propose in this book to discuss the ways different states police the institutions the state charters; some crack down on diploma mills, some do not!

siders the person adequately prepared to teach in a designated field and grade level.

This is, I recognize, a radical suggestion. While it does more sharply hold the colleges and universities responsible for attesting that the person is prepared *to teach* as well as being a "well-educated person," it removes all state requirements for specific courses except practice teaching and closely related special methods courses, and asks the state to rely on the good judgment and integrity of these institutions in determining what instruction is required prior to, or in addition to, practice teaching.

The adoption of such a policy by a state would, I believe, invigorate the institutions. To be sure, a competition between teacher-training colleges and universities would result; but as a consequence faculties would develop more pride in the quality of their graduates; there would be gradual recognition by superintendents and school boards that alumni of certain institutions tended to be better prepared than those of rival institutions. Such a change in the climate of opinion would affect the attitude of the professors. We tend to forget that faculties are made up of individuals whose personal reputations are affected by the quality of the instruction just as their own efforts determine that quality. When the state or an accrediting agency unduly restricts the program of teacher preparation (or any other program), the degree of freedom of each faculty member is thereby diminished, and individual professors do not or cannot put their creative energies into the building of a curriculum; teacher-education programs become increasingly sterile. Recommendation 1 would free the colleges without opening the doors to the appointment of incompetent teachers by the local boards.

Let me now face an objection that I am sure will spring up in many readers' minds. Those who have observed the slipshod conditions under which practice teaching is often done will be appalled at the suggestion that the state content itself with this device for certification. And unless the state authorities, the colleges, and the local school districts give very serious attention to these conditions, I, too, would find the prospects truly appalling. However, my subsequent comments will, I trust, make clear that I do not propose to perpetuate the present sometimes-chaotic system. Though the details of a practice-teaching program will have to be worked out by each state Department and each college and public school system with which it works, I would like to suggest some things that I believe must be assured if practice teaching is to serve adequately, either as a step in teacher preparation or as a basis for certification.

There must be enough time allotted to enable the student teacher to have the following experience: to participate in the overall planning of the semester's work; to observe critically for a week or so, with the guidance of someone who can tell him what to look for; to begin with simple instructional tasks involving individuals and small groups of children (note that I say "instructional tasks"—not filling out forms or pulling on rubbers); and, ultimately, to assume full responsibility for an extended period of instruction which he plans, executes, and evaluates. . . .

The regular teacher in whose classroom the future teacher works should be one known to his own school officials, the collegiate faculty, and the state Department as a highly competent teacher both of classroom pupils and of student teachers. Such persons, often called "cooperating teachers," should have time freed to aid the student teachers; they should also have increased compensation in recognition of added responsibility and special talent.

The college personnel directly involved should be of the type I shall call "clinical professors" (not to be confused with the cooperating teachers). The clinical professors must be master teachers who themselves periodically teach at the level of those being supervised, and who are given by the college full recognition in salary and rank of their essential function. They must not be treated as second-class citizens of the university. *The clinical professor will be the person responsible for teaching the "methods" course. Such courses, designed to guide student teachers to the best instructional material in the field as well as to assist them in the planning and conduct of instruction, should be part of the practice teaching experience.* The clinical professor must be a master of teaching methods and materials; he must also be up to date on advances in the educational sciences and know how to apply this knowledge to the concrete work in which his student teacher is involved.

The cooperating teacher, the clinical professor, and any others brought in to evaluate the practice teaching must be qualified to judge the candidate's mastery of the subject he teaches, his utilization of educational knowledge, his mastery of techniques of teaching, and his possession of the intellectual and personality traits relevant to effective teaching. It goes without saying that they must have opportunity to observe often enough and over a long-enough period so that the candidate has a chance for guided improvement, and, ultimately, a fair test. Ideally, I would hope that other professors in such fields as mathematics, science, social science, humanities, and education would observe student teachers and use their observations as a basis for revising the college curriculum as well as for judging the candidate's competence.

When I recommend, then, that practice teaching become the basis of certification, I assume that state certifying authorities will not approve practice-teaching programs that are inadequate either for certification purposes or for teacher-education purposes.

Recommendations 2 to 5 below attempt to spell out more fully—from the perspective of the colleges, the public school districts, and the state —the implications of this basic shift in certification policies.

> 2. *Each college or university should be permitted to develop in detail whatever program of teacher education it considers most desirable, subject only to two conditions: first, the president of the institution in behalf of the entire faculty involved—academic as well as professional—certifies that the candidate is adequately prepared to teach on a specific level or in specific fields, and second, the institution establishes in conjunction with a public school system a state-approved practice-teaching arrangement.*

This proposal calls for a contract between each college and one or more public school systems in the practice-teaching arrangements. Such a contract already exists in most cases. However, I believe that local school districts have not yet assumed the responsibility they ought to assume either for the initial training of teachers or for the introduction of teachers into service during a probationary period. To effect a full partnership among the state Departments, the universities or colleges, and the public schools, two further recommendations would have to be accepted.

> 3. *Public school systems that enter contracts with a college or university for practice teaching should designate, as classroom teachers working with practice teaching, only those persons in whose competence as teachers, leaders, and evaluators they have the highest confidence, and should give such persons encouragement by reducing their work loads and raising their salaries.*

To implement this recommendation, it would be necessary for the school board to formalize its relation with the institutions that send student teachers into its school. If no contract now exists, one should be prepared and signed. More important, the school board should adopt a policy that would show recognition of the continuing value of its responsibility. The board should direct the superintendent to have his principals see that the best teachers become cooperating teachers. The board should also require the superintendent to report from time to time on the way the arrangements for practice teaching are functioning.

The acceptance of Recommendation 3 and its full implementation would mean an increase in the budget. What I have in mind is a considerable raise in salary for the cooperating teacher. The board would be committed by its policy to recruiting some of its best teachers to participate in the education of future teachers. Since there is no assurance that those being thus educated will be employed by the board, it hardly seems fair to charge the extra expense to the local budget. In such an arrangement, the local board functions as an agency of the state, and plays an important part in discharging a state responsibility: the education of future teachers. If the citizens of the state want those enrolled in the teacher-preparation programs within the state (in private or public institutions) to be well educated, the role of the local board cannot be overlooked. If the job is to be well done, the state must provide the money out of state funds on a per-student basis, the money to be used for increasing the salary of the cooperating teachers. (One state at least has already made a modest step in this direction.) These considerations may be summed up in the following recommendation:

4. *The state should provide financial assistance to local boards to insure high-quality practice teaching as part of the preparation of teachers enrolled in either private or public institutions.*

So far I have left the colleges and universities free to define and control the paths to practice teaching. I assume—and in an increasing number of institutions the assumption is already fact—that professors of education and academic professors will share in designing programs leading to the teacher's diploma.

At the practice-teaching stage, I have urged that public school people become involved. And both public schools and colleges would be represented through the clinical professors. But since the state has an inescapable responsibility ultimately to certify, it, too, must act directly. I recommend that:

> 5. *The state should approve programs of practice teaching. It should, working cooperatively with the college and public school authorities, regulate the conditions under which practice teaching is done and the nature of the methods instruction that accompanies it. The state should require that the colleges and public school systems involved submit evidence concerning the competence of those appointed as cooperating teachers and clinical professors.*

In referring to "evidence" in Recommendation 5, I do not have in mind the offering of special courses and credits accumulated, a practice to be found in certain states, of which I heartily disapprove.

In making these recommendations, I have hoped to encourage flexibility in teacher-education programs, and to minimize conflict by restricting the focus of state control. I have left under state scrutiny that part of the program by which the entire program can be evaluated. If a potential teacher is seriously lacking in knowledge of his field, in information concerning the conduct of schooling, or in teaching skill, such inadequacies should show up when he actually teaches under the scrutiny of two experienced teachers, namely the clinical professor and the cooperating teacher. These teachers, both acting with the sanction of the state, must be prepared to reject those who are inadequate. This obligation is of special importance with respect to the candidate's mastery of the subject he teaches.

Though I trust that the colleges will already have screened out most of those candidates whose personality traits provide obvious handicaps to teaching, those missed should also show up at this time. I repeat, however, that those who evaluate practice teaching must include persons capable of judging *every* critical aspect of the candidate's preparation. I believe that if the state provides for a careful examination of the student teacher in the actual act of teaching, it will have the most effective device by which to insure itself of competent teachers.

Since the purpose of these proposals is to provide greater flexibility, their intent would be defeated if, through the influence of such groups as TEPS [National Council on Teacher Education and Professional Standards], all institutions preparing teachers for a given state prescribed the same path to practice teaching. The state should not remove the tariff barrier and then permit it to be reestablished as a private cartel. Should such a cartel develop, the state may have to set up special practice-teaching centers to insure reasonable flexibility.

By these proposals responsibility is sharply focused at three gates: first, the individual colleges, whose programs may vary widely, control entrance to practice teaching; second, the state, using state Department, collegiate (or university), and public school personnel, certifies on the basis of effectiveness in actual teaching during the practice-teaching operation; and third, the local board, choosing from persons who, without exception, are certified by the state but who may have been prepared under widely varying programs, is responsible for the final choice.

These, I believe, should be the limits of *legal restraints* within which experimentation, research, and persuasion should be free to operate. No *single* program of teacher education should be granted a legal monopoly, nor should it be necessary for those wishing to experiment or reform to secure legislative action or seek escape clauses in state regulations.

On the other hand, all programs of teacher education and all local school board employment policies should be subjected to more informed public scrutiny than has often in the past been possible. The state educational authorities have unique opportunity and responsibility for this scrutiny. I recommend, then, that:

6. *State Departments of Education should develop and make available to local school boards and colleges and universities data relevant to the preparation and employment of teachers. Such data may include information about the types of teacher-education programs of colleges or universities throughout the state and information concerning supply and demand of teachers at various grade levels and in various fields.*

• • • • •

Information placed by the state into the hands of local school boards can be useful, but it is not enough. No matter how well prepared a teacher is in one subject or for one grade level, he is likely to be incompetent when misassigned. Our survey of state laws and such evidence as that provided by the National Science Foundation study make it clear that local school boards are not only legally free to assign teachers in areas for which they are unprepared but actually do so in far too many cases. On this matter both tighter regulations and more rigorous enforcement are needed. I therefore recommend that:

7. *The state education authorities should give top priority to the development of regulations insuring that a teacher will be assigned only to those teaching duties for which he is specifically prepared, and should enforce these regulations rigorously.*

If my Recommendations 1 and 2 have been adopted, the state will have in its hands documents in which the college or university president attests that the teacher has, in the college's judgment, been prepared to teach specific subjects or at a specific grade level. It should then be possible for the state Department to check actual teaching assignments to make certain that they correspond to the attested preparation.

• • • • •

It must by now be clear that my recommendations so far are designed first, to insure that no teacher enters a classroom without having been tested and found competent in the actual act of teaching; second, to provide both teacher-educating institutions and local school boards with as free a market as is consistent with assurance that inept teachers are kept out of our schools; and third, to increase the range of information and opinion available to those who educate or hire teachers. The "free market" provides state Department personnel, teachers' organizations, and other interested groups with a greater, rather than a lesser, stake in educational leadership, but it calls them to bring this leadership to bear in the local communities and in the colleges and universities rather than in the state capitals. Those who are bested in the struggle in one community or campus can hope to prevail in another.

We have noted that an increasing number of states has given a quasi-legal status to NCATE, and that since 1957 the NEA [National Education Association] and its affiliates, working largely through TEPS, have conducted a widespread campaign on both the state and national levels to persuade states automatically to certify graduates of an NCATE-approved institution outside their own states. At present about half the states have given *some* weight to NCATE-accreditation in their approved-program approach to certification; in at least one state persons graduating from out-of-state NCATE-approved institutions receive automatic certification. Thus has NCATE become a quasi-legal body with tremendous national power.

We have also seen that the regional accrediting bodies, such as the North Central Association of Colleges and Secondary Schools, by selective accreditation of schools, use their power to insist that teachers be educated as these organizations believe they should be. They, too, tend to require a specific number of courses in specific fields.

Both NCATE and secondary school branches of regional accreditation agencies are controlled by people whose wide professional experience well qualifies them to *advise* colleges on how to prepare teachers and to *advise* local school boards on what kinds of teacher to hire. However, both are widely, and I believe somewhat justly, accused of representing only a narrow sector of those actively engaged in American public and higher education; in neither are the well-informed conscientious lay citizens—who, I believe, have an important role in determining educational policy—adequately represented. I, therefore, recommend that:

8. *The governing boards of NCATE and the regional associations should be significantly broadened to give greater power to (a) representatives of scholarly disciplines in addition to professional education, and to (b) informed representatives of the lay public.*

The governing council of NCATE, for example, should include distinguished citizens, scholars, and laymen.

But even given such enlarged representation, no strictly private group should have delegated to it, either directly or indirectly, the power to determine which institutions may or may not legally prepare candidates for state certification through the process I have described above. For this reason, I recommend that:

9. *NCATE and the regional associations should serve only as advisory bodies to teacher-preparing institutions and local school boards. They should, on the request of institutions, send in teams to study and make recommendations concerning the whole or any portion of a teacher-education program. They should, on the request of local boards, evaluate employment policies. They should provide a forum in which issues concerning teacher education and employment are debated.*

NCATE has been most widely used as a basis of reciprocity to facilitate the migration of teachers from state to state; this function has been one of the major reasons for its development. I strongly doubt that such an institution as NCATE is really needed to achieve this purpose.

Should my recommendations be followed, the certification requirements will be limited, but will also be more sharply defined. It should not be too difficult for state certification authorities to achieve comparable standards by negotiation. I do, however, recommend that:

10. *Whenever a teacher has been certified by one state under the provisions of Recommendations 1 and 2, his certificate should be accepted as valid in any other state.*

The above recommendations refer to the initial certification process. This process should insure a safe level of preparation for the initial assumption of full responsibility for a public school classroom. I believe this level of preparation can be achieved in a four-year program. However, no such program—in my judgment, no kind of preservice program—can prepare first-year teachers to operate effectively in the "sink-or-swim" situation in which they too often find themselves. Many local school boards have, I believe, been scandalously remiss in failing to give adequate assistance to new teachers. I recommend, therefore, that:

11. *During the initial probationary period, local school boards should take specific steps to provide the new teacher with every possible help in the form of: (a) limited teaching responsibility; (b) aid in gathering instructional materials; (c) advice of experienced teachers whose own load is reduced so that they can work with the new teacher in his own classroom; (d) shifting to more experienced teachers those pupils who create problems beyond the ability of the novice to handle effectively; and (e) specialized instruction concerning the characteristics of the community, the neighborhood, and the students he is likely to encounter.*

• • • • •

One way and possibly the most promising way of implementing Recommendation 11 would be to have the new teacher become part of a teaching team. The idea of team teaching has been widely discussed in recent years, but the phrase lacks clear-cut definition. As applied to the induction of a new teacher, I would define a teaching team as an arrangement by which one or more older and experienced teachers shared a teaching responsibility with the new teacher. There might be two junior members of the team. The most junior would be the brand-new teacher; the other would be a teacher in his second or third year of a probationary period. One can only suggest such arrangements, for the details would obviously differ from grade to grade and from subject to subject. The objectives to be achieved are summed up in the recommendation.

I have made one recommendation (11) that is essentially in the hands of local school boards, and two additional ones (3, 4) will affect them. Two of my recommendations (8, 9) affect NCATE and other accrediting bodies. I have no doubt that the TEPS groups and other professional organizations will be concerned with all the recommendations.

It is surely not my prerogative to tell the reader how to bring these changes to pass if he is persuaded that my recommendations should be followed. It should be clear that both the structure and the process of decision making vary too widely from state to state to admit of a uniform strategy of reform. However, I have expressed my conviction that each structure, though possessing unique qualities, is flexible enough so that responsible men willing to study and work within their own state's system can make their influence felt.

• • • • •

THE ACADEMIC PREPARATION OF TEACHERS
• • • • •

INSTRUCTION PROVIDED IN DIFFERENT TYPES OF INSTITUTIONS

For our purposes, it is neither desirable nor possible to assess the quality and performance of individual college and university instructors. They are as varied as the autumn leaves, and such wide differences in personnel are found within institutions, and even in very small departments, that one simply cannot make generalizations about them. It is, however, very much to the point to direct our attention to the institutions in which our teachers are educated. In so doing, we encounter at once several false assumptions held among the critics of the present situation.

The first, that teachers colleges supply most of our classroom teachers, is simply not the case. Only 20 per cent of our teachers come from colleges that can clearly be designated "teachers" colleges.[2] Indeed, the greatest number of teachers come from universities that fit neither the "teachers college" nor the "liberal arts" college stereotype. Three-quarters of the four-year colleges and universities in the nation, including nearly every type of institution, are in the business of preparing teachers. The universities involved can be divided into those that offer teacher training only on the graduate level, of which there are very few, and those that maintain both graduate and undergraduate teacher-training courses. Of the four-year colleges, there are four subcategories: private "liberal arts" colleges that have no vocational programs other than teacher training; private colleges that now offer several vocational programs, including teacher training; state colleges offering a variety of vocational programs; and state colleges in which 80 per cent or more of the students plan to teach.

• • • • •

Apart from comparable salary figures, names in *Who's Who,* and similar limited grounds for comparison, there is too little to go on. To be sure, the faculty of a great university would in general be superior to that of a small, struggling college; and it might be argued that an historian or a chemist would be more willing to take a position in a college with a liberal arts tradition than in a state college primarily concerned with training teachers. Statistically speaking, these considerations may be valid in broad comparisons. If one compared the academic professors in 100 institutions of one type or another, the professors in the universities and private prestige colleges might be better scholars more thoroughly acquainted with their fields than those in the teachers colleges. But by the same token, the better teachers colleges might in turn have more distinguished scholars than the poorer universities and private colleges. Moreover, excellence in scholarship is not necessarily identical with excellence in teaching. And it is also obviously true that many a strong faculty has some weak members, and many modestly staffed colleges can boast some gifted and dedicated professors. Thus,

---

[2] As a case in point, the reader may recall the shocking revelations contained in the 1961 NSF [National Science Foundation] survey on mathematics and science teachers. . . . Of the 3,000 teachers covered in that survey, 29 per cent received their bachelor's degrees from "teachers colleges" (presumably this includes state colleges primarily or exclusively concerned with teacher training), 39 per cent from "liberal arts" colleges, 20 per cent from university schools of education, 12 per cent from "other" institutions. (The distribution varied somewhat from region to region.)

anyone who asserted that a student would be "better taught" in a particular *type* of institution would be very bold indeed!

Another variable that complicates comparisons between types of institutions is the wide divergence in academic standards among institutions of every type. This factor is evident whenever scores on standardized examinations are made public. As an example, I quote from the reports of the Graduate Record Examinations—and specifically, from data on the natural science part—taken in a variety of colleges and universities by seniors who are candidates for graduate schools. In the institution with the highest mean score, something like 98 per cent made a score better than that made by only 25 per cent in the lowest-ranking institution. If this score had been taken as a passing score, only 2 per cent of the seniors in one institution would have failed, whereas 75 per cent would have failed in the other college—and, needless to say, in the second institution no such mortality rate was recorded.

Another example is afforded by the results on the National Teacher Examinations. Information I have seen pertaining to this examination shows that in one state, only 1 per cent of the seniors in the state university made a score of less than 500. In a private institution in the same state, 40 per cent made a score of less than 500, and in two other institutions 75 per cent made less than 500. Yet certainly all or almost all the seniors in all the institutions were graduated. If 500 had been the passing score, in the state university 1 per cent would have failed, in the private college 40 per cent would have failed, and in the two other institutions 75 per cent.

Nothing revealed by a close study of institutions designated as "teachers colleges," as compared to those designated as "liberal arts" colleges, justifies a sweeping assertion that one *type* of institution consistently gives the student a better education than the other. The belief that "liberal arts" colleges provide more "breadth and depth" than teachers colleges rests essentially on the notion that courses in education in teachers colleges displace general requirements, subject specialization, or both. My investigations have convinced me that this is simply not the case. The time devoted to education courses in teachers colleges, and in teacher-preparation programs in multipurpose institutions, is not taken away from academic requirements; rather, the courses that are displaced are electives, and such elective courses also give way in a "liberal arts" college that prepares students for certification. Thus one would be quite mistaken to believe that a student necessarily gets a better academic education in one or another type of institution.

There are certain basic procedures and policies in all types of institutions that could be improved; and it is in this area that colleges and universities should be attempting to raise their standards. For example, I should like to register my dissatisfaction with the way I have seen subjects studied in both colleges that train few teachers and those exclusively concerned with teacher training. The use of a textbook may be a necessary evil; but I hope that the dreary discussions I have heard in classes of thirty are the exception and not the rule. One would expect that a stimulating lecture could from time to time set the tone; the use of closed-circuit TV makes it possible to direct such lectures to an unlimited audience. Individual reading assignments resulting in short essays and conferences in *small* groups should, but rarely do, characterize the collegiate methods of instruction as contrasted with the high school methods, and would correspond to the increased maturity of the student.

I found other unfortunate practices in many colleges: the use of graduate students as teaching assistants placed in charge of "sections" of freshman courses; heavy dependence on anthologies and textbooks; pretentious reading lists, which only a few students take seriously; and lectures poorly delivered by uninspired teachers.

I am also far from pleased with the reliance of most colleges and universities on conventional patterns of courses. Just as the notion that education can only be measured out in units of semester hours has become a sacred cow, so has the concept of the "course." Higher education in America is course-ridden. I do not propose to drive these sacred cows from the pasture. The semester-hour system seems to be a necessary medium of exchange, and the "course" is a natural and logical way to organize a large part of collegiate education. My protest is against the supine acceptance of it as the *only* way and the exclusion of other ways. One need not cite the example of Abraham Lincoln by the fireside, or the practice of "reading law," to argue that independent study has always been, and should be, a legitimate road to the mastery of a subject. It is striking that with the exception of honors programs, of provisions for independent work in some institutions, and of scattered instances of the use of examinations in place of course work, American colleges and universities of all types seem to be almost totally committed to the shibboleth of the "course" involving a certain amount of time in a certain room. One might expect widespread use of examinations both to determine whether a student is prepared for a beginning college course and as a basis for bypassing required courses when he has by independent study already achieved mastery of the subject.

• • • • •

THE QUALITY OF THE STUDENT BODY

And this consideration brings us to the second element in the educational process, the students instructed. This is essentially the question of standards: who are admitted, allowed to continue, and given degrees.

I have heard a great deal of talk during the course of my study about upgrading the teaching profession. I have heard little discussion of the minimum level of scholastic aptitude to be required of candidates for teaching positions. I suggest that it is time this subject was examined and vigorously discussed state by state. The state boards of education, the state school boards' associations, and the highly influential state teachers' associations might well devote some time and energy to such an inquiry. At the outset this question would be faced: Is there a minimum level of intellectual ability we should set in this state for future teachers? I believe the answer should be yes.

I know it is often argued that there is no close correlation between teaching ability and intellectual ability (as measured by grades in courses or scholastic aptitude tests), and I am not unsympathetic to this argument. I realize that there are certainly many outstanding college students who for one reason or another would make poor schoolteachers and should be weeded out during the college course, and that there are also other college students, relatively slow in their academic work, who would yet make good teachers. This I grant, but I still maintain that *we should endeavor to recruit our teachers from the upper third of the graduating high school class on a national basis.* Why? Because the courses in the academic subjects that I believe important as part of a general education must not be pitched at too low a level or too slow a pace. The program I suggest in the following pages, which includes such subjects as college mathematics, science, and philosophy, would be too difficult for students whose intellectual ability placed them much below the top 30 per cent, in terms of the high school graduating class on a national basis.[3] In this chapter and hereafter, when I suggest the kind of educational programs that should be provided in a four-year course for teachers, I shall assume that all the students fall in the upper 30 per cent category. For those with much less aptitude for academic work, what I am recommending is too stiff a program both in high school and in college.

. . . We cannot at present hope to obtain all our teachers from the upper 30 per cent, although we may be able to do so in the future. For the time being, it is plain that there will be some colleges and universities that could not follow my suggestions . . . if they would; the students would not be up to it. Those who are interested in my specific suggestions about curricula must first examine the cutoff point in terms of academic ability for those enrolled in the teacher-training programs.

With this in mind, I suggest that if a state wishes to raise the intellectual level of those being trained within the state as teachers, it should establish for future teachers a loan policy *limited to students who can meet a certain level of scholastic aptitude.* A number of states have taken the matter in hand; some of the provisions of the NDEA [National Defense Education Act] are directed at helping future teachers to finance their education. But there has not been the emphasis on helping the more able that I should like. To establish any national standards of scholastic aptitude would be extremely difficult and totally unrealistic; therefore, my recommendation is for state-by-state action.

12. *Each state should develop a loan policy for future teachers aimed at recruiting into the profession the most able students; the requirements for admission to the teacher-training institutions within the state should be left to the institution, but the state should set a standard for the recipients in terms of scholastic aptitude; the amount of the loan should be sufficient to cover expenses, and the loan should be canceled after four or five years of teaching in the public schools of the state.*

[3] Techniques for measuring academic aptitude abound, and all of them are subject to some criticism. A 30 per cent pool selected by one set of criteria will leave out people who belong according to a second set. Different researchers use different criteria, and the experts in the field are constantly seeking to improve their tools for prediction. I do not propose to judge which are the best tools. Those who must in practice make the selections have to decide for themselves what criteria to use. My 30 per cent figure suggests a general category, and the overwhelming number of students who fall in that category by one criterion will also fall in it by most others. Obviously in using tools that are only statistically valid, one must use common sense in their application to particular cases.

Many will question such a recommendation; some will do so on the grounds that it is impossible to set up suitable standards; others will say that if this is done, there will not be teachers enough to meet the needs. Obviously, much depends on the pupil-teacher ratio, and much depends on the extent to which new developments can spread the effectiveness of the best teachers. These include team teaching, programmed instruction, television, and various ways of providing teachers with clerical and other assistance. It is beyond the scope of this book to examine the degree to which these new and highly important developments would enable a school system to change the teacher-student ratio. What I suggest is simply this: *If a state is faced with a shortage of teachers, it would be far better to push the new developments with the hope of decreasing the demand than to continue to·recruit teachers with very low intellectual ability, as some states do at the present moment.*

Over and above the talent of the would-be teachers, there is a second factor that teacher-training institutions should consider, and that is high school preparation. Today many young people with the requisite academic talent are graduating from high school without having studied as wide an academic program as I would recommend. Therefore, in my view, the improvement of the education of future teachers in many regions of the country must start with first, more rigorous selection of those who enter the collegiate programs, and second, the improvement of the high school programs.

Judging from what I have found, I believe that far too many students intending to become teachers enter college without sufficient academic preparation.

For future teachers, I believe that the content of general education in school and college should include certain essential ingredients. Let me start with a summary of what may be accomplished in school. For those planning to be teachers I would suggest the following high school program: [4]

[4] Readers of my earlier book, *The American High School Today,* will recall my recommendation that all students in the upper 15 to 20 per cent of an age group should be urged to take a similar program including four years of mathematics. A careful reader will also note that I did not suggest that such programs be *restricted* to the upper 15 per cent. I am quite convinced that what I recommend is possible for a substantial number of students in the upper 30 per cent of the high school graduating class (already a more select group than 30 per cent of the total age group), particularly if the fourth year of mathematics is dropped.

English (including frequent practice in writing)	4 years
Foreign language (one language studied consecutively)	4 years
Mathematics (four years preferred)	3 years
Natural science	3 years
History and social studies	3 years
Art and music	2 years

Remember, I am assuming that we are considering students whose scholastic aptitude places them in the category of the top 30 per cent of the high school graduating class on a national basis. Such students can, I believe, study with profit and without an excessive demand on time and energy the program I have suggested in high school. I would refer any who question this assumption to the academic inventories I have published in *Slums and Suburbs,* particularly that of the Newton High School in Newton, Massachusetts. The evidence there presented shows that over half the boys and girls in the I.Q. range 105–114 were taking and passing 18 academic courses in four years, including four years of mathematics. (The range I.Q. 111 and higher corresponds roughly to the upper 30 per cent of the high school graduating class on a national basis.)

I should be disposed to go even a step further, and urge that, for the most talented students, opportunities for advanced placement be extended. If these were widely enough offered, a great many students could do a good deal of general college work in high school.

• • • • •

WHAT CONSTITUTES GENERAL EDUCATION?

Assuming sufficient aptitude and an adequate secondary school preparation, what should be the general requirements for the bachelor's degree in a program of teacher education, and on what assumptions would such requirements rest? If I were advising a teacher-education institution, I should argue that the assumptions are neither new nor far to seek. They are: first, that there are certain areas of knowledge with which all future teachers should be acquainted; second, that in these areas of knowledge there are characteristic ways of grasping the subject; third, that in both the knowledge and the ways of understanding them there are basic principles; finally, that properly studied and taught, these subjects and the principles discoverable in them can further the *process* of a liberal education.

There is, moreover, an important practical reason for certain studies: almost any teacher inevitably faces the necessity of dealing with subjects outside his area of specialization, not only in his classroom but also in conversations with students. If he is largely ignorant or uninformed, he can do much harm. Moreover, if the teachers in a school system are to be a group of learned persons cooperating together, they should have as much intellectual experience in common as possible, and any teacher who has not studied in a variety of fields in college will always feel far out of his depth when talking with a colleague who is the high school teacher in a field other than his own.

And too, if teachers are to be considered as learned persons in their communities (as they are in certain European countries), and if they are to command the respect of the professional men and women they meet, they must be prepared to discuss difficult topics. This requires a certain level of sophistication. For example, to participate in any but the most superficial conversations about the impact of science on our culture, one must have at some time wrestled with the problems of the theory of knowledge. The same is true when it comes to the discussion of current issues.

What I am about to suggest in the way of a general education program would occupy half the student's time for four years, even assuming a good high school preparation. If one accepts my argument in the preceding paragraphs, this amount of time is not too much. Whether more time could be used profitably is a question that leads into the controversial issue of breadth versus depth, and I must postpone for a few pages weighing the particular pros and cons in this area. Here I am arguing for two years in college aimed at developing such a degree of competence in the usual academic areas that the teacher has some confidence in talking with a colleague who is a specialist in one of these areas. Such confidence is important for the elementary teacher as well as for the secondary. Even though the elementary teacher is directly concerned with arithmetic or relatively simple science or social science, he ought to know what kind of road eventually lies ahead.

General education for future teachers, then, should be a broad *academic* education. The limitation implied by the word academic is, I believe, a necessary restriction. Without it one can argue for all sorts of broadening educational experiences whose values I might or might not question. But with the time limits imposed upon formal education, I am ready to defend the restrictions implied in the word "academic."

What subjects should be included as academic? Of the fields usually studied in secondary schools, college programs should continue literature, history, government, mathematics, the natural sciences, geography, art, and music. How much further should these be pursued in college as part of a general education of teachers? One might say that ideally each subject should be studied until the student has attained enough competence to teach the subject to a 12th grade average class. But to demand any such degree of concentration in each field would be to extend the general education alone to far more than four years.

Foreign languages and mathematics, at least as they have been taught, have been the traditional stumbling blocks to many able students. I believe in the importance of having educated Americans at least bilingual by the time they graduate from high school. But I would not now push the claim that all future teachers should have something approaching a mastery of a foreign language. Such a goal is for the future.

Given time enough, good teaching, and a sufficient degree of interest, many more people could probably study mathematics in college than now do. Moreover, an understanding of much of modern science is heavily dependent on mathematics. Therefore, mathematics must be included in a college program. Further study in college is certainly a necessity in English, in literature, and in history, and probably in the natural sciences. The high school courses in art and music are so varied and the time devoted to them so uncertain that I hesitate to say what the exposure should be in college. It is enough to say that teachers should have a common background of knowledge and appreciation of our cultural heritage. Thus some time in college should be spent on increasing the understanding of literature, art, and music that was acquired in school.

In each of these fields, collegiate faculties should define the levels of knowledge and understanding or skill that should be required as the product of the total *general* education of the future teacher. *I should hope each institution that has serious concern with educating teachers would, through appropriate committees, define such levels, bearing in mind that the entire general education course should not require more than half the student's time during four years* (though the program need not be completed in the first two years . . .).

∙ ∙ ∙ ∙ ∙

There are five areas of knowledge that I believe can only be studied on the college level, namely, philosophy, sociology and anthropology, economics, political science, and psychology. I have in mind the introductory college course. In the time available only an introduction can be accomplished, but such an introduction I feel to be of the utmost importance. Properly taught, such introductory courses would lay the basis for further self-education based on reading. I shall not attempt to outline the nature of the introduction, for the essential matter is the person or persons who give the course and the way the study is conducted.

I consider it essential that a person of the maturity of a college student explore these areas of knowledge under the guidance of a person who has been trained as a scholar in these fields. All future teachers are not now required to study philosophy under a philosopher or psychology under a psychologist or sociology under a sociologist; in many cases students are first introduced to these subjects by members of a faculty of education who are by no means philosophers or psychologists or sociologists but who are experts in the application of principles from these fields to the educational process. . . . There is an important function to be performed by such people. But philosophy taught by a philosopher of education is definitely *not* what I have in mind in referring to philosophy as part of the general education of a teacher. This point I believe to be of some importance.

While I recognize that differences in faculties, in students, and in habits of thought and outlook in the 1,150 institutions that prepare teachers result in differences in actual practice, nevertheless I am bold enough to translate what I have just said into the following pattern of general education for future teachers. It is *not* a prescription but an illustration of my contention that, given a good high school preparation, an able student can receive a general education of some breadth in two years.

Subjects already studied in high school	NO. OF COURSES	EQUIVALENT SEM. HOURS
The English language and composition	2	6
The Western world's literary tradition	2	6
History (at least one-half other than American)	3	9
Art appreciation and music appreciation	2	6
Mathematics	2	6
Science (physical and biological, each studied consecutively)	4	12
Subjects not studied in school		
Introduction to general psychology	1	3
Introduction to sociology and anthropology	1	3
Introduction to the problems of philosophy	1	3
Introduction to economics	1	3
Introduction to political science	1	3
	20	60

This general education program for future teachers should occupy about one-half of the four years, or 60 out of 120 semester hours. Such an amount is considerably larger than the amount I found in most institutions, where something on the order of 30 to 45 semester hours, i.e., a year to a year and a half, is the usual prescription. Since, as we shall see, the amount of time given to major concentration and professional courses is not enough to fill the remaining two years, the question inevitably arises: Where does the rest go? The answer is, to a fetish of American higher education—elective courses.

When I refer to the concept of providing elective courses as a fetish, I am guilty of using a negative word to cover an area of collegiate study that may be deserving of more respect. Therefore, I should make clear that I am not denying the educational value of courses chosen solely on the basis of the student's interest. This would be ignoring the universal experience that we tend to devote our best efforts to the things that interest us. A student's field of concentration represents a relatively free choice, as does the curriculum or program he pursues, the institution he attends, and the career he follows. For the most part these are elected. Why, then, should the college student not *elect* some of his courses?

• • • • •

Any suggestion that the area of unrestricted election be reduced is likely to meet resistance by vocal segments of the faculties. Certain courses are likely to depend heavily on free elections for their enrollments. A professor who for some years has successfully given a popular elective course is not likely to welcome any change that would bring fewer students into his lecture room. He will argue, and it will be hard to disagree, that more rather than fewer students should take his course. He will find many allies in other departments who will close ranks with him to defend the areas of free election, for these are their professional bread and butter. I am not writing cynically, but only stating one of the facts of academic life, well known to anyone who has spent much time in the strange world of higher education. Of course, the argument for free electives is not usually carried on in these terms. The appeal is usually to the spirit of free inquiry, resistance to onrushing materialism, faith in the good sense of the students, and the importance of giving a person a broadened outlook so that he may face the responsibilities of citizenship. It is hard to seem to be opposed to all these fine things, especially when one is not opposed, and more especially when they are not the issue at all.

The real issue, in considering the collegiate education of students who are preparing for a vocation or a profession, is whether as much as one to two years of collegiate work can be permitted to be spread over a wide range of subjects, in no necessarily coherent pattern, entirely at the student's choice—and yet *required* for the bachelor's degree, which each year seems to be thought more of a necessity and each year becomes more expensive. While observing the varied patterns of higher education at a good many colleges and universities in America, I have been forcibly struck by the extreme looseness of the elective system as it has developed on most campuses. Accordingly, I feel bound to point out to my lay readers—especially to the parents who are supporting their children's education, often at considerable sacrifice, and to the taxpayers who support our public institutions—that a substantial part of what they are paying for may bear no relation at all to the student's field of concentration, his future occupation, or even to the pattern of a broad general education. Too often the student's random sampling of courses is dictated not by educational values, but by the courses' convenience or their reputation for ease or liveliness.

While it would be desirable for the future teacher to elect some courses of interest outside his chosen field and the subjects studied for breadth, in most of the programs that I shall describe later there will not be room for electives, *unless* the student has earned advanced placement at entrance, or wishes to add extra courses during a regular term or a summer session. To those who would protest against such a limitation, I reply that the future teacher is becoming an educated person, an example to his students, and of all people should be expected to continue his education on his own after receiving his degree. Earlier I stated my objections to the idea that a subject can be studied only by taking a course—by the student's being physically present in the classroom. Collateral studies pursued for their inherent interest need not come out of the teacher's formal educational program but should be a part of his continuing education, his own independent reading as an adult, as with any professional person. The argument that breadth should be narrowed, or depth made more shallow, in order to make room for one or two years' worth of elective courses does not seem to me to have any force.

CURRENT PROGRAMS IN SPECIALIZATION

Now let us turn to the question of subject specialization for the future teacher. Again, we shall begin by looking at some of the requirements now in effect, including specific programs in both a teachers college and a liberal arts college.

It would be too long a story to describe the full spectrum of requirements for concentration in American colleges and universities. One has only to turn the pages of the catalogs of the arts and sciences in almost any major university to see what wide differences there are just within one unit of an institution—quite apart from other colleges or schools of business administration, journalism, and agriculture, all offering a bachelor's degree. It may surprise some laymen to discover that among the subjects included in the major programs in the college of letters and science in a very distinguished institution are "Decorative Art," "Journalism," "Physical Education," and "Wildlife Conservation." This is not to argue that these offerings are wrongly conceived, or somehow improper. That is for the institution to determine. Such evidence (which could be duplicated in the catalogs of many large universities) is offered simply to show that possession of a bachelor of arts degree may signify a great many things indeed!

• • • • •

WHAT CONSTITUTES EDUCATION IN DEPTH?

For the future secondary school teacher, there is no argument about his devoting a considerable amount of time to the study of the subject to be taught. For such a person, the study in depth of a field might well be classified as special education, as is the study of science beyond the freshman year for the future doctor or the more advanced courses in physics and chemistry for the future chemist. If there were no other reason than a vocational one for a student's concentrating his efforts on one field during the college years, I might close this chapter here. But the history of college education in this country in this century shows that there is a rationale for the idea of studying a field in depth quite apart from the student's future profession or vocation, and though I must confess to a distrust of a good many high-flown statements that I have read in college catalogs, I subscribe in general to the rationale.

There is a way of stating the argument that has always appealed to me, although its validity is limited. It is this: Only through pursuing a subject well beyond the introductory level can the student gain a coherent picture of the subject, get a glimpse of the vast reaches of knowledge, feel the cutting edge of disciplined training, and discover the satisfactions of the scholarly habit of mind (so that if he becomes a teacher, he can communicate something of this spirit to others). Thousands of students each year wander through survey courses with only the shallowest knowledge of the subjects. I believe that if the student once has the experience of getting inside a subject, he is more likely to become so interested in it that he will wish to go on with it on his own (which I regard as one of the hallmarks of an "educated" person); at the same time he will be less likely to be timid in addressing himself to other complicated subjects, or to accept dogma, or to countenance nonsense on any subject.

• • • • •

. . . As I see it, to gain anything like a coherent grasp of a subject like English or biology or mathematics, any student should complete a minimum of 12 courses, that is, 36 semester hours, or the equivalent of more than a full college year's work, including 2 or more courses on the introductory level, carried as part of the general education requirement.

For the elementary teacher, a concentration of 36 hours is about all that can be included in a four-year program, and should suffice. For students intending to be high school teachers, I suggest more than the above minimum—in many cases a total concentration of 16 courses, or 48 semester hours, again including such introductory work as may have been taken as general education. To complete an honors program in most colleges, this amount of time must usually be devoted.

Admittedly, this is a fairly stiff prescription. Not one of the "prestige" colleges mentioned earlier requires as much.[5] Nevertheless, it is quite feasible within a four-year program. As we have seen, the requirements for breadth will occupy 60 hours or somewhat less, depending on the high school preparation; but these will include at least 6 hours of introductory work in the subject in which the student is concentrating. To meet my suggested minimum amount of concentration, 30 hours (plus the introductory 6) would be needed, leaving free 30 in the total of 120; to meet the maximum amount, 42 (plus the introductory 6) would be needed, leaving free 18 hours. All of this must be approximate, since I am attempting here only to indicate what the dimensions of a field of concentration should be.

• • • • •

What I have tried to do in this chapter is to show what ought to be achieved and could be achieved, in contrast to what actually takes place in a good many four-year efforts in American colleges and universities. While I have been writing with future teachers in mind, there is clearly a need for wide reforms generally, as many critics and experts assure us; and if some of the above views were to be accepted as having validity on a wider scale in our scheme of higher education, I should not be upset.

I have three recommendations to make to the boards of trustees of colleges and universities and the state boards responsible for state colleges, for I have long been convinced that higher education is far too important to be left exclusively to professors. At the risk of incurring

[5] Of the 20 prestige institutions, the time for a major ranged from 18 to 42 semester hours. Free electives 24 to 68.

the everlasting hostility of the American Association of University Professors, I suggest that the time is more than ripe for lay boards to ask searching questions of the experts. These questions, needless to say, should be addressed to the faculties through the president and deans. Depending on the answers, the lay board may or may not decide to use its influence. The important point is that the questions should be of a kind to elicit from the faculties valid reasons for the present policy, for everyone who has had experience with college faculties knows how often policy is determined by compromises of different academic disciplines. The chemists will argue, for example, that so much time should be devoted to their subject, the professors of English so much to theirs. Rarely is there a *joint* examination of the content and aims of the two proposals. What emerges is a timetable in which so many semester hours are allotted to each of the contending parties.

When in doubt, a board should refrain from action, and under no conditions should it attempt to dictate the content of specific courses once authorized, or attempt to take a hand directly in the appointments of members of the staff. I recommend that:

13. *If the institution is engaged in educating teachers, the lay board trustees should ask the faculty or faculties whether in fact there is a continuing and effective all-university (or interdepartmental) approach to the education of teachers; and if not, why not.*

Only through such an approach can the requirements of the departments of instruction—which must be concerned with all students, not only future teachers—be coordinated with the particular needs of teacher education, both in general education and in programs of concentration.

14. *The board of trustees should ask the faculty to justify the present requirements for a bachelor's degree for future teachers with particular reference to the breadth of the requirements and to spell out what in fact are the total educational exposures (school and college) demanded now in the fields of (a) mathematics, (b) physical science, (c) biological science, (d) social science, (e) English literature, (f) English composition, (g) history, (h) philosophy.*

15. *If courses are required in a foreign language, evidence of the degree of mastery obtained by fulfilling the minimum requirement for a degree should be presented to the board of trustees.*

THE THEORY AND PRACTICE OF TEACHING

I now come to a question many readers will have had in mind when they opened this volume: How about those courses in education? Do they deal with anything worth dealing with? A closely related query is: Why should the state require all teachers to take these courses? To this second question I have already given my reply. Without passing judgment either on courses in education or on courses in the arts and sciences, I have recommended that there be only *one state requirement* for future teachers. I would eliminate all course requirements by the state—all adding up of semester hours. I would have the competence of a future teacher tested by practice teaching under conditions set by the state and subject to state supervision. Beyond that I would put the responsibility squarely on the university or college for certifying that in the opinion of the institution the young man or woman is ready to enter upon a full-time teaching responsibility. The reputation of the institution would be at stake; no longer could the faculty dodge the issue "What should we require if there were no state certification rules?" They would then be forced to face up to the question of what professional information is desirable.

· · · · ·

Let us look, now, at what seems to be the subject matter of the education courses that are at present required by law in all states in the union. . . .

The minimum amount of time devoted to the professional sequence is determined by state law at present. The actual amount is far from constant throughout the United States, though I might risk the generalization that, with few exceptions, more time is devoted to the professional sequence in single-purpose state colleges than in universities, and more in both than in four-year multipurpose private colleges.

There do seem to be a few constants in professional education programs. All the programs I have examined include a study of educational psychology, at least one course in methods, and one course that treats historically or philosophically the relation of the school to society. In every institution some practice teaching is specified. But here the uniformity ends. Even in the area of practice teaching, great diversity is found in the actual provision for students. The number of clock hours of practice teaching differs from institution to institution. The minimum requirement I encountered was 90, the maximum 300. The translation of such teaching experience into academic bookkeeping is most confusing. One college, which specifies 110 clock hours, allots the same number of semester hours' credit as another, which requires 220. Therefore, when I report a range in the time devoted to practice teaching for secondary teachers from 4 to 11 semester hours, I have hardly recorded anything of quantitative significance even as a first approximation.

In an earlier [6] study of the education course requirements in 294 institutions, the range for elementary teachers was 18 to 69 semester hours, for secondary teachers 10 to 51 semester hours. In the institutions on which I have centered attention the corresponding ranges were 26 to 59 and 17 to 30. With such variation, the value of the median, of course, has no significance, though one often finds it quoted in surveys of teacher education.

As a matter of fact, the situation is even more confusing than the figures I have quoted indicate. There is a shadowy area, particularly in the program of future elementary teachers, where a course might be classified as an education course, or in an academic field of concentration, or in general education. Even in the training of secondary school teachers ambiguities in reporting can easily arise. For example, I visited a state college that announces only 15 semester hours devoted to education courses, but a careful examination of the catalogs reveals that the time devoted to practice teaching is not included. If it and several other courses my colleagues considered as "really education courses" were included, the figure is not 15 but 30 semester hours. Another complication arises from the fact that all or almost all institutions require a special methods course which may or may not involve a considerable amount of study of the subject to be taught.

One more variable is of some significance, and that is the stage at which the professional program begins. Here, I might hazard the generalization that the professional sequence is more likely to start as early as the sophomore year in single-purpose state colleges than in either universities or private colleges. However, there are exceptions to this generalization, and one of the many controversial issues among professors of education is when a future elementary or secondary teacher

[6] *Summary of Requirements in Teacher Education Curricula Offered by Institutions Accredited by NCATE,* 1958, Washington, D.C.

should be "introduced to the profession" and how. Students and teachers with whom I have talked likewise differ in their judgment as to when in the college course a future teacher should begin to have some inkling of what the career of a school teacher is really like.

In the majority of large institutions—large in terms of the number of graduates preparing to teach—the first professional course is taken in the junior year. Equally in dispute is how early in the college work a student should be exposed to some experiences in a classroom or with a child or children. I can think of a number of well-known institutions that place considerable emphasis on the importance of introducing the student to these experiences in the *first professional course,* so the student may come to understand something about the classroom by observation and something about the behavior of a child or children. On the other hand, I could identify many institutions where no such opportunities are provided until the second or third course of the sequence of professional courses. Often, but by no means always, there is a difference in respect to the point I have just raised between the program for future elementary teachers and that for future secondary teachers.

In the majority of the institutions I visited, the future teacher starts his or her sequence of professional courses by taking the same introductory courses irrespective of whether the eventual goal is to teach in an elementary or a secondary school. Sometimes the first course is a course in educational psychology, usually requiring as a prerequisite a course in general psychology; but often it is of the type I shall describe as "eclectic." Frequently the type I describe as "eclectic" carries the label "foundations of education."

Those in charge of these foundations courses often attempt to patch together scraps of history, philosophy, political theory, sociology, and pedagogical ideology. The professors are frequently not well trained in any one of the parent disciplines; certainly very few have such mastery of all the disciplines as to be able to talk about them except at a most superficial level. They are far from being the kind of intermediary or middleman professor I described a few pages back. Occasionally, to be sure, one encounters a mature scholar who has ranged so broadly and so deeply over the fields of philosophy and social science that he can organize data from many fields to give his students a clear and exciting picture of the relationships between formal schooling and other cultural patterns. If an institution has one of these rare scholars, it might wisely encourage him to offer a social foundations course. In general, however, I would advise the elimination of such eclectic courses, for not only are they usually worthless, but they give education departments a bad name. I have rarely talked with students or school teachers who had good words to say for an eclectic foundations course. Perhaps the kindest word used to describe most of these courses was "pathetic."

As an example of such an eclectic course I might cite a course entitled "American Foundations" in a large private metropolitan university. The course is described in the prospectus as follows:

> An introduction to the professional sequence. A field of study in which the student becomes acquainted with the development of the contemporary school; with the teaching profession, its opportunities, requirements, and expectations; with the beliefs and aspirations of our people as they apply to the school and other agencies; and with the fundamental problems in American education. The historical development of ideas, events, and laws are reviewed in relation to the organization, purpose, and program of today's school. Satisfies requirements for (1) American Public Education, and (2) Philosophy of Education. 4 semester hours.

One characteristic of this course and of similar courses with which I have become familiar is the very impressive list of reference books. In this particular course no fewer than 23 titles are listed under the heading "Personalities, Ideas, and Events"; the titles range from Ulich's *History of Educational Thought* to Rugg's *Foundations for American Culture*. In the third section of the course, which is entitled "Purposes of the School in Our Society," the suggested reading runs to 34 titles ranging from Counts' *Education and American Civilization* to Caswell & Foshay's *Education in the Elementary School*. Such lists are impressive indeed, but in the institutions I visited I found on inquiry that only one copy of each suggested book was available, and not by any conceivable stretch of the imagination would a student find time to read even two or three of the books listed for each section. It must be remembered that such a course is, as a rule, a one-semester course carrying three semester hours of credit.

Another sample of an eclectic course is one entitled "Introduction to

Teaching" at a well-known state university. This course is even more of a potpourri, since bits of educational psychology and references to the literature on instructional methods have been stewed in. The 18 main headings of the outline of the course, each of which has two or three subheadings, will indicate the range of material covered:

1. The Challenge of Being a Teacher
2. Planning a Career in Education
3. Competencies and Certification Standards for Educators
4. Preparation for Teaching
5. Opportunities in Teaching
6. School and Community Responsibilities of Teachers
7. Learning to Guide the Growth of Pupils
8. Professional Organizations and Publications
9. Salaries of Teachers
10. Other Economic Benefits
11. Historical Development of Our Schools
12. The Development of Modern Concepts of Education
13. Community Aspects of Education
14. Purposes of Education in American Democracy
15. Problems, Issues, and Inservice Professional Growth
16. Organization and Administration of Schools
17. Financing Our Schools
18. Moving Ahead

I have found little evidence that these courses stimulate a student to read either deeply or widely. Quite the contrary. The classes I have visited are far too reminiscent of the less satisfactory high school classes I have seen. The course is dominated by a textbook or a syllabus, and the instruction seems to be wedded to the dogma that a discussion must take place whether the talk is lively or the class is bored. The pace and the intellectual level seemed geared to students far less able than those in the top 30 per cent group from which we should recruit our teachers.

The eclectic courses may be said to be a conglomeration of bits of the history of American education, the philosophy of education, educational sociology, the economics and politics of the school, together with an introduction to education as a profession as well as a glimpse at the application of psychological phraseology in the observation and teaching of children. From the point of view of education, I see no reason for the existence of these courses. One suspects that they exist to meet (on paper) state requirements! Since virtually every state has differing course titles and descriptions in their requirements, one must respect the versatility of the professors of education in designing courses that they can reasonably argue meet these diversely defined requirements. I have found the type of foundations course I have described being given in institutions approved by NCATE. *I consider the existence of such courses, which is encouraged by the present certification requirements and accreditation practices, one of the arguments for the reforms I have recommended.*

Courses in the philosophy, history, or sociology of education are, unlike "eclectic" courses, intended to apply the disciplines of specific academic areas to education. But these, too, may be of limited value; the crucial question is how they are taught and by whom.

The word philosophy, as used by many professors of education, is like a thin sheet of rubber—it can be distorted and stretched to cover almost any aspect of a teacher's interest. Under the best conditions, it seems to me a course in the philosophy of education would legitimately presuppose that the students had been exposed to the basic issues of epistemology, ontology, and ethics in an introductory philosophy course required of all teachers as part of their general requirements. . . .

• • • • •

. . . If I were participating in faculty appointments in an institution that certifies future teachers, I should do all in my power to see to it that all who gave courses in the philosophy of education were approved by the philosophy department as well as the department or faculty of education. *Graduate schools of education should cease trying to train professors of the philosophy of education without the active and responsible participation of the departments of philosophy.* The latter should move into this field as fast as possible, though they have been unwilling to do so in the past. Well-trained philosophers who turn their attention to problems of American education have an opportunity to make a real contribution to overhauling the philosophic foundations of education, which today consist of crumbling pillars of the past placed on a sand of ignorance and pretension.

The future teacher, as I have said, would do well to study philosophy under a real philosopher. An additional course in the philosophy of education would be desirable but not essential. The same is true of a course in the history of education. Again, the professor should be an intermediary or middleman; he should be approved by a department of education and a department of history or an outside committee containing eminent historians. The explanation of the history of the schools of the United States under the guidance of a first-rate American historian would be a valuable experience for any teacher. It would strengthen his understanding of the political basis of our educational system and relate what he should have learned in his American history courses to his own professional work. Some of the material presented might be considered sociological rather than historical. If a competent sociologist is investigating social problems closely related to the schools and is ready to give a course in educational sociology, the desirability of such a course is evident. As to whether the present group of professors who consider themselves educational sociologists should perpetuate themselves, I have the gravest doubts. I would wish that all who claim to be working in sociology would get together in the graduate training and appointment of professors who claim to use sociological methods in discussing school and youth problems.

The discipline of psychology is . . . more closely related to the work of the teacher than are philosophy, history, and sociology. As one would therefore expect, every teacher-training institution with which I am familiar includes in the program a course in educational psychology (under one name or another). In addition, a few institutions require a course in general psychology. Advanced courses in various branches of educational psychology given in summer schools are popular among teachers and are often included in graduate programs.

• • • • •

My own classification of the psychological material I have seen treated in different courses would be as follows: individual differences, child growth and development, tests and measurements (evaluation), adolescent psychology, mental health and abnormal psychology, learning theory, results of animal experimentation (Pavlov's dogs, Thorndike's cats, Kohler's apes, Skinner's pigeons), and neurophysiology. In any introductory course, an account of psychology as a science based on experiment should include, of course, considerable space devoted to the description of animal experimentation and an evaluation of the evidence thus obtained.

If those who write and read books in psychology were not always concerned with finding the "key to the mystery every man faces" and keen to use it, a good introduction to the establishment of a new science might be presented with little or no reference to human beings. As it is, most authors make the extrapolation from animal experimentation to human behavior seem so self-evident as to blur some important philosophic and methodological issues. Having had some experience with attempting to explain to students what is involved in the advances of science, I can be sympathetic with the writers of the general texts in psychology. The focus of attention, they feel, must be not only on science but also on its applications—on what the reader is going to apply tomorrow in his day-to-day dealings with people. Yet it must be demonstrated that the statements made are "scientific," which implies careful evaluation and analysis of the evidence. Furthermore, a vast range of phenomena must be considered.

The role of psychology in the education of teachers is a subject of much controversy. This is the case not only in the United States but also in other countries. In a recent report of a joint working party appointed by the British Psychological Society and the Association of Teachers in Colleges of Education (in Great Britain), the following statement occurs:

• • • • •

There must always be a cautious use of psychological theory, particularly when arguing by analogy. This refers particularly to some of the more speculative suggestions emanating from learning theory based on animal studies or on human learning in situations much simpler than those of the classroom. . . . The language of psychology should be taken over with the full context of its psychological use. Often this language is taken over in a slipshod way and subsequent casual usage can see it applied in situations far removed from the originator's mind. . . . A further difficulty is in securing the effective transfer of psychological knowledge to classroom circumstances; that is, in teaching the subject in such a way as to cultivate a student's psychological insight and judgment in concrete situations.

For my part, on the basis of my observations and reading of textbooks on educational psychology, I would subscribe to what the British group has written. But by no means all American professors of education (as apart from professors of educational psychology) would agree with my emphasis on the importance of a course in educational psychology as such. Those who believe in a science of education, whose attitude I described earlier, would be particularly reluctant to accept my argument. To them the interpretation of the results of research, or perhaps even the carrying out of such research, can be left to those who are trained as "educators," not as educational psychologists.

It would be my contention that the validity of principles of psychology applicable to teaching depends on whether, from these principles, one can deduce such specific predictions as "If I (as a teacher) do so and so, such and such will probably happen" or "If he (the pupil) behaves in this or that way in situation X, he will behave in a certain way in situation Y."

What is at issue here is the applicability of the research work of psychologists in this century to what goes on in the classroom. Do the writings of psychologists help the teacher in understanding children? Are there principles of child growth and development that can be demonstrated by laboratory experience—that is, in a classroom? After listening to many arguments, eliciting the opinions of many teachers, and reading some of the textbooks used in courses in education, I have come to the conclusion that there are perhaps a few principles of psychology—as well as a considerable amount of purely descriptive material—which are relevant. They are particularly relevant to the total task of teachers for the kindergarten and the first six grades. My quotation from the British report indicates what those principles are likely to comprehend.

Despite the present limitations on the scientific aspect of psychology as applied to teachers, *I have been convinced, largely by the testimony of students and teachers, that for those who teach children, psychology has much to say that is so valuable as to warrant the label "necessary," at least for elementary teachers.* I believe that research will continue that will yield generalizations sufficiently wide as to be called scientific. As an introduction to the point of view of those concerned with the behavior of animals (including man), a general course in psychology would seem essential. One would hope for close coordination between those responsible for such a general course and those who were teaching and advancing the applied science of educational psychology.

The principal complaint I have heard from undergraduate students about psychology is that there is a great deal of duplication between what is presented in the general course and what is presented in the courses in educational psychology and sometimes in the "methods courses" (which I shall discuss later). In one institution, at least, a valiant attempt is being made to coordinate the teaching of general psychology and educational psychology. In some colleges or universities, on the other hand, those who give the two types of course are barely acquainted with one another.

Except for aspects of educational psychology that deal with the field of tests and measurements, I am doubtful about the significance of educational psychology for the teachers in a senior high school. I venture to question the width and solidity of the so-called scientific generalizations that some professors of education claim are the product of research.[7] If my conclusion is at all sound, the role of psychology in the education of future elementary teachers should be greater than in the education of teachers for secondary schools.

• • • • •

And now I come to a red-hot question: How about those terrible methods courses, which waste a student's time? If the reader agrees with my recommendations about drastic changes in state control, he will subscribe to the idea that methods courses, like all other courses, must prove their worth in a free competition. Yet since one type of methods course is tied closely to practice teaching, to which I have given a key role, I must do my best to clarify a complicated situation.

For our purposes, it may be helpful to distinguish between general methods courses and special methods courses. While all the institutions with which I am familiar required special methods courses for secondary teachers, by no means all required a general methods course. The more one is inclined to believe in a well-developed corpus of knowledge about how to teach (a science of education, if you will), the more one is ready to accept the idea of a general methods course. Yet in none of the 27 institutions whose programs I analyzed in detail was more than one course (3 semester hours) required.

The general methods course assumes the existence of a body of predictive generalizations valid wherever a teaching-learning situation exists. It follows from this assumption that these generalizations are not dependent on variables inhering in the specific material to be taught, or on the characteristics of a particular body of students. That is to say, the material offered is assumed to be equally relevant to history, French, mathematics, and all other subjects. I fail to see where such generalizations would differ from those developed by psychologists

---

[7] I am here discussing the preservice education of secondary school teachers. An experienced teacher may have sufficient insight to gain much from psychological instruction that would mislead the novice.

concerned with the study of classroom learning, and taught in the general psychology course or in a basic course in educational psychology. I conclude, therefore, that such general methods courses are unnecessary and duplicate material already studied.

My judgment of special courses in the use of particular instructional techniques (e.g., audio-visual methods) is equally negative, though for different reasons. The techniques involved in such courses are likely, given the rapid advance of technology, to become quickly obsolete. And, fortunately, they can also be rather quickly learned by one who so desires. While it is useful for teachers to know the techniques and the instructional material available for use with these techniques, this material is highly specific, subject by subject, grade by grade. It seems to me, therefore, that the methods and materials can best be presented in the context of special methods instruction, which accompanies and is closely related to the actual practice-teaching situation. . . .

· · · · ·

On the basis of . . . what my colleagues and I have seen, heard, and read, I can only reach one conclusion: *Professors of education have not yet discovered or agreed upon a common body of knowledge that they all feel should be held by school teachers before the student takes his first full-time job.* To put it another way, I find no reason to believe that students who have completed the sequence of courses in education in one college or university have considered the same, or even a similar, set of facts or principles as their contemporaries in another institution even in the same state.

Far from reflecting unfavorably upon the professors of education, their inability to reach consensus concerning the material to be universally required might be considered, by a friendly critic, an indication of their respect for evidence. They are well aware that to date there simply is no conclusive research proving beyond reasonable doubt the superiority of one pattern of teacher education (including general education and areas of specialization) over another.[8] Given this lack of evi-

---

[8] In preparing this chapter I have benefited from reading a chapter on "The Role of the Teacher in School Learning" from Prof. John Carroll's forthcoming book provisionally entitled *Educational Psychology and Educational Research.* Professor Carroll's treatment includes a review of published research on criteria of teacher performance and attempts to relate these criteria to patterns of teacher preparation. One problem that plagues the researchers on this matter is that to date it has proved extremely difficult to identify precisely measurable criteria of good teaching.

dence and consensus, one can only conclude that the time has not yet come when the educational sciences can play the same role in training teachers as the medical sciences do in training doctors. To me the conclusion (with which many professors of education agree) points clearly to the need for giving institutions freedom to experiment with different ways of training teachers. Except for practice teaching and the special methods work combined with it, I see no rational basis for a state prescription of the time to be devoted to education courses, whether or not an attempt is made to specify the content. I see even less excuse for prescription by a voluntary accrediting agency whose decisions become in one way or another assimilated by a state authority.

As we have seen, the one indisputably essential element in professional education is practice teaching. The professor of education who is to supervise this practice teaching is analogous to the person who, in some medical schools, is called a "clinical professor." Following the suggestion of Prof. Robert Bush of Stanford University,[9] I am taking the phrase and applying it to the field of education. In so doing, I remind the reader that a clinical professor of surgery is an outstanding surgeon who continues his practice and gives only part of his time to students. His status is equal to that of a professor of surgery or professor of medicine, both of whom nowadays are expected to be primarily research men. The clinical professor, on the other hand, is not expected to publish papers. His status is assured by his accomplishments as a practitioner. He keeps up to date on modern medicine, but in his contribution as a teacher the emphasis is on practice rather than theory.

I recommend that:

16. *The professor from the college or university who is to supervise and assess the practice teaching should have had much practical experience. His status should be analogous to that of a clinical professor in certain medical schools.*

He might carry the title of "Professor of the Theory and Practice of Elementary Teaching" or "Professor of the Teaching of Mathematics"

---

[9] *Professional Imperatives: Expertness and Self-Determination.* Report of the NCTEPS, Fort Collins, 1962. National Commission on Teacher Education and Professional Standards, NEA, Washington, D.C., 1962, p. 45: Prof. Robert N. Bush chapter on "Self-Determination and Self-Realization in the Profession of Teaching."

(or other field). The salary should be equal to that of any professor in the institution. There would be no junior or intermediary grades. The clinical professor must be an excellent school teacher; he would not be expected to do research or publish papers. He must from time to time return to the school classroom as a classroom teacher. He might *serve the college either on a part-time basis or on a full-time basis.*

Quite apart from increasing the effectiveness of practice teaching, the acceptance of this recommendation would go far to raise the prestige of the classroom teacher. There is an infinite amount of talk about making teaching a profession, and constant reference to the medical profession. But few if any universities have recognized that an excellent classroom teacher by his or her performance merits a position as a professor at top salary. In many schools of education, graduate courses occupy the attention of a large number of the staff. With this graduate work is apt to go an increasing interest in research, and with this comes pressure from colleagues to publish articles and books. For younger instructors promotion depends on publication. Thus their connection with the school classroom becomes more and more remote.

This recommendation, if accepted, would change all this. The clinical professors need not hold the Ph.D. degree and would not be expected to make contributions by research and writing. They would be generally recognized as superb teachers of children or youth and as skilled teachers of college students. Such persons might well be given term appointments of, say, three to five years, either taking leave from their school teaching positions or, if possible, serving both the university and the school at the same time. They would be under an obligation to renew continually their experience in the classroom, either by serving both the university and the school at the same time or by returning to the school classroom every few years.

A special word or two about preparing secondary teachers is in order. The title I have suggested might be "Professor of the Teaching of Subject X." I did not include the phrase "Theory and Practice," which I suggested for the clinical professor concerned with elementary teaching, since I believe that there is a difference between preparing elementary and secondary teachers. There is far less theory in the latter. The "Professor of the Teaching of Subject X" should be responsible for placing the student in the proper classroom, where the classroom teacher (cooperating teacher) is an experienced skillful teacher. In addition, in the seminars during the practice-teaching period, the professor will amplify and extend what the cooperating teacher is teaching. In the sciences, a laboratory should be available for setting up demonstrations and allowing the future teacher an opportunity to become familiar with high school equipment. Current textbooks would be reviewed in each field, and if there were a revolutionary wave passing through the subject (as in the sciences and mathematics today), the clinical professor would show to his students the bearing of the new approaches on the classroom work. *Most important of all, he can and should keep the subject-matter departments in the college or university alert in regard to what a future high school teacher needs to know.* To this end, the subject-matter departments would have to go more than half way to meet the clinical professors.

How children fail

JOHN HOLT

John Holt's *How Children Fail* is a highly readable book that is representative of the radical critics of the 1960's and 1970's who question society and see the schools as agents of society. When the radicals view schools, they see miseducation and, even worse, boredom, suppression, manipulation, propaganda, dehumanization, and the benumbing of the student's intellectual development. Indeed, Holt is one of the most popular of the radical critics and the one who at present seems to have the greatest influence on the radical philosophy. Thus, when we read Holt's work, we must read it in context with the educational radicals; in fact, *How Children Fail* forms a triagonal reference, with Paul Goodman's *Compulsory Mis-Education* and A. S. Neill's *Summerhill*, as one of the key books within this philosophy, which is growing into a movement—a movement that would dismantle the present educational system and reconstruct it on the basis of more free and humanistic models. Therefore, when the reader peruses Holt's descriptions of the classroom and school situation, he should be aware of the radical biases that filter through the author's observations. Hence, almost every one of Holt's references to teachers and schools is negative.

How Children Fail is a deeply moving and perceptive account of the classroom situation. The author has the luxury (or time) and ability to intellectualize the finest points in the classroom, many of which escape us and which teachers do not have time to analyze. Without

SOURCE: John Holt, *How Children Fail* (New York: Pitman Publishing Corporation, 1964), pp. 3–26, 32–34, 38–42, 44–49, 59, 61–62, 67–69, 155–159. Copyright © 1964 by Pitman Publishing Corporation. Reprinted by permission of Pitman Publishing Corporation.

question, both the preservice and inservice teacher will find the book interesting and useful. It is full of insights that all teachers can profit by reading, and, indeed, it should help them become aware of the many things they probably will be doing and probably are at present doing in the classroom. The fundamental procedures of teachers in the classroom are questioned, and it is up to the individual teacher to respond to the analysis.

The book uses a case-technique procedure, developed from a log Holt compiled as a teacher and observer of other teachers at Colorado Rocky Mountain School and Lesley-Ellis School (two private upper-middle-class schools) over a period of two and a half years. The analysis is based on the author's experience and informal observation; it is personal and subjective—not based on research or authority that can be substantiated or can stand up to criticism. For this reason, and because of the severity with which the author vilifies teachers and schools, the book has annoyed some readers. Nevertheless, for anyone who works with or cares about children, *How Children Fail* is a book that must be read and reflected upon, for Holt is describing us—our roles as adults, teachers, and educators—and the way we "turn off" and stupefy our children.

The book keenly describes how the child's intelligence, creativity, and interest in learning are discouraged and eventually terminated by the schooling process. Concrete and specific examples are provided: how children learn to be stupid, learn how not to learn, and adopt strategies of fear and failure so as to please their teachers and, moreover, the way teachers reinforce these sad practices.

Holt analyzes why most students develop only a small portion of the potential for creativity and learning with which they were born and of which they have made greater use in the first few years of their lives. He points out that the infant is actively curious about life, experimenting with and exploring his environment, soaking up new experiences, and trying to make sense of them. Even in the midst of failure, the infant is persistent and willing to attempt a new strategy if the original one fails. The infant rebounds; he is not afraid of failure; he does not feel shame or disgrace if he fails to comprehend something or someone; he does not need outside rewards or penalties to learn; he welcomes new experiences and embraces life with gusto.

Instead of building on this foundation, school tears it down. We make children stupid and uninterested in learning. We break down their curiosity and zest to experiment with and embrace life. We make them afraid to take a chance, to explore the unknown, to ask questions, to think out answers. We blur and eventually extinguish their potential for creativity and learning, which was evidenced during infancy. By the time children are midway through elementary school, they no longer ask questions and no longer care about learning; they are more afraid of not pleasing their teacher or not having the right answer. Indeed, we seem to like children who are afraid of us, who are docile and conform easily. The idea of the "good" student is, in effect, the one who gives us the answers we want, is afraid of us, and will do what we tell him to do. He is the one whom we have no reason to fear and who will not threaten our authority or ego in front of the class.

The selection that follows shows how the schooling process encourages *producers* (students who seek to please adults and obtain right answers and who, if they fail to obtain the right answers, plunge into despair) and how it discourages *thinkers* (students who are not so concerned with pleasing adults and who can grapple with ideas, cope with uncertainty, and solve problems under consideration). In a system that is run on right answers, those who are thinkers find school an unpleasant place. Indeed, school is a sad commentary. Many students cannot bear to be wrong; they must be right. They wait for the magic words "right" or "wrong." Those who are right are relieved and forget the problem. Those who are wrong no longer want to think about the problem; they give up. When the teacher asks a question and they know they do not know the right answer, they "gulp" and fear paralyzes their minds.

Holt points out that teachers and students talk but do not communicate with each other. Teachers are attuned to their own interests and students to their own interests, but the interests are quite different. The teacher attempts to teach the lesson, but the students are more concerned with what is the right answer. The teacher asks questions to stimulate thought, but the students have learned how not to think, to get the teacher to answer his own questions. If the teacher gives the students a problem they do not understand or cannot do, they just give up; the problem itself is meaningless. The teacher wishes to test the students to find out how much they have learned, but the students are more concerned with masking what they have not learned. Even worse, the teacher accommodates the students by announcing the test, coaching them on what will be on the test, or teaching the test—thus avoiding the harsh fact that the students have learned very little. The teacher assigns a task to help the students learn the material, but the students' main object is to dispose of the imposed task as soon as possible with the least amount of effort—thus defeating the purpose the teacher had in assigning the task.

The "successful" students become cunning strategists in a game of beating the system—figuring out their teacher and how they can outsmart him, what they can get away with, how they can get the answer out of him, how they can do the least amount of work and obtain the most credit, how they can give the teacher what he expects to hear and supply the right answer. Experience has taught these students that even illegal and dishonest methods pay off. Furthermore, the teachers are generally unaware of these strategies.

Holt also points out that what goes on in the classroom is often not what teachers think. For the most part, the students are bored and pay little attention to the lesson. Some daydream or gaze out the window. Others doodle on their papers or desks, whisper, or write and pass notes. Still others fiddle and squirm in their seats. (And others, the editors may add, read comic books or do their homework assignments when they are supposed to be listening to the teacher or copying their notes from the blackboard.) Writes Holt, "A teacher in class is like a man in the woods at night with a powerful flashlight in his hand. Wherever he turns his light, the creatures on whom it shines are aware of it, and do not behave as they do in the dark." Thus, the act of calling upon or watching the student changes his behavior. The student recognizes when the teacher's attention is on him, and his behavior changes to please the teacher, often to revert back to the original behavioral patterns when the teacher's spotlight is turned off or focuses in another direction.

To Holt, school is a place where students follow meaningless procedures to obtain meaningless answers to meaningless questions. School is a place where students learn not how to think but how to be stupid—to be docile and to conform. It is a kind of jail where the prisoners are the students, the prison guards are the teachers, and the warden is the principal. Students are in school not because they are eager to learn but because they have to be, and they are in the teacher's class either because they have to be or because otherwise they would have to be in another class. School is a place where, according to the students, "*they* make you go and where *they* tell you to do things and where *they* try to make your life unpleasant if you don't do them or don't do them right." School is a place where a student is coerced, manipulated, assimilated, and socialized into our society—one of the nuts and bolts of our working-class assembly line or middle-class bureaucracy. We can talk until we are blue or try to "con" our students about how good school is and how important their education is, but for the present all they are concerned with is how much it hurts, how much more punishment they must endure, and how much longer their imprisonment will last.

The majority of students adapt and become "good" subjects, caught in the web of fear—fear of failure, fear of not being right, fear of not having an answer (any old answer when you're desperate), fear of being laughed at or being called stupid, fear of failing the next test, fear of not pleasing the teacher, fear of being kept back. Many students become overwhelmed by fear and failure and consequently take refuge in total incompetence and failure. When a student is incompetent, others demand and expect little from him; the student also reduces what he expects and hopes of himself. By setting out to fail, the child cannot be disappointed or disgraced. Hence, the pressure of school is alleviated, and with it vanishes the fear that accompanies the pressure. Is this not one reason why some students appear to be stupid and incompetent in school? Is this not one reason why many bright students are under-achievers and why school fails the children we presently label disadvantaged?

Although Holt's insights are based on middle- and upper-middle-class students, they apply to the classroom situation with all students, even at the college and university level—wherever the teaching-learning process goes on and wherever teachers work with students. In the same vein, the literature is suffused with the plight of the disadvantaged child and his learning problems. The child's environment is blamed for the student's failure, but after reading Holt one cannot help but put the finger on the school, too, and on the way teachers and students relate to each other.

Although Holt is more concerned about stating the problems than presenting a strategy for reform or offering viable solutions, he does tell us indirectly what schools should be like: a place where students are not afraid of asking questions, not afraid of being wrong, not afraid of their teachers, and not afraid of taking risks and playing with ideas. School should be a place where the teacher-student interaction is humane and the pressure is minimized, where there is freedom for students to express their needs and problems, where they can explore ideas, where they can "learn what they want to know instead of what we think they ought to know." School should also be a place where each child can satisfy his curiosity, pursue his own interests, develop his own talents in his own way, learn how to think and learn on his own—where there are several options (athletic, artistic, creative, and intellectual) from which a student can choose as much as he wants, or as little. In short, school should be an interesting and exciting place where the student's human potential is fulfilled, and where the student gets into the habit of using his intelligence. Although Holt offers no practical method for implementing his ideas, if only a small portion of them could become reality, school would be transformed into a pleasant place—and many of the negative experiences the reader recalls about his own schooling would be images of the past, no longer relevant to today's schools.

I can't get Nell out of my mind. When she talked with me about fractions today, it was as if her mind rejected understanding. Isn't this unusual? Kids often resist understanding, make no effort to understand; but they don't often grasp an idea and then throw it away. Do they? But this seemed to be what Nell was doing. Several times she would make a real effort to follow my words, and did follow them, through a number of steps. Then, just as it seemed she was on the point of getting the idea, she would shake her head and say, "I don't get it." Can a child have a vested interest in failure? What on earth could it be? Martha, playing the number game, often acts the same way. She does not understand, does not want to understand, does not listen when you are explaining, and then says, "I'm all mixed up."

There may be a connection here with *producer-thinker* strategies. (We used the word *producer* to describe the student who was only interested in getting right answers, and who made more or less uncritical use of rules and formulae to get them; we called *thinker* the student who tried to think about the meaning, the reality, of whatever it was he was working on.) A student who jumps at the right answer and misses often falls back into defeatism and despair because he doesn't know what else to do. The thinker is more willing to plug on.

It is surprising to hear so many of these kids say, "I'm dumb." I thought this kind of thing came later, with the bogey, adolescence. Apparently not.

My room group did fairly well today at the number game. (At certain periods, two-thirds of the class was away at art or shop classes, and the rest stayed with me for "room period," a special class, invented by Bill Hull. We met in a small room just off the classroom. There we played various kinds of intellectual games, did puzzles, and held discussions in a way as little like ordinary classroom work as possible. On this occasion we played a game like Twenty Questions, in which the teacher thinks of a number, and the students try to find it by asking questions to which the teacher may answer "Yes" or "No.") Laura was consistently the poorest asker of questions. It happened that on several occasions her turn came when the choice of numbers had been narrowed down to three or four, and she guessed the number. This made her feel that she was the official number-guesser for the day. In one game she made her first guess at an individual number when there were still twelve numbers left to choose from—obviously a poor move. Once she guessed, others started doing the same, and wasted four turns on it. Later on Mary got the idea that she was a mind reader, and started trying to guess the numbers from the beginning. The rest of her team became infected with this strategy for a while, before they went back to the plan of closing in on the number.

On the whole they were poised and collected and worked well as a team, though they didn't eliminate enough numbers at a turn. Thus, knowing that the number was between 250 and 300, they would say, "Is it between 250 and 260?" instead of taking a larger bite.

Nancy played well; but after a point the tension of the game got to be too much for her, and her mind just stopped working. She didn't get frantic, like Nell or Martha, or make fantastic guesses; she just couldn't think of anything to say, and so said nothing. A safe policy.

Intelligence is a mystery. We hear it said that most people never develop more than a very small part of their latent intellectual capacity. Probably not, but *why* not? Most of us have our engines running at about ten percent of their power. Why no more? And how do some people manage to keep revved up to twenty percent or thirty percent of their full power—or even more?

What turns the power off, or keeps it from ever being turned on?

During these past four years at the Colorado Rocky Mountain School my nose has been rubbed in the problem. When I started, I thought that some people were just born smarter than others and that not much could be done about it. This seems to be the official line of most of the psychologists. It isn't hard to believe, if all your contacts with students are in the classroom or the psychological testing room. But if you live at a small school, seeing students in class, in the dorms, in their private lives, at their recreations, sports, and manual work, you can't escape the conclusion that some people are much smarter part of the time than they are at other times. Why? Why should a boy or girl, who under some circumstances is witty, observant, imaginative, analytical, in a word, *intelligent,* come into the classroom and, as if by magic, turn into a complete dolt?

The worst student we had, the worst I have ever encountered, was in his life outside the classroom, as mature, intelligent, and interesting a student as anyone at the school. What went wrong? Experts muttered to his parents about brain damage—a handy way to end a mystery that you can't explain otherwise. Somewhere along the line, his intelligence became disconnected from his schooling. Where? Why?

This past year I had some terrible students. I failed more kids, mostly in French and Algebra, than did all the rest of the teachers in the school together. I did my best to get them through, goodness knows. Before every test we had a big cram session of practice work, politely known as "review." When they failed the exam, we had post-mortems, then more review, then a make-up test (always easier than the first), which they almost always failed again.

I thought I knew how to deal with the problem: make the work interesting and the classroom a lively and enthusiastic place. It was, too, some of the time at least; many of these failing students actually liked my classes. Overcome children's fear of saying what they don't understand, and keep explaining until they do understand. Keep a steady and resolute pressure on them. These things I did. Result? The good students stayed good, and some may have got better; but the bad students stayed bad, and some of them seemed to get worse. If they were failing in November they were still failing in June. There must be a better answer. Maybe we can prevent kids from becoming chronic failers in the first place.

OBSERVING IN BILL HULL'S CLASS

In today's work period three or four people came up to you for help. All were stuck on that second math problem. None of them had made any effort to listen when you were explaining it at the board. I had been watching George, who had busied himself during the explanation by trying, with a pencil, to ream and countersink a hole in the side of his desk, all the while you were talking. He indignantly denied this. I showed him the hole, which silenced him. Gerald was in dreamland; so for the most part was Nancy, though she made a good recovery when asked a question. Unusual for her. Don listened about half the time, Laura about the same. Martha amused herself by turning her hand into an animal and having it crawl around her desk.

Watching older kids study, or try to study, I saw after a while that they were not sufficiently self-aware to know when their minds had wandered off the subject. When, by speaking his name, I called a day-dreamer back to earth, he was always startled, not because he had thought I wouldn't notice that he had stopped studying, but because *he* hadn't noticed.

Except by inflicting real pain on myself, I am never able to stay awake when a certain kind of sleepiness comes over me. The mind plays funny tricks at such times. I remember my own school experience of falling asleep in class while listening to the teacher's voice. I used to find that the "watchman" part of my mind that was saying, "Keep awake, you fool!" would wake me when the teacher's voice began to fade. But the part of my mind that wanted or needed sleep was not so easily beaten. It used to (and still does) counterfeit a voice, so that as I fell asleep an imaginary voice continued to sound in my head, long enough to fool me until the watchman no longer had the power to awaken me. The watchman learned, in turn, that this counterfeit voice was liable to be talking about something different, or pure nonsense, and thus learned to recognize it as counterfeit. Many times, I have dozed off with a voice sounding inside my head, only to have the watchman say, "Hey! Wake up! That voice is a phoney!"

Most of us have very imperfect control over our attention. Our minds slip away from duty before we realize that they are gone. Part of being a good student is learning to be aware of the state of one's own mind and the degree of one's own understanding. The good student may be one who often says that he does not understand, simply because he keeps a constant check on his understanding. The poor student, who does not, so to speak, watch himself trying to understand, does not know most of the time whether he understands or not. Thus the problem is not to get students to ask us what they don't know; the problem is to make them aware of the difference between what they know and what they don't.

All this makes me think of Herb. I saw the other day why his words so often run off the paper. When he is copying a word, he copies about two letters at a time. I doubt whether he looks beyond them, or that he could tell you, in the middle of a word, what the whole word was. He has no idea, when he begins to copy a word, how long the word is going to be, or how much room it may take up.

• • • • •

Remember when Emily, asked to spell "microscopic," wrote MINCO-PERT? That must have been several weeks ago. Today I wrote MINCO-PERT on the board. To my great surprise, she recognized it. Some of the kids, watching me write it, said in amazement, "What's that for?" I said, "What do you think?" Emily answered, "It's supposed to be 'microscopic.'" But she gave not the least sign of knowing that she was the person who had written MINCOPERT.

On the diagnostic spelling test, she spelled "tariff" as TEARERFIT. Today I thought I would try her again on it. This time she wrote TEAR-FIT. What does she do in such cases? Her reading aloud gives a clue. She closes her eyes and makes a dash for it, like someone running past a graveyard on a dark night. No looking back afterward, either.

Reminds me of a fragment of the Ancient Mariner—perhaps the world's best short ghost story:

> Like one, that on a lonesome road
> Doth walk in fear and dread,
> And having once turned round walks on,
> And turns no more his head;
> Because he knows, a frightful fiend
> Doth close behind him tread.

Is this the way some of these children make their way through life?

MEMO TO THE RESEARCH COMMITTEE
· · · · ·

I am curious about the ability of children to turn things around in their minds. One day, in room period, I asked the children to write on paper certain words that I had showed them, and then write what these would look like if seen in a mirror. I told them to be sure to write the words exactly as I did, with the same use of capital or lower case letters. First I wrote CAT. Emily wrote CAt. It didn't trouble her that two letters were capitals, and one lower case—if she noticed it at all. She assumed that seen in a mirror the order of letters would be reversed, so she wrote TaC. The lower-case *t* became capital; the *A* became lower case. The next word was BIRD. She completely forgot what she had just done about reversing the order of the letters. This time she assumed that the trick was to write each letter backwards, while keeping them in the original order. On her paper she had written BIrD. She reversed the *B* correctly, wrote the *I,* then looked at the lower-case *r,* which must have looked to her like an upside-down *L,* decided, "I must turn this right side up," and wrote *L.* Then she decided that the letters *B* and *D* should not be reversed, so her final answer was BILD. Answer to what question? She hadn't the faintest idea. Whatever task she had set out to do at the beginning had gone from her mind long before she got to the end of it; it had become changed into something else, something to do with writing letters upside down, or backwards, or something.

This child *must* be right. She cannot bear to be wrong, or even to imagine that she might be wrong. When she is wrong, as she often is, the only thing to do is to forget it as quickly as possible. Naturally she will not tell herself that she is wrong; it is bad enough when others tell her. When she is told to do something, she does it quickly and fearfully, hands it to some higher authority, and awaits the magic words, "right," or "wrong." If the word is "right," she does not have to think about that problem any more; if the word is "wrong," she does not want to, cannot bring herself to think about it.

This fear leads her to other strategies, which other children use as well. She knows that in a recitation period the teacher's attention is divided among twenty students. She also knows the teacher's strategy of

asking questions of students who seem confused, or not paying attention. She therefore feels safe waving her hand in the air, as if she were
bursting to tell the answer, whether she really knows it or not. This is
her safe way of telling me that she, at least, knows all about whatever
is going on in class. When someone else answers correctly she nods her
head in emphatic agreement. Sometimes she even adds a comment,
though her expression and tone of voice show that she feels this is
risky. It is also interesting to note that she does not raise her hand
unless there are at least half a dozen other hands up.

Sometimes she gets called on. The question arose the other day,
"What is half of forty-eight?" Her hand was up; in the tiniest whisper
she said, "Twenty-four." I asked her to repeat it. She said, loudly, "I
said," then whispered "twenty-four." I asked her to repeat it again,
because many couldn't hear her. Her face showing tension, she said,
very loudly, "I said that one-half of forty-eight is . . ." and then, very
softly, "twenty-four." Still, not many of the students heard. She said,
indignantly, "OK, I'll shout." I said that that would be fine. She shouted,
in a self-righteous tone, "The question is, what is half of forty-eight.
Right?" I agreed. And once again, in a voice scarcely above a whisper,
she said, "Twenty-four." I could not convince her that she had shouted
the question but not the answer.

Of course, this is a strategy that often pays off. A teacher who asks
a question is tuned to the right answer, ready to hear it, eager to hear it,
since it will tell him that his teaching is good and that he can go on to
the next topic. He will assume that anything that sounds close to the
right answer is meant to be the right answer. So, for a student who is not
sure of the answer, a mumble may be his best bet. If he's not sure
whether something is spelled with an *a* or an *o,* he writes a letter that
could be either one of them.

The mumble strategy is particularly effective in language classes. In
my French classes, the students used to work it on me, without my
knowing what was going on. It is particularly effective with a teacher
who is finicky about accents and proud of his own. To get such a teacher
to answer his own questions is a cinch. Just make some mumbled,
garbled, hideously un-French answer, and the teacher, with a shudder,
will give the correct answer in elegant French. The student will have to
repeat it after him, but by that time he is out of the worst danger.

Game theorists have a name for the strategy which maximizes your
chances of winning and minimizes your losses if you should lose. They

call it "minimax." Kids are expert at finding such strategies. They can always find ways to hedge, to cover their bets. . . .

• • • • •

Children are often quite frank about the strategies they use to get answers out of a teacher. I once observed a class in which the teacher was testing her students on parts of speech. On the blackboard she had three columns, headed Noun, Adjective, and Verb. As she gave each word, she called on a child and asked in which column the word belonged.

Like most teachers, she hadn't thought enough about what she was doing to realize, first, that many of the words given could fit into more than one column; and secondly, that it is often the way a word is used that determines what part of speech it is.

There was a good deal of the tried-and-true strategy of *guess-and-look,* in which you start to say a word, all the while scrutinizing the teacher's face to see whether you are on the right track or not. With most teachers, no further strategies are needed. This one was more poker-faced than most, so *guess-and-look* wasn't working very well. Still, the percentage of hits was remarkably high, especially since it was clear to me from the way the children were talking and acting that they hadn't a notion of what Nouns, Adjectives, and Verbs were. Finally one child said, "Miss —, you shouldn't point to the answer each time." The teacher was surprised, and asked what she meant. The child said, "Well, you don't exactly *point,* but you kind of stand next to the answer." This was no clearer, since the teacher had been standing still. But after a while, as the class went on, I thought I saw what the girl meant. Since the teacher wrote each word down in its proper column, she was, in a way, getting herself ready to write, pointing herself at the place where she would soon be writing. From the angle of her body to the blackboard the children picked up a subtle clue to the correct answer.

This was not all. At the end of every third word, her three columns came out even, that is, there were an equal number of nouns, adjectives, and verbs. This meant that when she started off a new row, you had one chance in three of getting the right answer by a blind guess; but for the next word, you had one chance in two, and the last word was a dead giveaway to the lucky student who was asked it. Hardly any missed this opportunity; in fact, they answered so quickly that the teacher (brighter than most) caught on to their system and began keeping her columns uneven, making the strategist's job a bit harder.

In the midst of all this, there came a vivid example of the kind of thing we say in school that makes no sense, that only bewilders and confuses the thoughtful child who tries to make sense out of it. The teacher, whose specialty, by the way, was English, had told these children that a verb is a word of action—which is not always true. One of the words she asked was "dream." She was thinking of the noun, and apparently did not remember that "dream" can as easily be a verb. One little boy, making a pure guess, said it was a verb. Here the teacher, to be helpful, contributed one of those "explanations" that are so much more hindrance than help. She said, "But a verb has to have action; can you give me a sentence, using 'dream', that has action?" The child thought a bit, and said, "I had a dream about the Trojan War." Now it's pretty hard to get much more action than that. But the teacher told him he was wrong, and he sat silent, with an utterly baffled and frightened expression on his face. She was so busy thinking about what she wanted him to say, she was so obsessed with that *right answer* hidden in her mind, that she could not think about what he was really saying and thinking, could not see that his reasoning was logical and correct, and that the mistake was not his, but hers.

At one of our leading prep schools I saw, the other day, an example of the way in which a teacher may not know what is going on in his own class.

This was a math class. The teacher, an experienced man, was doing the day's assignment on the blackboard. His way of keeping attention was to ask various members of the class, as he did each step, "Is that right?" It was a dull class, and I found it hard to keep my mind on it. It seemed to me that most students in the class had their minds elsewhere, with a mental sentry posted to alert them when their names were called. As each name was called, the boy who was asked if something or other was right answered "Yes." The class droned on. In time my mind slipped away altogether, I don't know for how long. Suddenly something snapped me to attention. I looked at the teacher. Every boy in the class was looking at him, too. The boy who had been asked if what had just been written was right, was carefully looking at the blackboard. After a moment he said, "No, sir, that isn't right, it ought to be so-and-so." The teacher chuckled appreciatively and said, "You're right, it should be." He made the change, and the class and I settled back into our private thoughts for the rest of the period.

After the boys had left, I thanked the teacher for letting me visit. He said, "You notice I threw them a little curve ball there. I do that every now and then. Keeps them on their toes." I said something in agreement. It didn't seem the time or place to tell him that when he threw his little curve ball the expression in his voice changed enough so that it warned, not only the boys, but also a complete stranger, that something was coming up and that attention had better be paid.

I've been reading over all the memos from last winter and spring. It is a curious and unsettling process, the business of changing your mind on a subject about which you had very positive convictions. After all I have said and written about the need for keeping children under pressure, I find myself coming to realize that what hampers their thinking, what drives them into these narrow and defensive strategies, is a feeling that they must please the grownups at all costs. The really able thinkers in our class turn out to be, without exception, children who don't feel so strongly the need to please grownups. Some of them are good students, some not so good; but good or not, they don't work to please us, but to please themselves.

Here is Walter, just the opposite, very eager to do whatever people want him to do, and very good at doing it. (By conventional standards he was a very able pupil, so much so that people called him brilliant, which he most assuredly was not.)

We had the problem, "If you are travelling at 40 miles per hour, how long will it take you to go 10 miles?"

WALTER: 4 minutes.
JH (me): How did you get it?
W: Divided the 40 by the 10.
  A quick look at my face told him that this would not do. After a while he wrote, "15 minutes." I wanted to check this understanding.
JH: If you were going 50 miles per hour, how far would you go in 24 minutes?
W (quickly): 36 miles.
JH: How did you get that?
W: Subtracted 24 from 60.
  He still hadn't gotten it: I tried again.
JH: If you were going 50 miles per hour, how far would you go in 30 minutes?
W: 25 miles. 30 minutes is half an hour, and half of 50 is 25.

It sounded as if he knew what he was doing at last. I thought he would have no trouble with the 24 minutes problem. But it took a long time, with some hinting from me, before he saw that 24 minutes was ⅖ of an hour, and therefore, that he would go ⅖ of 50 miles, or 20 miles, in 24 minutes. Would he have discovered it if I had not paved the way with leading questions? Hard to tell.

Most teachers would have assumed, as I would have once, that when he got the 15-minutes problem, he knew what he was doing. Even the skeptical would have been convinced when he gave his explanation about the 30-minutes problem. Yet in each case he showed that he had not really understood what he was doing, and it is not at all certain that he understands yet.

• • • • •

OBSERVING IN BILL HULL'S CLASS

Of all I saw and learned this past half-year, one thing stands out. What goes on in class is not what teachers think—certainly not what I had always thought. For years now I have worked with a picture in mind of what my class was like. This reality, which I felt I knew, was partly physical, partly mental or spiritual. In other words, I thought I knew, in general, what the students were doing, and also what they were thinking and feeling. I see now that my picture of reality was almost wholly false. Why didn't I see this before?

Sitting at the side of the room, watching these kids, not so much to check up on them as to find out what they were like and how they differed from the teen-agers I have worked with and know, I slowly became aware of something. You can't find out what a child does in class by looking at him only when he is called on. You have to watch him for long stretches of time without his knowing it.

During many of the recitation classes, when the class supposedly is working as a unit, most of the children paid very little attention to what was going on. Those who most needed to pay attention usually paid the least. The kids who knew the answer to whatever question you were asking wanted to make sure that you knew they knew, so their hands were always waving. Also, knowing the right answer, they were in a position to enjoy to the full the ridiculous answers that might be given by their less fortunate colleagues. But, as in all classes, these able students are a minority. What of the unsuccessful majority? Their attention depended on what was going on in class. Any raising of the emotional temperature made them prick up their ears. If an argument was going on, or someone was in trouble, or someone was being laughed at for a foolish answer, they took notice. Or, if you were explaining to a slow student something so simple that all the rest knew it, they would wave their arms and give agonized, half-suppressed cries of "O-o-o-o-oh! O-o-o-o-oh!" But most of the time, when explaining, questioning, or discussing was going on, the majority of children paid little attention or none at all. Some daydreamed, and no amount of calling them back to earth with a crash, much as it amused everyone else, could break them of the habit. Others wrote and passed notes, or whispered, or held conversations in sign language, or made doodles or pictures on their papers or desks, or fiddled with objects.

There doesn't seem to be much a teacher can do about this, if he is really teaching and not just keeping everyone quiet and busy. A teacher in class is like a man in the woods at night with a powerful flashlight in his hand. Wherever he turns his light, the creatures on whom it shines are aware of it, and do not behave as they do in the dark. Thus the mere fact of his watching their behavior changes it into something very different. Shine where he will, he can never know very much of the night life of the woods.

So, in class, the teacher can turn the spotlight of his attention, now on this child, now on that, now on them all; but the children know when his attention is on them, and do not act at all as they do when it is elsewhere. A teacher who is really thinking about what a particular child is doing or asking, or about what he, himself, is trying to explain, will not be able to know what all the rest of the class is doing. And if he does notice that other children are doing what they should not, and tells them to stop, they know they have only to wait until he gets back, as he must, to his real job. Classroom observers don't seem to see much of this. Why not? Some of them do not stay with a class long enough for the children to begin to act naturally in their presence. But even those who are with a class for a long time make the mistake of watching the teacher too much and the children too little. Student teachers in training spend long periods of time in one classroom, but they think they are in there to learn *How To Teach,* to pick up the tricks of child management from watching a *Master At*

Work. Their concern is with manipulating and controlling children rather than understanding them. So they watch the teacher, see only what the teacher sees, and thus lose most of what could be a valuable experience.

• • • • •

Teachers feel, as I once did, that their interests and their students' are fundamentally the same. I used to feel that I was guiding and helping my students on a journey that they wanted to take but could not take without my help. I knew the way looked hard, but I assumed they could see the goal almost as clearly as I and that they were almost as eager to reach it. It seemed very important to give students this feeling of being on a journey to a worthwhile destination. I see now that most of my talk to this end was wasted breath. Maybe *I* thought the students were in my class because they were eager to learn what I was trying to teach, but they knew better. They were in school because they had to be, and in my class either because they had to be, or because otherwise they would have had to be in another class, which might be even worse.

Children in school are like children at the doctor's. He can talk himself blue in the face about how much good his medicine is going to do them; all they think of is how much it will hurt or how bad it will taste. Given their own way, they would have none of it.

So the valiant and resolute band of travelers I thought I was leading toward a much-hoped-for destination turned out instead to be more like convicts in a chain gang, forced under threat of punishment to move along a rough path leading nobody knew where and down which they could see hardly more than a few steps ahead. School feels like this to children: it is a place where *they* make you go and where *they* tell you to do things and where *they* try to make your life unpleasant if you don't do them or don't do them right.

For children, the central business of school is not learning, whatever this vague word means; it is getting these daily tasks done, or at least out of the way, with a minimum of effort and unpleasantness. Each task is an end in itself. The children don't care how they dispose of it. If they can get it out of the way by doing it, they will do it; if experience has taught them that this does not work very well, they will turn to other means, illegitimate means, that wholly defeat whatever purpose the task-giver may have had in mind.

They are very good at this, at getting other people to do their tasks for them. I remember the day not long ago when Ruth opened my eyes. We had been doing math, and I was pleased with myself because, instead of telling her answers and showing her how to do problems, I was "making her think" by asking her questions. It was slow work. Question after question met only silence. She said nothing, did nothing, just sat and looked at me through those glasses, and waited. Each time, I had to think of a question easier and more pointed than the last, until I finally found one so easy that she would feel safe in answering it. So we inched our way along until suddenly, looking at her as I waited for an answer to a question, I saw with a start that she was not at all puzzled by what I had asked her. In fact, she was not even thinking about it. She was coolly appraising me, weighing my patience, waiting for that next, sure-to-be-easier question. I thought, "I've been had!" The girl had learned how to make me do her work for her, just as she had learned to make all her previous teachers do the same thing. If I wouldn't tell her the answers, very well, she would just let me question her right up to them.

Schools and teachers seem generally to be as blind to children's strategies as I was. Otherwise, they would teach their courses and assign their tasks so that students who really thought about the meaning of the subject would have the best chance of succeeding, while those who tried to do the tasks by illegitimate means, without thinking or understanding, would be foiled. But the reverse seems to be the case. Schools give every encouragement to *producers,* the kids whose idea is to get "right answers" by any and all means. In a system that runs on "right answers," they can hardly help it. And these schools are often very discouraging places for *thinkers.*

Until recently it had not occurred to me that poor students thought differently about their work than good students; I assumed they thought the same way, only less skillfully. Now it begins to look as if the expectation and fear of failure, if strong enough, may lead children to act and think in a special way, to adopt strategies different from those of more confident children. Emily is a good example. She is emotionally as well as intellectually incapable of checking her work, of comparing her ideas against reality, of making any kind of judgment about the value of her thoughts. She makes me think of an animal fleeing danger—go like the wind, don't look back, remember where that danger was, and stay away from it as far as you can. Are there many other children who react to their fears in this way?

· · · · ·

Here are some notes from the other day, when the fourth graders were playing Twenty Questions.

Many of them are very anxious when their turn comes to ask a question. We ask them to play Twenty Questions in the hope that, wanting to find the hidden thought, they will learn to ask more informative and useful questions.

They see the game quite differently: "When my turn comes, I have to ask a question." They are not the least interested in the object of the game, or whether their question gains useful information. The problem is simply to think of a question, any old question. The first danger is that you will just be sitting there, unable to think of a question. The next danger is that when you ask a question, other kids will think it is silly, laugh at it, say, "That's no good."

So the problem becomes not just thinking up a question, but thinking up a question that will sound good. The best way to do this is to listen to kids that you know are pretty sharp, and ask questions that sound like theirs. Thus, a child who found in one game that "Is it water?" was a useful question, went on asking it in game after game, even when other questions had established that the information sought for had nothing to do with water.

Many of our kids play the same way. Pat, Rachel, and some others never have any idea what the object of the game is, or what information has been gained by questions already asked. All they want, when their turn comes, is to have a question that won't be laughed at. Jessie plays it even safer than that. She just refuses to ask a question, says, "I pass," and looks very pleased with herself after she says it, too.

Another popular strategy is the disguised blind guess. When kids first play this game, every question is a guess. Then some of them see that it is silly to guess right at the beginning, and that the sensible thing to do is narrow down the possibilities. They criticize very severely teammates who start guessing too soon. So the trick becomes to ask a guessing question that doesn't sound like a guess, like Nat's classic, "Was he killed by Brutus?" This has become something of a joke in his group. Still, every question he asks conceals a guess.

One day we were using the atlas, and the field of the game was geographical locations. Sam wanted to ask if it was Italy, but that was a guess, so he said, "Does it look like a boot?" Every time it is his turn, he says, "Can I make a guess?" The strategy of narrowing down possibilities has not occured to him, or if it has, he does not know how to make use of it.

Betty makes multiple guesses. Thinking of either Corsica or Sardinia, she asked, "Does it begin with *C* or *S?*" Another time she said, "Does it begin with *B, D, C, P,* or *T?*" This is not bad strategy. On another occasion she said to a cautious teammate, "Don't say 'Could it be?'; say 'Is it?' " She's a positive little critter.

Sometimes we try to track down a number with Twenty Questions. One day I said I was thinking of a number between 1 and 10,000. Children who use a good narrowing-down strategy to find a number between 1 and 100, or 1 and 500, go all to pieces when the number is between 1 and 10,000. Many start guessing from the very beginning. Even when I say that the number is very large, they will try things like 65, 113, 92. Other kids will narrow down until they find that the number is in the 8,000's; then they start guessing, as if there were now so few numbers to choose from that guessing became worthwhile. Their confidence in these shots in the dark is astonishing. They say, "We've got it this time!" They are always incredulous when they find they have not got it.

They still cling stubbornly to the idea that the only good answer is a *yes* answer. This, of course, is the result of their miseducation, in which "right answers" are the only ones that pay off. They have not learned how to learn from a mistake, or even that learning from mistakes is possible. If they say, "Is the number between 5,000 and 10,000?" and I say *yes,* they cheer; if I say *no,* they groan, even though they get exactly the same amount of information in either case. The more anxious ones will, over and over again, ask questions that have already been answered, just for the satisfaction of hearing a *yes.* Their more sophisticated teammates point out in vain that it is silly to ask a question when you already know the answer.

FEAR AND FAILURE
· · · · ·

The other day I decided to talk to the other section about what happens when you don't understand what is going on. We had been chatting about something or other, and everyone seemed in a relaxed frame of mind, so I said, "You know, there's something I'm curious about, and I wonder if you'd tell me." They said, "What?" I said, "What do you think, what goes through your mind, when the teacher asks you a question and you don't know the answer?"

It was a bombshell. Instantly a paralyzed silence fell on the room. Everyone stared at me with what I have learned to recognize as a tense expression. For a long time there wasn't a sound. Finally Ben, who is bolder than most, broke the tension, and also answered my question, by saying in a loud voice, "Gulp!"

He spoke for everyone. They all began to clamor, and all said the same thing, that when the teacher asked them a question and they didn't know the answer they were scared half to death. I was flabbergasted—to find this in a school which people think of as progressive; which does its best not to put pressure on little children; which does not give marks in the lower grades; which tries to keep children from feeling that they're in some kind of race.

I asked them why they felt gulpish. They said they were afraid of failing, afraid of being kept back, afraid of being called stupid, afraid of feeling themselves stupid. Stupid. Why is it such a deadly insult to these children, almost the worst thing they can think of to call each other? Where do they learn this?

Even in the kindest and gentlest of schools, children are afraid, many of them a great deal of the time, some of them almost all the time. This is a hard fact of life to deal with. What can we do about it?

All fall long, I wondered why Jack fell down so much playing soccer. He is an agile, well-coordinated boy. His balance is good. People don't knock him over. Why was he on the ground so often? Suddenly, the other day, I had the answer.

I discovered it while trying to learn to control the tension that builds up in me when I practice the flute. Music is a good thing for teachers to study, because it creates in us the kind of tension that children live under all the time in the classroom, and that most adults have long forgotten. . . .

I have observed many times that children who can do one or two problems of a certain kind, with no trouble, collapse when given a big sheet of them. Something like this is true of exercises in music. When I am trying to play an exercise at (for me) high speed, I am under tension. If the exercise is short, I feel that I can get through it before tension gets the better of me. But if it is long, I am less confident from the start that I can get through without a mistake. . . .

I haven't forgotten Jack and his falling down. One thing I have discovered is that there is a peculiar kind of relief, a lessening of tension, when you make a mistake. For when you make one, you no longer have to worry about whether you are going to make one. Walking a tightrope, you worry about falling off; once fallen off, you don't have to worry. Children, to whom making mistakes is acutely painful, are therefore under great tension when doing something correctly. Worrying about the mistakes they might make is as bad—no, worse— than worrying about the mistakes they have made. Thus, when you tell a child that he has done a problem wrong, you often hear a sigh of relief. He says, "I *knew* it would be wrong." He would rather *be* wrong, and know it, than not know whether he was wrong or not.

Well, the reason Jack falls down is that this relieves him, for a few seconds, of the great tension he is under when he plays soccer. Being small, he is afraid of crashing into bigger boys, but he is also afraid of showing his fear, and resolutely tries to play the game as he feels he should. This puts his nervous system under a strain that is too much for it. Being a boy, he can't pull out of the game, as a girl might do, or just get out of the way of bigger boys when they come at him. So, every now and then, he falls down, and thus gets an honorable rest period for a second or two.

• • • • •

. . . It used to puzzle me that the students who made the most mistakes and got the worst marks were so often the first ones to hand in their papers. I used to say, "If you finish early, take time to check your work, do some problems again." Typical teacher's advice; I might as well have told them to flap their arms and fly. When the paper was in, the tension was ended. Their fate was in the lap of the gods. They might still worry about flunking the paper, but it was a fatalistic kind of worry, it didn't contain the agonizing element of choice, there was nothing more they could do about it. Worrying about whether you did the right thing, while painful enough, is less painful than worrying about the right thing to do.

One way to keep down tension is to be aware of it. I told the math class that to let something go by in class without knowing what it means, and without saying anything, is like leaving something in Howard Johnson's on a long car trip. You are going to have to go back for it eventually, so the sooner the better. This foolish metaphor has helped the kids, or so they say. They have learned to recognize, if only a little, the feeling of panicky confusion that slowly gets hold of them. To be able to say, "I'm getting left at Howard Johnson's" helps them to control this feeling, and if it gets too much for them they can always tell me that they have been left behind; then I can do something about picking them up.

We must set a limit to the tension that we put children under. If we don't, they will set their own limits by not paying attention, by fooling around, by saying unnecessarily, "I don't get it." We should let them know in advance that they will not have to be under tension for an entire period, and that, if need be, they have the means to bring it to a stop.

* * * * *

Someone asked the other day, "Why do we go to school?" Pat, with a vigor unusual in her, said "So when we grow up we won't be stupid." These children equate stupidity with ignorance. Is this what they mean when they call themselves stupid? Is this one of the reasons why they are so ashamed of not knowing something? If so, have we, perhaps unknowingly, taught them to feel this way? We should clear up this distinction, show them that it is possible to know very few facts, but make very good use of them. Conversely, one can know many facts and still act stupidly. The learned fool is by no means rare in this country.

* * * * *

One thing we see in our intelligent children is that they are intensely involved with life. Rachel, Pat, Elaine, Garry, all are daydreamers. But Barbara, Betty, Maria, Ralph, and Hal don't withdraw from life; they embrace it. We spoke once of a love affair with learning. These children seem to have a love affair with life. Think of the gusto with which Betty, or Barbara, or Sam tell even the simplest story about themselves.

Intelligent children act as if they thought the universe made some sense. They check their answers and their thoughts against common sense, while other children, not expecting answers to make sense, not knowing what is sense, see no point in checking, no way of checking. Yet the difference may go deeper than this. It seems as if what we call intelligent children feel that the universe can be trusted even when it does not seem to make any sense, that even when you don't understand it you can be fairly sure that it is not going to play dirty tricks on you. How close this is in spirit to the remark of Einstein's, "I cannot believe that God plays dice with the universe."

On page 54 in the July 1958 *Scientific American,* in the article "Profile of Creativity," there is the following apt comparison:

The creative scientist analyzes a problem slowly and carefully, then proceeds rapidly with a solution. The less creative man is apt to flounder in disorganized attempts to get a quick answer.

Indeed he is! How often have we seen our answer-grabbers get into trouble. The fact is that problems and answers are simply different ways of looking at a relationship, a structure, an order. A problem is a picture with a piece missing; the answer is the missing piece. The children who take time to see, and feel, and grip the problem, soon find that the answer is there. The ones who get in trouble are the ones who see a problem as an order to start running at top speed from a given starting point, in an unknown direction, to an unknown destination. They dash after the answer before they have considered the problem. What's their big hurry?

Here are Elaine, the answer-grabber, and Barbara, the thinker, at work on the problem $\frac{3}{4} + \frac{2}{5} = ?$

Elaine (adding tops and bottoms, as is her usual custom): Why not $\frac{5}{9}$?

Barbara: $\frac{5}{9}$ is less than $\frac{3}{4}$. She saw that since $\frac{2}{5}$ was added to $\frac{3}{4}$, the answer would have to be bigger than $\frac{3}{4}$; so $\frac{5}{9}$ could not be it. But this went right over Elaine's head.

Elaine: Where's the $\frac{3}{4}$?

Barbara: In the problem!

Yet I doubt that any amount of explaining could have made Elaine understand what Barbara was saying, far less enable her to do the same kind of thinking for herself.

The poor thinker dashes madly after an answer; the good thinker takes his time and looks at the problem. Is the difference merely a matter of a skill in thought, a technique which, with ingenuity and luck, we might teach and train into children? I'm afraid not. The good thinker can take his time because he can tolerate uncertainty, he can stand not knowing. The poor thinker can't stand not knowing; it drives him crazy.

This cannot be completely explained by the fear of being wrong. No doubt this fear puts, say, Monica under heavy pressure; but Hal is under the same pressure, and maybe I am as well. Monica is not alone in wanting to be right and fearing to be wrong. What is involved here is another insecurity, the insecurity of not having *any* answer to a problem. Monica wants the right answer, yes; but what she wants, first of all, is an answer, any old answer, and she will do almost anything to get some kind of answer. Once she gets it, a large part of the pressure is off. Rachel was like this; so was Gerald, and many others. They can't stand a problem without a solution, even if they know that their solution will probably be wrong. This panicky search for certainty, this inability to tolerate unanswered questions and unsolved problems seems to lie at the heart of many problems of intelligence. . . .

• • • • •

A year ago I was wondering how a child's fears might influence his strategies. This year's work has told me. The strategies of most of these kids have been consistently self-centered, self-protective, aimed above all else at avoiding trouble, embarrassment, punishment, disapproval, or loss of status. This is particularly true of the ones who have had a tough time in school. When they get a problem, I can read their thoughts on their faces, I can almost hear them, "Am I going to get this right? Probably not; what'll happen to me when I get it wrong? Will the teacher get mad? Will the other kids laugh at me? Will my mother and father hear about it? Will they keep me back this year? Why am I so dumb?" And so on.

Even in the room periods, where I did all I could to make the work non-threatening, I was continually amazed and appalled to see the children hedging their bets, covering their losses in advance, trying to fix things so that whatever happened they could feel they had been right, or if wrong, no more wrong than anyone else. "I think it will sort of balance." They are fence-straddlers, afraid ever to commit themselves—and at the age of ten. Playing games like Twenty Questions, which one might have expected them to play for fun, many of them were concerned only to put up a good front, to look as if they knew what they were doing, whether they did or not.

• • • • •

What is most surprising of all is how much fear there is in school. Why is so little said about it? Perhaps most people do not recognize fear in children when they see it. They can read the grossest signs of fear; they know what the trouble is when a child clings howling to his mother; but the subtler signs of fear escape them. It is these signs, in children's faces, voices, and gestures, in their movements and ways of working, that tell me plainly that most children in school are scared most of the time, many of them very scared. Like good soldiers, they control their fears, live with them, and adjust themselves to them. But the trouble is, and here is a vital difference between school and war, that the adjustments children make to their fears are almost wholly bad, destructive of their intelligence and capacity. The scared fighter may be the best fighter, but the scared learner is always a poor learner.

• • • • •

Children who depend heavily on adult approval may decide that, if they can't have total success, their next-best bet is to have total failure. Perhaps, in using the giving or withholding of approval as a way of making children do what we want, we are helping to make these deliberate failers. I think of a sixteen-year-old boy I once knew who, unable to fulfill all his father's very high expectations for him, decided to fulfill none of them. The father was a pillar of the community, good at everything he did; the boy became a playboy and a drunk. One night, at a party, the father was watching his son doing a very drunken and quite funny tango alone in the middle of the dance floor, before a laughing and admiring crowd. The thought flashed through my mind, "Well, that's one thing he can do better than you can."

It is often said that alcoholics may be very able people who feel they cannot meet the high standards they have set for themselves, and hence don't try. Perhaps children find, or try to find, in hopeless incompetence the kind of refuge that an alcoholic finds in liquor. But how do we get children to kick the failure habit? Do we organize a society of Failers Anonymous?

Incompetence has one other advantage. Not only does it reduce what others expect and demand of you, it reduces what you expect or even hope for yourself. When you set out to fail, one thing is certain—you can't be disappointed. As the old saying goes, you can't fall out of bed when you sleep on the floor.

• • • • •

My seventeen-month-old niece caught sight of my ball point pen the other day, and reached out for it. It has a plastic cap that fits over the point. She took hold of it, and after some pushing and pulling, got the cap off. After looking it over, she put it back on. Then off again; then on again. A good game! Now, if I want to be able to use my pen, I have to keep it out of sight, or when she sees it, she wants to play with it. She is so deft in putting it back on that it makes me wonder about all I've read about the lack of coordination in infants and the imprecision of their movements. Under the right circumstances —when they are interested—they may be much more skillful than we think.

These quiet summer days I spend many hours watching this baby. What comes across most vividly is that she is a kind of scientist. She is always observing and experimenting. She is hardly ever idle. Most of her waking time she is intensely and purposefully active, soaking up experience and trying to make sense out of it, trying to find how things around her behave, and trying to make them behave as she wants them to.

In the face of what looks like unbroken failure, she is so persistent. Most of her experiments, her efforts to predict and control her environment, don't work. But she goes right on, not the least daunted. Perhaps this is because there are no penalties attached to failure, except nature's—usually, if you try to step on a ball, you fall down. A baby does not react to failure as an adult does, or even a five-year-old, because she has not yet been made to feel that failure is shame, disgrace, a crime. Unlike her elders, she is not concerned with protecting herself against everything that is not easy and familiar; she reaches out to experience, she embraces life.

Watching this baby, it is hard to credit the popular notion that without outside rewards and penalties children will not learn. There are some rewards and penalties in her life; the adults approve of some things she does, and disapprove of others. But most of the time she lives beyond praise or blame, if only because most of her learning experiments are unobserved. After all, who thinks about the meaning of what a baby is doing, so long as she is quiet and contented? But watch a while and think about it, and you see that she has a strong desire to make sense of the world around her. Her learning gives her great satisfaction, whether anyone else notices it or not.

• • • • •

Today Andy had a long, tough session with me. He finally solved the problem I had given him. But I can't help wondering what he learned. Not much; he certainly didn't gain any insight into the property of multiplication in which I was interested. All that he had to show for his time was the memory of a long and painful experience, full of failure, frustration, anxiety, and tension. He did not even feel satisfaction when he had done the problem correctly, only relief at not having to think about it any more.

He is not stupid. In spite of his nervousness and anxiety, he is curious about some things, bright, enthusiastic, perceptive, and in his writing highly imaginative. But he is, literally, scared out of his wits. He cannot learn math because his mind moves so slowly from one thought to another that the connections between them are lost. His memory does not hold what he learns, above all else because he won't trust it. Every day he must figure out, all over again, that $9 + 7 = 16$, because how can he be sure that it has not changed, or that he has not made another in an endless series of mistakes? How can you trust any of your own thoughts when so many of them have proved to be wrong?

I can see no kind of life for him unless he can break out of the circle of failure, discouragement, and fear in which he is trapped. But I can't see how he is going to break out. Worst of all, I'm not sure that we, his elders, really want him to break out. It is no accident that this boy is afraid. We have made him afraid, consciously, deliberately, so that we might more easily control his behavior and get him to do whatever we wanted him to do.

I am horrified to realize how much I myself use fear and anxiety as instruments of control. I think, or at least hope, that the kids in my class are somewhat more free of fear than they have been in previous classes, or than most children are in most classes. I try to use a minimum of controls and pressures. Still, the work must be done —mustn't it?—and there must be some limits to what they can be allowed to do in class, and the methods I use for getting the work done and controlling the behavior rest ultimately on fear, fear of getting in wrong with me, or the school, or their parents.

Here is Andy, whose fears make him almost incapable of most kinds of constructive thinking and working. On the one hand, I try to dissipate those fears. But on the other, I have to do something to get him to do the work he so hates doing. What I do boils down to a series of penalties, which are effective in exactly the proportion that they rouse the kind of fears that I have been trying to dispel. Also, when children feel a little relieved of the yoke of anxiety that they are so used to bearing, they behave just like other people freed from yokes, like prisoners released, like victors in a revolution, like small-town businessmen on American Legion conventions. They cut up;

they get bold and sassy; they may for a while try to give a hard time to those adults who for so long have been giving them a hard time. So, to keep him in his place, to please the school and his parents, I have to make him fearful again. The freedom from fear that I try to give with one hand I almost instantly take away with the other.

What sense does this make?

HOW SCHOOLS FAIL
. . . . .

Some time ago, in an article on race stereotypes, I read something that stuck in my mind, but that only recently has seemed to have anything to do with children.

The author spent some time in a German concentration camp during the war. He and his fellow prisoners, trying to save both their lives and something of their human dignity, and to resist, despite their impotence, the demands of their jailers, evolved a kind of camp personality as a way of dealing with them. They adopted an air of amiable dullwittedness, of smiling foolishness, of cooperative and willing incompetence—like the good soldier Schweik. Told to do something, they listened attentively, nodded their heads eagerly, and asked questions that showed they had not understood a word of what had been said. When they could not safely do this any longer, they did as far as possible the opposite of what they had been told to do, or did it, but as badly as they dared. They realized that this did not much impede the German war effort, or even the administration of the camp; but it gave them a way of preserving a small part of their integrity in a hopeless situation.

After the war, the author did a good deal of work, in many parts of the world, with subject peoples; but not for some time did he recognize, in the personality of the "good black boy" of many African colonies, or the "good nigger" of the American South, the camp personality adopted during the war by himself and his fellow prisoners. When he first saw the resemblance, he was startled. Did these people, as he had done, put on this personality deliberately? He became convinced that this was true. Subject peoples both appease their rulers and satisfy some part of their desire for human dignity by putting on a mask, by acting much more stupid and incompetent than they really are, by denying their rulers the full use of their intelligence and ability, by declaring their minds and spirits free of their enslaved bodies.

Does not something very close to this happen often in school? Children are subject peoples. School for them is a kind of jail. Do they not, to some extent, escape and frustrate the relentless, insatiable pressure of their elders by withdrawing the most intelligent and creative parts of their minds from the scene? Is this not at least a partial explanation of the extraordinary stupidity that otherwise bright children so often show in school? The stubborn and dogged "I don't get it" with which they meet the instructions and explanations of their teachers—may it not be a statement of resistance as well as one of panic and flight?

I think this is almost certainly so. Whether children do this consciously and deliberately depends on the age and character of the child. Under pressure that they want to resist but don't dare to resist openly, some children may quite deliberately *go stupid;* I have seen it and felt it. Most of them, however, are probably not this aware of what they are doing. They deny their intelligence to their jailers, the teachers, not so much to frustrate them but because they have other and more important uses for it. Freedom to live and to think about life for its own sake is important and even essential to a child. He will only give so much time and thought to what others want him to do; the rest he demands and takes for his own interests, plans, worries, dreams. The result is that he is not all there during most of his hours in school. Whether he is afraid to be there, or just does not want to be there, the result is the same. Fear, boredom, resistance —they all go to make what we call stupid children.

To a very great degree, school is a place where children learn to be stupid. A dismal thought, but hard to escape. Infants are not stupid. Children of one, two, or even three throw the whole of themselves into everything they do. They embrace life, and devour it; it is why they learn so fast, and are such good company. Listlessness, boredom, apathy—these all come later. Children come to school *curious;* within a few years most of that curiosity is dead, or at least silent. Open a first or third grade to questions, and you will be deluged; fifth graders say nothing. They either have no questions or will not ask them. They think, "What's this leading up to? What's the catch?" Last year, thinking that self-consciousness and embarrassment might be silencing the children, I put a question box in the classroom, and said that I would answer any questions they put into it. In four months I got one question—"How long does a bear live?" While I was talking about the life span of bears and other creatures, one child said impatiently, "Come on, get to the point." The expressions on the children's faces seemed to say, "You've got us here in school; now make us do whatever it is that you want us to do." Curiosity, questions, speculation—these are for outside school, not inside.

Boredom and resistance may cause as much stupidity in school as fear. Give a child the kind of task he gets in school, and whether he is afraid of it, or resists it, or is willing to do it but bored by it, he will do the task with only a small part of his attention, energy, and intelligence. In a word, he will do it stupidly—even if correctly. This soon becomes a habit. He gets used to working at low power, he develops strategies to enable him to get by this way. In time he even starts to think of himself as being stupid, which is what most fifth graders think of themselves, and to think that his low-power way of coping with school is the only possible way.

It does no good to tell such students to pay attention and think about what they are doing. I can see myself now, in one of my ninth-grade algebra classes in Colorado, looking at one of my flunking students, a boy who had become frozen in his school stupidity, and saying to him in a loud voice, "Think! Think! Think!" Wasted breath; he had forgotten how. The stupid way—timid, unimaginative, defensive, evasive—in which he met and dealt with the problems of algebra were, by that time, the only way he knew of dealing with them. His strategies and expectations were fixed; he couldn't even imagine any others. He really was doing his dreadful best.

We ask children to do for most of a day what few adults are able to do even for an hour. How many of us, attending, say, a lecture that doesn't interest us, can keep our minds from wandering? Hardly any. Not I, certainly. Yet children have far less awareness of and control of their attention than we do. No use to shout at them to pay attention. If we want to get tough enough about it, as many schools do, we can terrorize a class of children into sitting still with their hands folded and their eyes glued on us, or somebody; but their minds will be far away. The attention of children must be lured, caught, and held, like a shy wild animal that must be coaxed with bait to come close. If the situations, the materials, the problems before a child do not interest him, his attention will slip off to what does interest him, and no amount of exhortation or threats will bring it back.

A child is most intelligent when the reality before him arouses in him a high degree of attention, interest, concentration, involvement —in short, when he cares most about what he is doing. This is why we should make schoolrooms and schoolwork as interesting and exciting as possible, not just so that school will be a pleasant place, but so that children in school will act intelligently and get into *the habit* of acting intelligently. The case against boredom in school is the same as the case against fear; it makes children behave stupidly, some on purpose, most because they cannot help it. If this goes on long enough, as it does in school, they forget what it is like to grasp at something, as they once grasped at everything, with all their minds and senses; they forget how to deal positively and aggressively with life and experience, to think and say, "I see it! I get it! I can do it!"

Democracy and education

JOHN DEWEY

If the measure of a man's greatness and influence is somehow related to the amount of criticism and abuse his works provoke, then John Dewey is surely to be counted as a great and influential American. Unfortunately, the majority of Dewey's critics have based their criticism upon the educational movement—progressive education—with which Dewey's name is associated, and not upon the philosophical basis of his thought. Not only Dewey's critics, but also his proponents, often fail to understand the philosophical and educational significance of his work. Indeed, in 1938 Dewey wrote *Experience and Education* in order to clarify his theoretical position in relation to that of the "progressive" educators and to dissociate himself from many of the educational practices which had become synonymous with progressivism.

For an understanding and appraisal of Dewey's contribution to educational thought, his *Democracy and Education,* published in 1916, is of the first importance. In *Democracy and Education* can be found all the elements of Dewey's philosophy, as well as its implications for the educational process. Dewey himself insisted that there could be no distinction drawn between a philosophy and a general theory of education. Further, although the book reveals much about formal schooling as it was practiced during the first fifteen years of this century *Democracy and Education* raises such

SOURCE: John Dewey, *Democracy and Education: An Introduction to the Philosophy of Education* (New York: Free Press, 1966), pp. 76–79, 100–110, 164–179, 180–193. Copyright 1916 by The Macmillan Company; renewed 1944 by John Dewey. Reprinted by permission of The Macmillan Company.

fundamental issues that its educational prescriptions may prove more relevant in the immediate years ahead than they were in the past. For example, Dewey was concerned with the increasing depersonalization of the productive process in an industrial society. He felt that the individual was being forced to work at tasks whose place in the entire productive scheme he could neither understand nor experience. Without rejecting the industrial society, Dewey considered depersonalization a problem whose solution must be found within the society creating it.

A brief overview of *Democracy and Education* may assist the reader in interpreting and evaluating the selections that follow. The book represents Dewey's attempt to link scientific inquiry, democratic social order, and the enterprise of formal education. Scientific inquiry constitutes the human organism's most successful attempt to deal effectively with the physical dimension of its environment. "Success" in this context refers to man's ability to provide for himself, from his physical surroundings, those needs essential to growth and well-being. It also constitutes man's successful attempt to define and live within the social dimension of his environment. The result of applying scientific methodology to social environment is, in Dewey's thought, the effecting of a democratic social order; that is, an order in which those needs essential to the social and psychological growth of the human organism are efficiently met.

In *Democracy and Education,* Dewey establishes education as the vehicle by which life and growth are carried forward in the social dimension. The increasing complexity of the social environment has made the need to formalize education an imperative. While random encounters with the physical environment may suffice to "educate," random encounters with our present complex social order are inadequate to prepare the young to grow and sustain themselves effectively.

Formal education, according to Dewey, must not only transmit socially relevant information to the young, but must also provide them with opportunities to participate *actively* in the acquisition of relevant information. Only by doing so will the young acquire that sense of their own abilities and the mastery of those materials so essential to their future social functioning.

Dewey insists that formal education in an open and democratic society must provide the young with simulated aspects of the larger society, in which they may develop the techniques and powers to deal with social relationships and to bring about social changes without creating social disorder. And with these same techniques and powers, the individual may realize the fullest meaning of his experience and gain increasing control over the pattern his life takes.

In all cases, however, the aims of formal education must be operational; that is, must be guides for the educator's observation of behavioral changes in the pupils and of their growing power to function effectively within the demanding social framework of the classroom. When educational aims are put into an operational context, with the classroom accepted as a societal entity, both teacher and pupil become directly involved in the "experiencing" of a developing social relationship. As the student changes, grows, and adapts in his social role, he is acquiring that most viable form of discipline, self-discipline, and thus contributing to the teacher's creation of a socially relevant order.

For Dewey, this "experiencing" is a process with both active and passive phases. The student is helped to make his experience educative, to internalize it, noting its sources, components, and consequences. With a growing commitment to this method of dealing with the self and others comes the beginning of intellectual commitment, reflected in such personal attitudes as "directness," "open-mindedness," "wholeheartedness," and "responsibility." The behavioral, and thus the social value of these attitudes is, of course, immense.

Finally, the "content" of this method, or what we might call the subject matter of formal schooling, is the creation of an environment which both stimulates and directs the pupil's educational development; that is, his intellectual habits and positive attitudes. Traditional subjects such as history and other organized bodies of knowledge serve the teacher as resources that assist in creating the desirable classroom environment, but they do not constitute the subject matter for the learner. For example, both history and geography prove invaluable sources *for the teacher,* by means of which he can assist the pupil in expanding *his* immediate experiences both temporally and spatially. A distinction must be drawn, in

Dewey's theory, between the psychological process or processes of learning and the logical form in which learned material can be stored for effective reuse. The two are not the same.

In *Democracy and Education,* Dewey argues that studies cannot be placed in a value hierarchy and that attempts to do so are misguided. To the extent that any study or body of knowledge is capable of expanding and extending the meaning of any experience, so in that particular instance it becomes intrinsically valuable and incomparable. Neither can studies be classed into the categories of labor and leisure; such a distinction is educationally irrelevant. Leisure must be considered as an opportunity to inquire freely, and not as freedom from all thinking and its attendant responsibilities.

Dewey maintains that the individual develops most fully when the power of authority derived from custom and tradition is reduced as a source of belief. Philosophy of education serves to point out obsolete educational values; it must criticize educational aims that are inconsistent with new knowledge and understandings derived from science. If formal education is essential to the growth of the democratic social order, if the principles of social environment are derived from scientific inquiry, then the value of educational philosophy is in its recognition of classroom procedure that is outmoded or sentimental and of new ways to forge the strong links of American culture. Such was Dewey's progressivism.

A few words now about the selections included here. The first selection represents an initial attempt to define "education"; the full definition of education is evolved throughout the entire text of *Democracy and Education.* Perhaps its most salient point is that education is a *process;* therefore, its meaning cannot be ascertained from a formal definition, but must be sought in a description of the process. The subject of the following selections is the definition of this process.

Every process must have its aim or goal; it must have a method by which it proceeds; and it must have an **outcome**, a desired result. Dewey is convinced of the interrelatedness of these three aspects of the process of education. The method of educating cannot be separated from the materials used; method merely states the way in which certain outcomes or products are effectively obtained. And for Dewey, the outcome or result of the process of educating *is* its true subject matter. It is the meanings, the significance, the habits and attitudes derived from having experienced the process. And such meanings are not separable from the aims and methods used in their development.

If we remember that both teacher and student are "experiencing" the educational process in its acute social form—the classroom—then it is clear that aim, method, and subject matter are not the same for both. This fact is essential to understanding and applying Dewey's general theory of education.

To what extent does *Democracy and Education* remain relevant today? Rarely in our history have the basic tenets of a democratic society been so severely challenged. Political and social institutions have become the focus of the challenge, with the nation's schools at the center. In *Democracy and Education* the challenge to our educational institutions was spelled out over fifty years ago, but it will be in the decade of the 1970's that education will have to answer that challenge. Seldom have the American people been forced into a position in which our choices may determine, once and for all, whether or not we are willing and able to support an open, democratic society. If we opt in favor of this, as we must, then Dewey provides us with a valuable guide to all that will be required to render our educational structures relevant.

What is relevant to educating an individual to function well as a free man in a free society remains constant. Therefore, Dewey's emphasis upon the "method of inquiry," which is really synonymous with "intelligent behavior," is quite as valid today as it was fifty years ago.

John Dewey was not dogmatic, even regarding his own views. When he speaks of production and productive individuals, he has in mind the assembly lines of 1910. That the schools must respond so as to assist the young in finding meaning in this sort of task was a guiding emphasis in Dewey's suggestions for curriculum design. However, the "productive" member of society today faces quite different requirements. The specific curriculum content recommended by Dewey in *Democracy and Education* must be revised in the light of new social demands and conditions—a revision in which Dewey would concur. But the question yet to be answered is: What will be the requirements for a productive individual in the 1970's and beyond?

EDUCATION AS CONSERVATIVE
AND PROGRESSIVE

• • • • •

We thus reach a technical definition of education: It is that reconstruction or reorganization of experience which adds to the meaning of experience, and which increases ability to direct the course of subsequent experience. (1) The increment of meaning corresponds to the increased perception of the connections and continuities of the activities in which we are engaged. The activity begins in an impulsive form; that is, it is blind. It does not know what it is about; that is to say, what are its interactions with other activities. An activity which brings education or instruction with it makes one aware of some of the connections which had been imperceptible. To recur to our simple example, a child who reaches for a bright light gets burned. Henceforth he *knows* that a certain act of touching in connection with a certain act of vision (and *vice-versa*) means heat and pain; or, a certain light means a source of heat. The acts by which a scientific man in his laboratory learns more about flame differ no whit in principle. By doing certain things, he makes perceptible certain connections of heat with other things, which had been previously ignored. Thus his acts in relation to these things get more meaning; he knows better what he is doing or "is about" when he has to do with them; he can *intend* consequences instead of just letting them happen—all synonymous ways of saying the same thing. At the same stroke, the flame has gained in meaning; all that is known about combustion, oxidation, about light and temperature, may become an intrinsic part of its intellectual content.

(2) The other side of an educative experience is an added power of subsequent direction or control. To say that one knows what he is about, or can intend certain consequences, is to say, of course, that he can better anticipate what is going to happen; that he can, therefore, get ready or prepare in advance so as to secure beneficial consequences and avert undesirable ones. A genuinely educative experience, then, one in which instruction is conveyed and ability increased, is contradistinguished from a routine activity on one hand, and a capricious activity on the other. (*a*) In the latter one "does not care what

happens"; one just lets himself go and avoids connecting the consequences of one's act (the evidences of its connections with other things)
with the act. It is customary to frown upon such aimless random activity,
treating it as willful mischief or carelessness or lawlessness. But there
is a tendency to seek the cause of such aimless activities in the youth's
own disposition, isolated from everything else. But in fact such activity
is explosive, and due to maladjustment with surroundings. Individuals
act capriciously whenever they act under external dictation, or from
being told, without having a purpose of their own or perceiving the
bearing of the deed upon other acts. One may learn by doing something
which he does not understand; even in the most intelligent action, we
do much which we do not mean, because the largest portion of the
connections of the act we consciously intend are not perceived or
anticipated. But we learn only because after the act is performed we
note results which we had not noted before. But much work in school
consists in setting up rules by which pupils are to act of such a sort that
even after pupils have acted, they are not led to see the connection
between the result—say the answer—and the method pursued. So far as
they are concerned, the whole thing is a trick and a kind of miracle.
Such action is essentially capricious, and leads to capricious habits.
(*b*) Routine action, action which is automatic, may increase skill to do
a *particular* thing. In so far, it might be said to have an educative
effect. But it does not lead to new perceptions of bearings and connections; it limits rather than widens the meaning-horizon. And since the
environment changes and our way of acting has to be modified in order
successfully to keep a balanced connection with things, an isolated
uniform way of acting becomes disastrous at some critical moment.
The vaunted "skill" turns out gross ineptitude.

The essential contrast of the idea of education as continuous reconstruction with the other one-sided conceptions . . . is that it identifies the
end (the result) and the process. This is verbally self-contradictory,
but only verbally. It means that experience as an active process occu-
pies time and that its later period completes its earlier portion; it
brings to light connections involved, but hitherto unperceived. The later
outcome thus reveals the meaning of the earlier, while the experience as
a whole establishes a bent or disposition toward the things possessing
this meaning. Every such continuous experience or activity is educative, and all education resides in having such experiences.

It remains only to point out . . . that the reconstruction of experience may be social as well as personal. For purposes of simplification we have spoken in the earlier chapters somewhat as if the education of the immature which fills them with the spirit of the social group to which they belong, were a sort of catching up of the child with the aptitudes and resources of the adult group. In static societies, societies which make the maintenance of established custom their measure of value, this conception applies in the main. But not in progressive communities. They endeavor to shape the experiences of the young so that instead of reproducing current habits, better habits shall be formed, and thus the future adult society be an improvement on their own. Men have long had some intimation of the extent to which education may be consciously used to eliminate obvious social evils through starting the young on paths which shall not produce these ills, and some idea of the extent in which education may be made an instrument of realizing the better hopes of men. But we are doubtless far from realizing the potential efficacy of education as a constructive agency of improving society, from realizing that it represents not only a development of children and youth but also of the future society of which they will be the constituents.

· · · · ·

AIMS IN EDUCATION

THE NATURE OF AN AIM

The account of education given in our earlier chapters virtually anticipated the results reached in a discussion of the purport of education in a democratic community. For it assumed that the aim of education is to enable individuals to continue their education—or that the object and reward of learning is continued capacity for growth. Now this idea cannot be applied to *all* the members of a society except where intercourse of man with man is mutual, and except where there is adequate provision for the reconstruction of social habits and institutions by means of wide stimulation arising from equitably distributed interests. And this means a democratic society. In our search for aims in education, we are not concerned, therefore, with finding an end outside of the educative process to which education is subordinate.

Our whole conception forbids. We are rather concerned with the contrast which exists when aims belong within the process in which they operate and when they are set up from without. And the latter state of affairs must obtain when social relationships are not equitably balanced. For in that case, some portions of the whole social group will find their aims determined by an external dictation; their aims will not arise from the free growth of their own experience, and their nominal aims will be means to more ulterior ends of others rather than truly their own.

Our first question is to define the nature of an aim so far as it falls within an activity, instead of being furnished from without. We approach the definition by a contrast of mere *results* with *ends*. Any exhibition of energy has results. The wind blows about the sands of the desert; the position of the grains is changed. Here is a result, an effect, but not an *end*. For there is nothing in the outcome which completes or fulfills what went before it. There is mere spatial redistribution. One state of affairs is just as good as any other. Consequently there is no basis upon which to select an earlier state of affairs as a beginning, later as an end, and to consider what intervenes as a process of transformation and realization.

Consider for example the activities of bees in contrast with the changes in the sands when the wind blows them about. The results of the bees' actions may be called ends not because they are designed or consciously intended, but because they are true terminations or completions of what has preceded. When the bees gather pollen and make wax and build cells, each step prepares the way for the next. When cells are built, the queen lays eggs in them; when eggs are laid, they are sealed and bees brood them and keep them at a temperature required to hatch them. When they are hatched, bees feed the young till they can take care of themselves. Now we are so familiar with such facts that we are apt to dismiss them on the ground that life and instinct are a kind of miraculous thing anyway. Thus we fail to note what the essential characteristic of the event is; namely, the significance of the temporal place and order of each element; the way each prior event leads into its successor while the successor takes up what is furnished and utilizes it for some other stage, until we arrive at the end, which, as it were, summarizes and finishes off the process.

Since aims relate always to results, the first thing to look to when it is a question of aims, is whether the work assigned possesses intrinsic continuity. Or is it a mere serial aggregate of acts, first doing one thing and then another? To talk about an educational aim when approximately each act of a pupil is dictated by the teacher, when the only order in the sequence of his acts is that which comes from the assignment of lessons and the giving of directions by another, is to talk nonsense. It is equally fatal to an aim to permit capricious or discontinuous action in the name of spontaneous self-expression. An aim implies an orderly and ordered activity, one in which the order consists in the progressive completing of a process. Given an activity having a time span and cumulative growth within the time succession, an aim means foresight in advance of the end or possible termination. If bees anticipated the consequences of their activity, if they perceived their end in imaginative foresight, they would have the primary element in an aim. Hence it is nonsense to talk about the aim of education —or any other undertaking—where conditions do not permit of foresight of results, and do not stimulate a person to look ahead to see what the outcome of a given activity is to be.

In the next place the aim as a foreseen end gives direction to the activity; it is not an idle view of a mere spectator, but influences the steps taken to reach the end. The foresight functions in three ways. In the first place, it involves careful observation of the given conditions to see what are the means available for reaching the end, and to discover the hindrances in the way. In the second place, it suggests the proper order or sequence in the use of means. It facilitates an economical selection and arrangement. In the third place, it makes choice of alternatives possible. If we can predict the outcome of acting this way or that, we can then compare the value of the two courses of action; we can pass judgment upon their relative desirability. If we know that stagnant water breeds mosquitoes and that they are likely to carry disease, we can, disliking that anticipated result, take steps to avert it. Since we do not anticipate results as mere intellectual onlookers, but as persons concerned in the outcome, we are partakers in the process which produces the result. We intervene to bring about this result or that.

Of course these three points are closely connected with one another. We can definitely foresee results only as we make careful scrutiny of present conditions, and the importance of the outcome supplies the motive for observations. The more adequate our observations, the more varied is the scene of conditions and obstructions that presents itself, and the more numerous are the alternatives between which choice may be made. In turn, the more numerous the recognized possibilities of the situation, or alternatives of action, the more meaning does the chosen activity possess, and the more flexibly controllable is it. Where only a single outcome has been thought of, the mind has nothing else to think of; the meaning attaching to the act is limited. One only steams ahead toward the mark. Sometimes such a narrow course may be effective. But if unexpected difficulties offer themselves, one has not as many resources at command as if he had chosen the same line of action after a broader survey of the possibilities of the field. He cannot make needed readjustments readily.

The net conclusion is that acting with an aim is all one with acting intelligently. To foresee a terminus of an act is to have a basis upon which to observe, to select, and to order objects and our own capacities. To do these things means to have a mind—for mind is precisely intentional purposeful activity controlled by perception of facts and their relationships to one another. To have a mind to do a thing is to foresee a future possibility; it is to have a plan for its accomplishment; it is to note the means which make the plan capable of execution and the obstructions in the way,—or, if it is really a *mind* to do the thing and not a vague aspiration—it is to have a plan which takes account of resources and difficulties. Mind is capacity to refer present conditions to future results, and future consequences to present conditions. And these traits are just what is meant by having an aim or a purpose. A man is stupid or blind or unintelligent—lacking in mind—just in the degree in which in any activity he does not know what he is about, namely, the probable consequences of his acts. A man is imperfectly intelligent when he contents himself with looser guesses about the outcome than is needful, just taking a chance with his luck, or when he forms plans apart from study of the actual conditions, including his own capacities. Such relative absence of mind means to make our feelings the measure of what is to happen. To be intelligent we must "stop, look, listen" in making the plan of an activity.

To identify acting with an aim and intelligent activity is enough to show its value—its function in experience. We are only too given to making an entity out of the abstract noun "consciousness." We forget that it comes from the adjective "conscious." To be conscious is to be aware of what we are about; conscious signifies the deliberate, observant, planning traits of activity. Consciousness is nothing which we have which gazes idly on the scene around one or which has impressions made upon it by physical things; it is a name for the purposeful quality of an activity, for the fact that it is directed by an aim. Put the other way about, to have an aim is to act with meaning, not like an automatic machine; it is to *mean* to do something and to perceive the meaning of things in the light of that intent.

THE CRITERIA OF GOOD AIMS

We may apply the results of our discussion to a consideration of the criteria involved in a correct establishing of aims. (1) The aim set up must be an outgrowth of existing conditions. It must be based upon a consideration of what is already going on; upon the resources and difficulties of the situation. Theories about the proper end of our activities—educational and moral theories—often violate this principle. They assume ends lying *outside* our activities; ends foreign to the concrete makeup of the situation; ends which issue from some outside source. Then the problem is to bring our activities to bear upon the realization of these externally supplied ends. They are something for which we *ought* to act. In any case such "aims" limit intelligence; they are not the expression of mind in foresight, observation, and choice of the better among alternative possibilities. They limit intelligence because, given ready-made, they must be imposed by some authority external to intelligence, leaving to the latter nothing but a mechanical choice of means.

(2) We have spoken as if aims could be completely formed prior to the attempt to realize them. This impression must now be qualified. The aim as it first emerges is a mere tentative sketch. The act of striving to realize it tests its worth. If it suffices to direct activity successfully, nothing more is required, since its whole function is to set a mark in advance; and at times a mere hint may suffice. But usually—at least in complicated situations—acting upon it brings to light conditions which had been overlooked. This calls for revision of the original aim; it has to be added to and subtracted from. An aim must, then, be *flexible;* it must be capable of alteration to meet circumstances. An end established externally to the process of action is always rigid. Being inserted or imposed from without, it is not supposed to have a working relationship to the concrete conditions of the situation. What happens in the

course of action neither confirms, refutes, nor alters it. Such an end can only be insisted upon. The failure that results from its lack of adaptation is attributed simply to the perverseness of conditions, not to the fact that the end is not reasonable under the circumstances. The value of a legitimate aim, on the contrary, lies in the fact that we can use it to change conditions. It is a method for dealing with conditions so as to effect desirable alterations in them. A farmer who should passively accept things just as he finds them would make as great a mistake as he who framed his plans in complete disregard of what soil, climate, etc., permit. One of the evils of an abstract or remote external aim in education is that its very inapplicability in practice is likely to react into a haphazard snatching at immediate conditions. A good aim surveys the present state of experience of pupils, and forming a tentative plan of treatment, keeps the plan constantly in view and yet modifies it as conditions develop. The aim, in short, is experimental, and hence constantly growing as it is tested in action.

(3) The aim must always represent a freeing of activities. The term *end in view* is suggestive, for it puts before the mind the termination or conclusion of some process. The only way in which we can define an activity is by putting before ourselves the objects in which it terminates —as one's aim in shooting is the target. But we must remember that the *object* is only a mark or sign by which the mind specifies the *activity* one desires to carry out. Strictly speaking, not the target but *hitting* the target is the end in view; one *takes* aim by means of the target, but also by the sight on the gun. The different objects which are thought of are means of *directing* the activity. Thus one aims at, say, a rabbit; what he wants is to shoot straight: a certain kind of activity. Or, if it is the rabbit he wants, it is not rabbit apart from his activity, but as a factor in activity; he wants to eat the rabbit, or to show it as evidence of his marksmanship—he wants to do something with it. The doing with the thing, not the thing in isolation, is his end. The object is but a phase of the active end,—continuing the activity successfully. This is what is meant by the phrase, used above, "freeing activity."

In contrast with fulfilling some process in order that activity may go on, stands the static character of an end which is imposed from without the activity. It is always conceived of as fixed; it is *something* to be attained and possessed. When one has such a notion, activity is a mere unavoidable means to something else; it is not significant or important on its own account. As compared with the end it is but a necessary evil; something which must be gone through before one can reach the object which is alone worth while. In other words, the external idea of the aim leads to a separation of means from end, while an end which grows up within an activity as plan for its direction is always both ends and means, the distinction being only one of convenience. Every means is a temporary end until we have attained it. Every end becomes a means of carrying activity further as soon as it is achieved. We call it end when it marks off the future direction of the activity in which we are engaged; means when it marks off the present direction. Every divorce of end from means diminishes by that much the significance of the activity and tends to reduce it to a drudgery from which one would escape if he could. A farmer has to use plants and animals to carry on his farming activities. It certainly makes a great difference to his life whether he is fond of them, or whether he regards them merely as means which he has to employ to get something else in which alone he is interested. In the former case, his entire course of activity is significant; each phase of it has its own value. He has the experience of realizing his end at every stage; the postponed aim, or end in view, being merely a sight ahead by which to keep his activity going fully and freely. For if he does not look ahead, he is more likely to find himself blocked. The aim is as definitely a *means* of action as is any other portion of an activity.

APPLICATIONS IN EDUCATION

There is nothing peculiar about educational aims. They are just like aims in any directed occupation. The educator, like the farmer, has certain things to do, certain resources with which to do, and certain obstacles with which to contend. The conditions with which the farmer deals, whether as obstacles or resources, have their own structure and operation independently of any purpose of his. Seeds sprout, rain falls, the sun shines, insects devour, blight comes, the seasons change. His aim is simply to utilize these various conditions; to make his activities and their energies work together, instead of against one another. It would be absurd if the farmer set up a purpose of farming, without any reference to these conditions of soil, climate, characteristic of plant growth, etc. His purpose is simply a foresight of the consequences of his energies connected with those of the things about him, a foresight used to direct his movements from day to day. Foresight of possible consequences leads to more careful and extensive observation of the nature and performances of the things he had to do with, and to laying out a plan—that is, of a certain order in the acts to be performed.

It is the same with the educator, whether parent or teacher. It is as absurd for the latter to set up his "own" aims as the proper objects of the growth of the children as it would be for the farmer to set up an ideal of farming irrespective of conditions. Aims mean acceptance of responsibility for the observations, anticipations, and arrangements required in carrying on a function—whether farming or educating. Any aim is of value so far as it assists observation, choice, and planning in carrying on activity from moment to moment and hour to hour; if it gets in the way of the individual's own common sense (as it will surely do if imposed from without or accepted on authority) it does harm.

And it is well to remind ourselves that education as such has no aims. Only persons, parents, and teachers, etc., have aims, not an abstract idea like education. And consequently their purposes are indefinitely varied, differing with different children, changing as children grow and with the growth of experience on the part of the one who teaches. Even the most valid aims which can be put in words will, as words, do more harm than good unless one recognizes that they are not aims, but rather suggestions to educators as to how to observe, how to look ahead, and how to choose in liberating and directing the energies of the concrete situations in which they find themselves. As a recent writer has said: "To lead this boy to read Scott's novels instead of old Sleuth's stories; to teach this girl to sew; to root out the habit of bullying from John's make-up; to prepare this class to study medicine,—these are samples of the millions of aims we have actually before us in the concrete work of education."

Bearing these qualifications in mind, we shall proceed to state some of the characteristics found in all good educational aims. (1) An educational aim must be founded upon the intrinsic activities and needs (including original instincts and acquired habits) of the given individual to be educated. The tendency of such an aim as preparation is, as we have seen, to omit existing powers, and find the aim in some remote accomplishment or responsibility. In general, there is a disposition to take considerations which are dear to the hearts of adults and set them up as ends irrespective of the capacities of those educated. There is also an inclination to propound aims which are so uniform as to neglect the specific powers and requirements of an individual, forgetting that all learning is something which happens to an individual at a given time and place. The larger range of perception of the adult is of great value in observing the abilities and weaknesses of the young, in deciding what they may amount to. Thus the artistic capacities of the adult exhibit what certain tendencies of the child are capable of; if we did not have the adult achievements we should be without assurance as to the significance of the drawing, reproducing, modeling, coloring activities of childhood. So if it were not for adult language, we should not be able to see the import of the babbling impulses of infancy. But it is one thing to use adult accomplishments as a context in which to place and survey the doings of childhood and youth; it is quite another to set them up as a fixed aim without regard to the concrete activities of those educated.

(2) An aim must be capable of translation into a method of coöperating with the activities of those undergoing instruction. It must suggest the kind of environment needed to liberate and to organize *their* capacities. Unless it lends itself to the construction of specific procedures, and unless these procedures test, correct, and amplify the aim, the latter is worthless. Instead of helping the specific task of teaching, it prevents the use of ordinary judgment in observing and sizing up the situation. It operates to exclude recognition of everything except what squares up with the fixed end in view. Every rigid aim just because it is rigidly given seems to render it unnecessary to give careful attention to concrete conditions. Since it *must* apply anyhow, what is the use of noting details which do not count?

The vice of externally imposed ends has deep roots. Teachers receive them from superior authorities; these authorities accept them from what is current in the community. The teachers impose them upon children. As a first consequence, the intelligence of the teacher is not free; it is confined to receiving the aims laid down from above. Too rarely is the individual teacher so free from the dictation of authoritative supervisor, textbook on methods, prescribed course of study, etc., that he can let his mind come to close quarters with the pupil's mind and the subject matter. This distrust of the teacher's experience is then reflected in lack of confidence in the responses of pupils. The latter receive their aims through a double or treble external imposition, and are constantly confused by the conflict between the aims which are natural to their own experience at the time and those in which they are taught to acquiesce. Until the democratic criterion of the intrinsic significance of every growing experience is recognized, we shall be intellectually confused by the demand for adaptation to external aims.

(3) Educators have to be on their guard against ends that are alleged to be general and ultimate. Every activity, however specific, is, of course, general in its ramified connections, for it leads out indefinitely into other things. So far as a general idea makes us more alive to these connections, it cannot be too general. But "general" also means "abstract," or detached from all specific context. And such abstractness means remoteness, and throws us back, once more, upon teaching and learning as mere means of getting ready for an end disconnected from the means. That education is literally and all the time its own reward means that no alleged study or discipline is educative unless it is worth while in its own immediate having. A truly general aim broadens the outlook; it stimulates one to take more consequences (connections) into account. This means a wider and more flexible observation of means. The more interacting forces, for example, the farmer takes into account, the more varied will be his immediate resources. He will see a greater number of possible starting places, and a greater number of ways of getting at what he wants to do. The fuller one's conception of possible future achievements, the less his present activity is tied down to a small number of alternatives. If one knew enough, one could start almost anywhere and sustain his activities continuously and fruitfully.

Understanding then the term general or comprehensive aim simply in the sense of a broad survey of the field of present activities, we shall take up some of the larger ends which have currency in the educational theories of the day, and consider what light they throw upon the immediate concrete and diversified aims which are always the educator's real concern. We premise (as indeed immediately follows from what has been said) that there is no need of making a choice among them or regarding them as competitors. When we come to act in a tangible way we have to select or choose a particular act at a particular time, but any number of comprehensive ends may exist without competition, since they mean simply different ways of looking at the same scene. One cannot climb a number of different mountains simultaneously, but the views had when different mountains are ascended supplement one another: they do not set up incompatible, competing worlds. Or, putting the matter in a slightly different way, one statement of an end may suggest certain questions and observations, and another statement another set of questions, calling for other observations. Then the more general ends we have, the better. One statement will emphasize what another slurs over. What a plurality of hypotheses does for the scientific investigator, a plurality of stated aims may do for the instructor.

SUMMARY

An aim denotes the result of any natural process brought to consciousness and made a factor in determining present observation and choice of ways of acting. It signifies that an activity has become intelligent. Specifically it means foresight of the alternative consequences attendant upon acting in a given situation in different ways, and the use of what is anticipated to direct observation and experiment. A true aim is thus opposed at every point to an aim which is imposed upon a process of action from without. The latter is fixed and rigid; it is not a stimulus to intelligence in the given situation, but is an externally dictated order to do such and such things. Instead of connecting directly with present activities, it is remote, divorced from the means by which it is to be reached. Instead of suggesting a freer and better balanced activity, it is a limit set to activity. In education, the currency of these externally imposed aims is responsible for the emphasis put upon the notion of preparation for a remote future and for rendering the work of both teacher and pupil mechanical and slavish.

THE NATURE OF METHOD

THE UNITY OF SUBJECT MATTER AND METHOD

The trinity of school topics is subject matter, methods, and administration or government. . . . It remains to disentangle them from the context in which they have been referred to, and discuss explicitly their nature. We shall begin with the topic of method. . . . Before taking it up, it may be well, however, to call express attention to one implication of our theory; the connection of subject matter and method with each other. The idea that mind and the world of things and persons are two separate and independent realms—a theory which philosophically is known as dualism—carries with it the conclusion that method and subject matter of instruction are separate affairs. Subject matter then becomes a ready-made systematized classification of the facts and principles of the world of nature and man. Method then has for its province a consideration of the ways in which this antecedent subject matter may be best presented to and impressed upon the mind; or, a consideration of the ways in which the mind may be externally brought to bear upon the matter so as to facilitate its acquisition and possession. In theory, at least, one might deduce from a science of the mind as something existing by itself a complete theory of methods of learning, with no knowledge of the subjects to which the methods are to be applied. Since many who are actually most proficient in various branches of subject matter are wholly innocent of these methods, this state of affairs gives opportunity for the retort that pedagogy, as an alleged science of methods of the mind in learning, is futile;—a mere screen for concealing the necessity a teacher is under of profound and accurate acquaintance with the subject in hand.

But since thinking is a directed movement of subject matter to a completing issue, and since mind is the deliberate and intentional phase of the process, the notion of any such split is radically false. The fact that the material of a science is organized is evidence that it has already been subjected to intelligence; it has been methodized, so to say. Zoölogy as a systematic branch of knowledge represents crude, scattered facts of our ordinary acquaintance with animals after they have been subjected to careful examination, to deliberate supplementation, and to arrangement to bring out connections which assist observation, memory, and further inquiry. Instead of furnishing a starting point for learning, they mark out a consummation. Method means that arrangement *of* subject matter which makes it most effective in use. Never is method something outside of the material.

How about method from the standpoint of an individual who is dealing with subject matter? Again, it is not something external. It is simply an effective treatment *of* material—efficiency meaning such treatment as utilizes the material (puts it to a purpose) with a minimum of waste of time and energy. We can distinguish a *way* of acting, and discuss it by itself; but the way *exists* only as way-of-dealing-with-material. Method is not antithetical to subject matter; it is the effective direction of subject matter to desired results. It is antithetical to random and ill-considered action,—ill-considered signifying ill-adapted.

The statement that method means directed movement of subject matter towards ends is formal. An illustration may give it content. Every artist must have a method, a technique, in doing his work. Piano playing is not hitting the keys at random. It is an orderly way of using them, and the order is not something which exists ready-made in the musician's hands or brain prior to an activity dealing with the piano. Order is found in the disposition of acts which use the piano and the hands and brain so as to achieve the result intended. It is the action of the piano directed to accomplish the purpose of the piano as a musical instrument. It is the same with "pedagogical" method. The only difference is that the piano is a mechanism constructed in advance for a single end; while the material of study is capable of indefinite uses. But even in this regard the illustration may apply if we consider the infinite variety of kinds of music which a piano may produce, and the variations in technique required in the different musical results secured. Method in any case is but an effective way of employing some material for some end.

These considerations may be generalized by going back to the conception of experience. Experience as the perception of the connection between something tried and something undergone in consequence is a process. Apart from effort to control the course which the process takes, there is no distinction of subject matter and method. There is simply an activity which includes both what an individual does and what the environment does. A piano player who had perfect mastery of his instrument would have no occasion to distinguish between his contribution and that of the piano. In well-formed, smooth-running functions of any sort—skating, conversing, hearing music, enjoying a landscape—there is no consciousness of separation of the method of the person and of the subject matter. In whole-hearted play and work there is the same phenomenon.

When we reflect upon an experience instead of just having it, we inevitably distinguish between our own attitude and the objects toward which we sustain the attitude. When a man is eating, he is eating *food*. He does not divide his act into eating *and* food. But if he makes a scientific investigation of the act, such a discrimination is the first thing he would effect. He would examine on the one hand the properties of the nutritive material, and on the other hand the acts of the organism in appropriating and digesting. Such reflection upon experience gives rise to a distinction of *what* we experience (the experienc*ed*) and the experienc*ing*—the *how*. When we give names to this distinction we have subject matter and method as our terms. There is the thing seen, heard, loved, hated, imagined, and there is the act of seeing, hearing, loving, hating, imagining, etc.

This distinction is so natural and so important for certain purposes, that we are only too apt to regard it as a separation in existence and not as a distinction in thought. Then we make a division between a self and the environment or world. This separation is the root of the dualism of method and subject matter. That is, we assume that knowing, feeling, willing, etc., are things which belong to the self or mind in its isolation, and which then may be brought to bear upon an independent subject matter. We assume that the things which belong in isolation to the self or mind have their own laws of operation irrespective of the modes of active energy of the object. These laws are supposed to furnish method. It would be no less absurd to suppose that men can eat without eating something, or that the structure and movements of the jaws, throat muscles, the digestive activities of stomach, etc., are not what they are *because* of the material with which their activity is engaged. Just as the organs of the organism are a continuous part of the very world in which food materials exist, so the capacities of seeing, hearing, loving, imagining are intrinsically connected with the subject matter of the world. They are more truly ways in which the environment enters into experience and functions there than they are independent acts brought to bear upon things. Experience, in short, is not a combination of mind and world, subject and object, method and subject matter, but is a single continuous interaction of a great diversity (literally countless in number) of energies.

For the purpose of *controlling* the course or direction which the moving unity of experience takes we draw a mental distinction between the how and the what. While there is no *way* of walking or of eating or of learning over and above the actual walking, eating, and studying, there are certain elements in the act which give the key to its more effective control. Special attention to these elements makes them more obvious to perception (letting other factors recede for the time being from conspicuous recognition). Getting an idea of *how* the experience proceeds indicates to us what factors must be secured or modified in order that it may go on more successfully. This is only a somewhat elaborate way of saying that if a man watches carefully the growth of several plants, some of which do well and some of which amount to little or nothing, he may be able to detect the special conditions upon which the prosperous development of a plant depends. These conditions, stated in an orderly sequence, would constitute the method or way or manner of its growth. There is no difference between the growth of a plant and the prosperous development of an experience. It is not easy, in either case, to seize upon just the factors which make for its best movement. But study of cases of success and failure, and minute and extensive comparison, helps to seize upon causes. When we have arranged these causes in order, we have a method of procedure or a technique.

A consideration of some evils in education that flow from the isolation of method from subject matter will make the point more definite. (*i*) In the first place, there is the neglect (of which we have spoken) of concrete situations of experience. There can be no discovery of a method without cases to be studied. The method is derived from observation of what actually happens, with a view to seeing that it happen better next time. But in instruction and discipline, there is rarely sufficient opportunity for children and youth to have the direct normal experiences from which educators might derive an idea of method or order of best development. Experiences are had under conditions of such constraint that they throw little or no light upon the normal course of an experience to its fruition. "Methods" have then to be authoritatively recommended to teachers, instead of being an expression of their own intelligent observations. Under such circumstances, they have a mechanical uniformity, assumed to be alike for all minds. Where flexible personal experiences are promoted by providing an environment which calls out directed occupations in work and play, the methods ascertained will vary with individuals—for it is certain that each individual has something characteristic in his way of going at things.

(*ii*) In the second place, the notion of methods isolated from subject matter is responsible for the false conceptions of discipline and interest already noted. When the effective way of managing material is treated as something ready-made apart from material, there are just three possible ways in which to establish a relationship lacking by assumption. One is to utilize excitement, shock of pleasure, tickling the palate. Another is to make the consequences of not attending painful; we may use the menace of harm to motivate concern with the alien subject matter. Or a direct appeal may be made to the person to put forth effort without any reason. We may rely upon immediate strain of "will." In practice, however, the latter method is effectual only when instigated by fear of unpleasant results.

(*iii*) In the third place, the act of learning is made a direct and conscious end in itself. Under normal conditions, learning is a product and reward of occupation with subject matter. Children do not set out, consciously, to learn walking or talking. One sets out to give his impulses for communication and for fuller intercourse with others a show. He learns in consequence of his direct activities. The better methods of teaching a child, say, to read, follow the same road. They do not fix his attention upon the fact that he has to learn something and so make his attitude self-conscious and constrained. They engage his activities, and in the process of engagement he learns: the same is true of the more successful methods in dealing with number or whatever. But when the subject matter is not used in carrying forward impulses and habits to significant results, it is just something to be learned. The pupil's attitude to it is just that of having to learn it. Conditions more unfavorable to an alert and concentrated response would be hard to devise. Frontal attacks are even more wasteful in learning than in war. This does not mean, however, that students are to be seduced unaware into preoccupation with lessons. It means that they shall be occupied with them for real reasons or ends, and not just as something to be learned. This is accomplished whenever the pupil perceives the place occupied by the subject matter in the fulfilling of some experience.

(*iv*) In the fourth place, under the influence of the conception of the separation of mind and material, method tends to be reduced to a cut and dried routine, to following mechanically prescribed steps. No one can tell in how many schoolrooms children reciting in arithmetic or grammar are compelled to go through, under the alleged sanction of method, certain preordained verbal formulae. Instead of being encouraged to attack their topics directly, experimenting with methods that seem promising and learning to discriminate by the consequences that accrue, it is assumed that there is one fixed method to be followed. It is also naïvely assumed that if the pupils make their statements and explanations in a certain form of "analysis," their mental habits will in time conform. Nothing has brought pedagogical theory into greater disrepute than the belief that it is identified with handing out to teachers recipes and models to be followed in teaching. Flexibility and initiative in dealing with problems are characteristic of any conception to which method is a way of managing material to develop a conclusion. Mechanical rigid woodenness is an inevitable corollary of any theory which separates mind from activity motivated by a purpose.

METHOD AS GENERAL AND AS INDIVIDUAL

In brief, the method of teaching is the method of an art, of action intelligently directed by ends. But the practice of a fine art is far from being a matter of extemporized inspirations. Study of the operations and results of those in the past who have greatly succeeded is essential. There is always a tradition, or schools of art, definite enough to impress beginners, and often to take them captive. Methods of artists in every branch depend upon thorough acquaintance with materials and tools; the painter must know canvas, pigments, brushes, and the technique of manipulation of all his appliances. Attainment of this knowledge requires persistent and concentrated attention to objective materials. The artist studies the progress of his own attempts to see what succeeds and what fails. The assumption that there are no alternatives between following ready-made rules and trusting to native gifts, the inspiration of the moment and undirected "hard work," is contradicted by the procedures of every art.

Such matters as knowledge of the past, of current technique, of materials, of the ways in which one's own best results are assured, supply the material for what may be called *general* method. There exists a cumulative body of fairly stable methods for reaching results, a body authorized by past experience and by intellectual analysis, which an individual ignores at his peril. As was pointed out in the discussion of habit-forming . . . , there is always a danger that these methods will become mechanized and rigid, mastering an agent instead of being powers at command for his own ends. But it is also true that the innovator who achieves anything enduring, whose work is more than a passing sensation, utilizes classic methods more than may appear to himself or to his critics. He devotes them to new uses, and in so far transforms them.

Education also has its general methods. And if the application of this remark is more obvious in the case of the teacher than of the pupil, it is equally real in the case of the latter. Part of his learning, a very important part, consists in *becoming* master of the methods which the experience of others has shown to be more efficient in like cases of getting knowledge. These general methods are in no way opposed to individual initiative and originality—to personal ways of doing things. On the contrary they are reinforcements of them. For there is radical difference between even the most general method and a prescribed rule. The latter is a *direct* guide to action; the former operates indirectly through the enlightenment it supplies as to ends and means. It operates, that is to say, through intelligence, and not through conformity to orders externally imposed. Ability to use even in a masterly way an established technique gives no warranty of artistic work, for the latter also depends upon an animating idea.

If knowledge of methods used by others does not directly tell us what to do, or furnish ready-made models, how does it operate? What is meant by calling a method intellectual? Take the case of a physician. No mode of behavior more imperiously demands knowledge of established modes of diagnosis and treatment than does his. But after all, cases are *like,* not identical. To be used intelligently, existing practices, however authorized they may be, have to be adapted to the exigencies of particular cases. Accordingly, recognized procedures indicate to the physician what inquiries to set on foot for himself, what measures to *try*. They are standpoints from which to carry on investigations; they economize a survey of the features of the particular case by suggesting the things to be especially looked into. The physician's own personal attitudes, his own ways (individual methods) of dealing with the situation in which he is concerned, are not subordinated to the general principles of procedure, but are facilitated and directed by the latter. The instance may serve to point out the value to the teacher of a knowledge of the psychological methods and the empirical devices found useful in the past. When they get in the way of his own common sense, when they come between him and the situation in which he has to act, they are worse than useless. But if he has acquired them as intellectual aids in sizing up the needs, resources, and difficulties of the unique experiences in which he engages, they are of constructive value. In the last resort, just because *everything* depends upon his own methods of response, *much* depends upon how far he can utilize, in making his own response, the knowledge which has accrued in the experience of others.

As already intimated, every word of this account is directly applicable also to the method of the pupil, the way of learning. To suppose that students, whether in the primary school or in the university, can be supplied with models of method to be followed in acquiring and expounding a subject is to fall into a self-deception that has lamentable consequences. . . . One must make his own reaction in any case. Indications of the standardized or general methods used in like cases by others—particularly by those who are already experts—are of worth or of harm according as they make his personal reaction more intelligent or as they induce a person to dispense with exercise of his own judgment.

If what was said earlier . . . about originality of thought seemed overstrained, demanding more of education than the capacities of average human nature permit, the difficulty is that we lie under the incubus of a superstition. We have set up the notion of mind at large, of intellectual method that is the same for all. Then we regard individuals as differing in the *quantity* of mind with which they are charged. Ordinary persons are then expected to be ordinary. Only the exceptional are allowed to have originality. The measure of difference between the average student and the genius is a measure of the absence of originality in the former. But this notion of mind in general is a fiction. How one person's abilities compare in quantity with those of another is none of the teacher's business. It is irrelevant to his work. What is required is that every individual shall have opportunities to employ his own powers in activities that have meaning. Mind, individual method, originality (these are convertible terms) signify the *quality* of purposive or directed action. If we act upon this conviction, we shall secure more originality even by the conventional standard than now develops. Imposing an alleged uniform general method upon everybody breeds mediocrity in all but the very exceptional. And measuring originality by deviation from the mass breeds eccentricity in them. Thus we stifle the distinctive quality of the many, and save in rare instances (like, say, that of Darwin) infect the rare geniuses with an unwholesome quality.

THE TRAITS OF INDIVIDUAL METHOD

The most general features of the method of knowing have been given in our chapter on thinking. They are the features of the reflective situation: Problem, collection and analysis of *data,* projection and elaboration of suggestions or ideas, experimental application and testing; the resulting conclusion or judgment. The specific elements of an individual's method or way of attack upon a problem are found ultimately in his native tendencies and his acquired habits and interests. The method of one will vary from that of another (and *properly* vary) as his original instinctive capacities vary, as his past experiences and his preferences vary. Those who have already studied these matters are in possession of information which will help teachers in understanding the responses different pupils make, and help them in guiding these responses to greater efficiency. Child-study, psychology, and a knowledge of social environment supplement the personal acquaintance gained by the teacher. But methods remain the personal concern, approach, and attack of an individual, and no catalogue can ever exhaust their diversity of form and tint.

Some attitudes may be named, however, which are central in effective intellectual ways of dealing with subject matter. Among the most important are directness, open-mindedness, single-mindedness (or whole-heartedness), and responsibility.

1. It is easier to indicate what is meant by directness through negative terms than in positive ones. Self-consciousness, embarrassment, and constraint are its menacing foes. They indicate that a person is not immediately concerned with subject matter. Something has come between which deflects concern to side issues. A self-conscious person is partly thinking about his problem and partly about what others think of his performances. Diverted energy means loss of power and confusion of ideas. Taking an attitude is by no means identical with being conscious of one's attitude. The former is spontaneous, naïve, and simple. It is a sign of whole-souled relationship between a person and what he is dealing with. The latter is not of

necessity abnormal. It is sometimes the easiest way of correcting a false method of approach, and of improving the effectiveness of the means one is employing,—as golf players, piano players, public speakers, etc., have occasionally to give especial attention to their position and movements. But this need *is* occasional and temporary. When it is effectual a person thinks of himself in terms of what is to be done, as one means among others of the realization of an end—as in the case of a tennis player practicing to get the "feel" of a stroke. In abnormal cases, one thinks of himself not as part of the agencies of execution, but as a separate object—as when the player strikes an attitude thinking of the impression it will make upon spectators, or is worried because of the impression he fears his movements give rise to.

Confidence is a good name for what is intended by the term directness. It should not be confused, however, with *self*-confidence which may be a form of self-consciousness—or of "cheek." Confidence is not a name for what one thinks or feels about his attitude; it is not reflex. It denotes the straightforwardness with which one goes at what he has to do. It denotes not *conscious* trust in the efficacy of one's powers but unconscious faith in the possibilities of the situation. It signifies rising to the needs of the situation.

We have already pointed out . . . the objections to making students emphatically aware of the fact that they are studying or learning. Just in the degree in which they are induced by the conditions to be so aware, they are *not* studying and learning. They are in a divided and complicated attitude. Whatever methods of a teacher call a pupil's attention off from what he has to do and transfer it to his own attitude towards what he is doing impair directness of concern and action. Persisted in, the pupil acquires a permanent tendency to fumble, to gaze about aimlessly, to look for some clew of action beside that which the subject matter supplies. Dependence upon extraneous suggestions and directions, a state of foggy confusion, take the place of that sureness with which children (and grown-up people who have not been sophisticated by "education") confront the situations of life.

2. Open-mindedness. Partiality is, as we have seen, an accompaniment of the existence of interest, since this means sharing, partaking, taking sides in some movement. All the more reason, therefore, for an attitude of mind which actively welcomes suggestions and relevant information from all sides. In the chapter on Aims it was shown that foreseen ends are factors in the development of a changing situation.

They are the means by which the direction of action is controlled. They are subordinate to the situation, therefore, not the situation to them. They are not ends in the sense of finalities to which everything must be bent and sacrificed. They are, as foreseen, *means* of guiding the development of a situation. A target is not the future goal of shooting; it is the centering factor in a present shooting. Openness of mind means accessibility of mind to any and every consideration that will throw light upon the situation that needs to be cleared up, and that will help determine the consequences of acting this way or that. Efficiency in accomplishing ends which have been settled upon as unalterable can coexist with a narrowly opened mind. But intellectual growth means constant expansion of horizons and consequent formation of new purposes and new responses. These are impossible without an active disposition to welcome points of view hitherto alien; an active desire to entertain considerations which modify existing purposes. Retention of capacity to grow is the reward of such intellectual hospitality. The worst thing about stubbornness of mind, about prejudices, is that they arrest development; they shut the mind off from new stimuli. Openmindedness means retention of the childlike attitude; closed-mindedness means premature intellectual old age.

Exorbitant desire for uniformity of procedure and for prompt external results are the chief foes which the open-minded attitude meets in school. The teacher who does not permit and encourage diversity of operation in dealing with questions is imposing intellectual blinders upon pupils—restricting their vision to the one path the teacher's mind happens to approve. Probably the chief cause of devotion to rigidity of method is, however, that it seems to promise speedy, accurately measurable, correct results. The zeal for "answers" is the explanation of much of the zeal for rigid and mechanical methods. Forcing and overpressure have the same origin, and the same result upon alert and varied intellectual interest.

Open-mindedness is not the same as empty-mindedness. To hang out a sign saying "Come right in; there is no one at home" is not the equivalent of hospitality. But there is a kind of passivity, willingness to let experiences accumulate and sink in and ripen, which is an essential of development. Results (external answers or solutions) may be hurried; processes may not be forced. They take their own time to mature. Were all instructors to realize that the quality of mental process, not the production of correct answers, is the measure of educative growth something hardly less than a revolution in teaching would be worked.

3. Single-mindedness. So far as the word is concerned, much that was said under the head of "directness" is applicable. But what the word is here intended to convey is *completeness* of interest, unity of purpose; the absence of suppressed but effectual ulterior aims for which the professed aim is but a mask. It is equivalent to mental integrity. Absorption, engrossment, full concern with subject matter for its own sake, nurture it. Divided interest and evasion destroy it.

Intellectual integrity, honesty, and sincerity are at bottom not matters of conscious purpose but of quality of active response. Their acquisition is fostered of course by conscious intent, but self-deception is very easy. Desires are urgent. When the demands and wishes of others forbid their direct expression they are easily driven into subterranean and deep channels. Entire surrender, and wholehearted adoption of the course of action demanded by others are almost impossible. Deliberate revolt or deliberate attempts to deceive others may result. But the more frequent outcome is a confused and divided state of interest in which one is fooled as to one's own real intent. One tries to serve two masters at once. Social instincts, the strong desire to please others and get their approval, social training, the general sense of duty and of authority, apprehension of penalty, all lead to a half-hearted effort to conform, to "pay attention to the lesson," or whatever the requirement is. Amiable individuals want to do what they are expected to do. Consciously the pupil thinks he is doing this. But his own desires are not abolished. Only their evident exhibition is suppressed. Strain of attention to what is hostile to desire is irksome; in spite of one's *conscious* wish, the underlying desires determine the main course of thought, the deeper emotional responses. The mind wanders from the nominal subject and devotes itself to what is intrinsically more desirable. A systematized divided attention expressing the duplicity of the state of desire is the result.

One has only to recall his own experiences in school or at the present time when outwardly employed in actions which do not engage one's desires and purposes, to realize how prevalent is this attitude of divided attention—double-mindedness. We are so used to it that we take it for granted that a considerable amount of it is necessary. It may be; if so, it is the more important to face its bad intellectual effects. Obvious is the loss of energy of thought immediately available when one is consciously trying (or trying to seem to try) to attend to one matter, while unconsciously one's imagination is spontaneously going out to more congenial affairs. More subtle and more permanently crippling to efficiency of intellectual activity is a fostering of habitual self-deception, with the confused sense of reality which accompanies it. A double standard of reality, one for our own private and more or less concealed interests, and another for public and acknowledged concerns, hampers, in most of us, integrity and completeness of mental action. Equally serious is the fact that a split is set up between conscious thought and attention and impulsive blind affection and desire. Reflective dealings with the material of instruction is constrained and half-hearted; attention wanders. The topics to which it wanders are unavowed and hence intellectually illicit; transactions with them are furtive. The discipline that comes from regulating response by deliberate inquiry having a purpose fails; worse than that, the deepest concern and most congenial enterprises of the imagination (since they center about the things dearest to desire) are casual, concealed. They enter into action in ways which are unacknowledged. Not subject to rectification by consideration of consequences, they are demoralizing.

School conditions favorable to this division of mind between avowed, public, and socially responsible undertakings, and private, ill-regulated, and suppressed indulgences of thought are not hard to find. What is sometimes called "stern discipline," *i.e.*, external coercive pressure, has this tendency. Motivation through rewards extraneous to the thing to be done has a like effect. Everything that makes schooling merely preparatory . . . works in this direction. Ends being beyond the pupil's present grasp, other agencies have to be found to procure immediate attention to assigned tasks. Some responses are secured, but desires and affections not enlisted must find other outlets. Not less serious is exaggerated emphasis upon drill exercises designed to produce skill in action, independent of any engagement of thought—exercises have no purpose but the production of automatic skill. Nature abhors a mental vacuum. What do teachers imagine is happening to thought and emotion when the latter get no outlet in the things of immediate activity? Were they merely kept in temporary abeyance, or even only calloused, it would not be a matter of so much moment. But they are not abolished; they are not suspended; they are not suppressed—save with reference to the task in question. They follow their own chaotic and undisciplined course. What is native, spontaneous, and vital in mental reaction goes unused and untested, and the habits formed are such that these qualities become less and less available for public and avowed ends.

4. Responsibility. By responsibility as an element in intellectual attitude is meant the disposition to consider in advance the probable consequences of any projected step and deliberately to accept them: to accept them in the sense of taking them into account, acknowledging them in action, not yielding a mere verbal assent. Ideas, as we have seen, are intrinsically standpoints and methods for bringing about a solution of a perplexing situation; forecasts calculated to influence responses. It is only too easy to think that one accepts a statement or believes a suggested truth when one has not considered its implications; when one has made but a cursory and superficial survey of what further things one is committed to by acceptance. Observation and recognition, belief and assent, then become names for lazy acquiescence in what is externally presented.

It would be much better to have fewer facts and truths in instruction —that is, fewer things supposedly accepted,—if a smaller number of situations could be intellectually worked out to the point where conviction meant something real, some identification of the self with the type of conduct demanded by facts and foresight of results. The most permanent bad results of undue complication of school subjects and congestion of school studies and lessons are not the worry, nervous strain, and superficial acquaintance that follow (serious as these are), but the failure to make clear what is involved in really knowing and believing a thing. Intellectual responsibility means severe standards in this regard. These standards can be built up only through practice in following up and acting upon the meaning of what is acquired.

Intellectual *thoroughness* is thus another name for the attitude we are considering. There is a kind of thoroughness which is almost purely physical: the kind that signifies mechanical and exhausting drill upon all the details of a subject. Intellectual thoroughness is *seeing a thing through*. It depends upon a unity of purpose to which details are subordinated, not upon presenting a multitude of disconnected details. It is manifested in the firmness with which the full meaning of the purpose is developed, not in attention, however "conscientious" it may be, to the steps of action externally imposed and directed.

SUMMARY

Method is a statement of the way the subject matter of an experience develops most effectively and fruitfully. It is derived, accordingly, from observation of the course of experiences where there is no conscious distinction of personal attitude and manner from material dealt with. The assumption that method is something separate is connected with the notion of the isolation of mind and self from the world of things. It makes instruction and learning formal, mechanical, constrained. While methods are individualized, certain features of the normal course of an experience to its fruition may be discriminated, because of the fund of wisdom derived from prior experiences and because of general similarities in the materials dealt with from time to time. Expressed in terms of the attitude of the individual the traits of good method are straightforwardness, flexible intellectual interest or open-minded will to learn, integrity of purpose, and acceptance of responsibility for the consequences of one's activity including thought.

THE NATURE OF SUBJECT MATTER

SUBJECT MATTER OF EDUCATION AND OF LEARNER

. . . The nature of subject matter . . . consists of the facts observed, recalled, read, and talked about, and the ideas suggested, in course of a development of a situation having a purpose. This statement needs to be rendered more specific by connecting it with the materials of school instruction, the studies which make up the curriculum. What is the significance of our definition in application to reading, writing, mathematics, history, nature study, drawing, singing, physics, chemistry, modern and foreign languages, and so on?

. . . The educator's part in the enterprise of education is to furnish the environment which stimulates responses and directs the learner's course. In last analysis, *all* that the educator can do is modify stimuli so that response will as surely as is possible result in the formation of desirable intellectual and emotional dispositions. Obviously studies or the subject matter of the curriculum have intimately to do with this business of supplying an environment. The other point is the necessity of a social environment to give meaning to habits formed. In what we have termed informal education, subject matter is carried directly in the matrix of social intercourse. It is what the persons with whom an individual associates do and say. This fact gives a clew to the understanding of the subject matter of formal or deliberate instruction. A connecting link is found in the stories, traditions, songs, and liturgies which accompany the doings and rites of a primitive social group. They represent the stock of meanings which have been precipitated out of previous experience, which are so prized by the group as to be identified with their conception of their own collective life. Not being obviously a part of the skill exhibited in the daily occupations of eating, hunting, making war and peace, constructing rugs, pottery, and baskets, etc., they are consciously impressed upon the young; often, as in the initiation ceremonies, with intense emotional fervor. Even more pains are consciously taken to perpetuate the myths, legends, and sacred verbal formulae of the group than to transmit the directly useful customs of the group just because they cannot be picked up, as the latter can be in the ordinary processes of association.

As the social group grows more complex, involving a greater number of acquired skills which are dependent, either in fact or in the belief of the group, upon standard ideas deposited from past experience, the content of social life gets more definitely formulated for purposes of instruction. As we have previously noted, probably the chief motive for consciously dwelling upon the group life, extracting the meanings which are regarded as most important and systematizing them in a coherent arrangement, is just the need of instructing the young so as to perpetuate group life. Once started on this road of selection, formulation, and organization, no definite limit exists. The invention of writing and of printing gives the operation an immense impetus. Finally, the bonds which connect the subject matter of school study with the habits and ideals of the social group are disguised and covered up. The ties are so loosened that it often appears as if there were none; as if subject matter existed simply as knowledge on its own independent behoof, and as if study were the mere act of mastering it for its own sake, irrespective of any social values. Since it is highly important for practical reasons to counteract this tendency . . . the chief purposes of our theoretical discussion are to make clear the connection which is so readily lost from sight, and to show in some detail the social content and function of the chief constituents of the course of study.

The points need to be considered from the standpoint of instructor and of student. To the former, the significance of a knowledge of subject matter, going far beyond the present knowledge of pupils, is to supply definite standards and to reveal to him the possibilities of the crude activities of the immature. (*i*) The material of school studies translates into concrete and detailed terms the meanings of current social life which it is desirable to transmit. It puts clearly before the instructor the essential ingredients of the culture to be perpetuated, in such an organized form as to protect him from the haphazard efforts he would be likely to indulge in if the meanings had not been standardized. (*ii*) A knowledge of the ideas which have been achieved in the past as the outcome of activity places the educator in a position to perceive the meaning of the seeming impulsive and aimless reactions of the young, and to provide the stimuli needed to direct them so that they will amount to something. The more the educator knows of music the more he can perceive the possibilities of the inchoate musical impulses of a child. Organized subject matter represents the ripe fruitage of experiences like theirs, experiences involving the same world, and powers and needs similar to theirs. It does not represent perfection or infallible wisdom; but it is the best at command to further new experiences which may, in some respects at least, surpass the achievements embodied in existing knowledge and works of art.

From the standpoint of the educator, in other words, the various studies represent working resources, available capital. Their remoteness from the experience of the young is not, however, seeming; it is real. The subject matter of the learner is not, therefore, it cannot be, identical with the formulated, the crystallized, and systematized subject matter of the adult; the material as found in books and in works of art, etc. The latter represents the *possibilities* of the former; not its existing state. It enters directly into the activities of the expert and the educator, not into that of the beginner, the learner. Failure to bear in mind the difference in subject matter from the respective standpoints of teacher and student is responsible for most of the mistakes made in the use of texts and other expressions of preëxistent knowledge.

The need for a knowledge of the constitution and functions, in the concrete, of human nature is great just because the teacher's attitude to subject matter is so different from that of the pupil. The teacher presents in actuality what the pupil represents only in *posse*. That is, the teacher already knows the things which the student is only learning. Hence the problem of the two is radically unlike. When engaged in the direct act of teaching, the instructor needs to have subject matter at his fingers' ends; his attention should be upon the attitude and response of the pupil. To understand the latter in its interplay with subject matter is his task, while the pupil's mind, naturally, should be not on itself but on the topic in hand. Or to state the same point in a somewhat different manner: the teacher should be occupied not with subject matter in itself but in its interaction with the pupils' present needs and capacities. Hence simple scholarship is not enough. In fact, there are certain features of scholarship or mastered subject matter—taken by itself—which get in the way of effective teaching *unless* the instructor's habitual attitude is one of concern with its interplay in the pupil's own experience. In the first place, his knowledge extends indefinitely beyond the range of the pupil's acquaintance. It involves principles which are beyond the immature pupil's understanding and interest. In and of itself, it may no more represent the living world of the pupil's experience than the astronomer's knowledge of Mars represents a baby's acquaintance with the room in which he stays. In the second place, the method of organization of the material of achieved scholarship differs from that of the beginner. It is not true that the experience of the young is unorganized—that it consists of isolated scraps. But it is organized in connection with direct practical centers of interest. The child's home is, for example, the organizing center of his geographical knowledge. His own movements about the locality, his journeys abroad, the tales of his friends, give the ties which hold his items of information together. But the geography of the geographer, of the one who has already developed the implications of these smaller experiences, is organized on the basis of the relationship which the various facts bear to one another—not the relations which they bear to his house, bodily movements, and friends. To the one who is learned, subject matter is extensive, accurately defined, and logically interrelated. To the one who is learning, it is fluid, partial, and connected through his personal occupations.[1] The problem of teaching is to keep the experience of the student moving in the direction of what the expert already knows.

[1] Since the learned man should also still be a learner, it will be understood that these contrasts are relative, not absolute. But in the earlier stages of learning at least they are practically all-important.

Hence the need that the teacher know both subject matter and the characteristic needs and capacities of the student.

THE DEVELOPMENT OF SUBJECT MATTER IN THE LEARNER

It is possible, without doing violence to the facts, to mark off three fairly typical stages in the growth of subject matter in the experience of the learner. In its first estate, knowledge exists as the content of intelligent ability—power to do. This kind of subject matter, or known material, is expressed in familiarity or acquaintance with things. Then this material gradually is surcharged and deepened through communicated knowledge or information. Finally, it is enlarged and worked over into rationally or logically organized material—that of the one who, relatively speaking, is expert in the subject.

I. The knowledge which comes first to persons, and that remains most deeply ingrained, is knowledge of *how to do;* how to walk, talk, read, write, skate, ride a bicycle, manage a machine, calculate, drive a horse, sell goods, manage people, and so on indefinitely. The popular tendency to regard instinctive acts which are adapted to an end as a sort of miraculous knowledge, while unjustifiable, is evidence of the strong tendency to identify intelligent control of the means of action with knowledge. When education, under the influence of a scholastic conception of knowledge which ignores everything but scientifically formulated facts and truths, fails to recognize that primary or initial subject matter always exists as matter of an active doing, involving the use of the body and the handling of material, the subject matter of instruction is isolated from the needs and purposes of the learner, and so becomes just a something to be memorized and reproduced upon demand. Recognition of the natural course of development, on the contrary, always sets out with situations which involve learning by doing. Arts and occupations form the initial stage of the curriculum, corresponding as they do to knowing how to go about the accomplishment of ends.

Popular terms denoting knowledge have always retained the connection with ability in action lost by academic philosophies. Ken and can are allied words. Attention means caring for a thing, in the sense of both affection and of looking out for its welfare. Mind means

carrying out instructions in action—as a child minds his mother—
and taking care of something—as a nurse minds the baby. To be
thoughtful, considerate, means to heed the claims of others. Apprehension means dread of undesirable consequences, as well as intellectual grasp. To have good sense or judgment is to know the conduct
a situation calls for; discernment is not making distinctions for the
sake of making them, an exercise reprobated as hair splitting, but is
insight into an affair with reference to acting. Wisdom has never lost
its association with the proper direction of life. Only in education,
never in the life of farmer, sailor, merchant, physician, or laboratory
experimenter, does knowledge mean primarily a store of information
aloof from doing.

Having to do with things in an intelligent way issues in acquaintance
or familiarity. The things we are best acquainted with are the things
we put to frequent use—such things as chairs, tables, pen, paper,
clothes, food, knives and forks on the commonplace level, differentiating into more special objects according to a person's occupations in
life. Knowledge of things in that intimate and emotional sense suggested by the word acquaintance is a precipitate from our employing
them with a purpose. We have acted with or upon the thing so frequently that we can anticipate how it will act and react—such is the
meaning of familiar acquaintance. We are ready for a familiar thing;
it does not catch us napping, or play unexpected tricks with us.
This attitude carries with it a sense of congeniality or friendliness, of
ease and illumination; while the things with which we are not accustomed to deal are strange, foreign, cold, remote, "abstract."

II. But it is likely that elaborate statements regarding this primary
stage of knowledge will darken understanding. It includes practically
all of our knowledge which is not the result of deliberate technical
study. Modes of purposeful doing include dealings with persons as
well as things. Impulses of communication and habits of intercourse
have to be adapted to maintaining successful connections with others;
a large fund of social knowledge accrues. As a part of this intercommunication one learns much from others. They tell of their experiences and of the experiences which, in turn, have been told them.
In so far as one is interested or concerned in these communications,
their matter becomes a part of one's own experience. Active connections with others are such an intimate and vital part of our own concerns that it is impossible to draw sharp lines, such as would enable

us to say, "Here my experience ends; there yours begins." In so far as we are partners in common undertakings, the things which others communicate to us as the consequences of their particular share in the enterprise blend at once into the experience resulting from our own special doings. The ear is as much an organ of experience as the eye or hand; the eye is available for reading reports of what happens beyond its horizon. Things remote in space and time affect the issue of our actions quite as much as things which we can smell and handle. They really concern us, and, consequently, any account of them which assists us in dealing with things at hand falls within personal experience.

Information is the name usually given to this kind of subject matter. The place of communication in personal doing supplies us with a criterion for estimating the value of informational material in school. Does it grow naturally out of some question with which the student is concerned? Does it fit into his more direct acquaintance so as to increase its efficacy and deepen its meaning? If it meets these two requirements, it is educative. The amount heard or read is of no importance—the more the better, *provided* the student has a need for it and can apply it in some situation of his own.

But it is not so easy to fulfill these requirements in actual practice as it is to lay them down in theory. The extension in modern times of the area of intercommunication; the invention of appliances for securing acquaintance with remote parts of the heavens and bygone events of history; the cheapening of devices, like printing, for recording and distributing information—genuine and alleged—have created an immense bulk of communicated subject matter. It is much easier to swamp a pupil with this than to work it into his direct experiences. All too frequently it forms another strange world which just overlies the world of personal acquaintance. The sole problem of the student is to learn, for school purposes, for purposes of recitations and promotions, the constituent parts of this strange world. Probably the most conspicuous connotation of the word knowledge for most persons to-day is just the body of facts and truths ascertained by others; the material found in the rows and rows of atlases, cyclopedias, histories, biographies, books of travel, scientific treatises, on the shelves of libraries.

The imposing stupendous bulk of this material has unconsciously influenced men's notions of the nature of knowledge itself. The statements, the propositions, in which knowledge, the issue of active concern with problems, is deposited, are taken to be themselves knowledge. The record of knowledge, independent of its place as an outcome of inquiry and a resource in further inquiry, is taken to *be* knowledge. The mind of man is taken captive by the spoils of its prior victories; the spoils, not the weapons and the acts of waging the battle against the unknown, are used to fix the meaning of knowledge, of fact, and truth.

If this identification of knowledge with propositions stating information has fastened itself upon logicians and philosophers, it is not surprising that the same ideal has almost dominated instruction. The "course of study" consists largely of information distributed into various branches of study, each study being subdivided into lessons presenting in serial cutoff portions of the total store. In the seventeenth century, the store was still small enough so that men set up the ideal of a complete encyclopedic mastery of it. It is now so bulky that the impossibility of any one man's coming into possession of it all is obvious. But the educational ideal has not been much affected. Acquisition of a modicum of information in each branch of learning, or at least in a selected group, remains the principle by which the curriculum, from elementary school through college, is formed; the easier portions being assigned to the earlier years, the more difficult to the later.

The complaints of educators that learning does not enter into character and affect conduct; the protests against memoriter work, against cramming, against gradgrind preoccupation with "facts," against devotion to wire-drawn distinctions and ill-understood rules and principles, all follow from this state of affairs. Knowledge which is mainly second-hand, other men's knowledge, tends to become merely verbal. It is no objection to information that it is clothed in words; communication necessarily takes place through words. But in the degree in which what is communicated cannot be organized into the existing experience of the learner, it becomes *mere* words: that is, pure sense-stimuli, lacking in meaning. Then it operates to call out mechanical reactions, ability to use the vocal organs to repeat statements, or the hand to write or to do "sums."

To be informed is to be posted; it is to have at command the subject matter needed for an effective dealing with a problem, and for giving added significance to the search for solution and to the solution itself. Informational knowledge is the material which can be fallen back upon as given, settled, established, assured in a doubtful situation. It is a kind of bridge for mind in its passage from doubt to discovery. It has the office of an intellectual middleman. It condenses and records in available form the net results of the prior experiences of mankind, as an agency of enhancing the meaning of new experiences. When one is told that Brutus assassinated Caesar, or that the length of the year is three hundred sixty-five and one fourth days, or that the ratio of the diameter of the circle to its circumference is 3.1415 . . . one receives what is indeed knowledge for others, but for him it is a stimulus to knowing. His acquisition of *knowledge* depends upon his response to what is communicated.

SCIENCE OR RATIONALIZED KNOWLEDGE

Science is a name for knowledge in its most characteristic form. It represents in its degree, the perfected outcome of learning,—its consummation. What is known, in a given case, is what is sure, certain, settled, disposed of; that which we think *with* rather than that which we think about. In its honorable sense, knowledge is distinguished from opinion, guesswork, speculation, and mere tradition. In knowledge, things are *ascertained;* they are *so* and not dubiously otherwise. But experience makes us aware that there is difference between intellectual certainty of *subject matter* and *our* certainty. We are made, so to speak, for belief; credulity is natural. The undisciplined mind is averse to suspense and intellectual hesitation; it is prone to assertion. It likes things undisturbed, settled, and treats them as such without due warrant. Familiarity, common repute, and congeniality to desire are readily made measuring rods of truth. Ignorance gives way to opinionated and current error,—a greater foe to learning than ignorance itself. A Socrates is thus led to declare that consciousness of ignorance is the beginning of effective love of wisdom, and a Descartes to say that science is born of doubting.

We have already dwelt upon the fact that subject matter, or data, and ideas have to have their worth tested experimentally: that in themselves they are tentative and provisional. Our predilection for premature acceptance and assertion, our aversion to suspended judgment, are signs that we tend naturally to cut short the process of testing. We are satisfied with superficial and immediate shortvisioned applications. If these work out with moderate satisfactoriness, we are content to suppose that our assumptions have been confirmed. Even in the case of failure, we are inclined to put the blame not on the inadequacy and incorrectness of our data and thoughts, but upon our hard luck and the hostility of circumstance. We charge the evil consequence not to the error of our schemes and our incomplete inquiry into conditions (thereby getting material for revising the former and stimulus for extending the latter) but to untoward fate. We even plume ourselves upon our firmness in clinging to our conceptions in spite of the way in which they work out.

Science represents the safeguard of the race against these natural propensities and the evils which flow from them. It consists of the special appliances and methods which the race has slowly worked out in order to conduct reflection under conditions whereby its procedures and results are tested. It is artificial (an acquired art), not spontaneous; learned, not native. To this fact is due the unique, the invaluable place of science in education, and also the dangers which threaten its right use. Without initiation into the scientific spirit one is not in possession of the best tools which humanity has so far devised for effectively directed reflection. One in that case not merely conducts inquiry and learning without the use of the best instruments, but fails to understand the full meaning of knowledge. For he does not become acquainted with the traits that mark off opinion and assent from authorized conviction. On the other hand, the fact that science marks the perfecting of knowing in highly specialized conditions of technique renders its results, taken by themselves, remote from ordinary experience—a quality of aloofness that is popularly designated by the term abstract. When this isolation appears in instruction, scientific information is even more exposed to the dangers attendant upon presenting ready-made subject matter than are other forms of information.

Science has been defined in terms of method of inquiry and testing. At first sight, this definition may seem opposed to the current conception that science is organized or systematized knowledge. The opposition, however, is only seeming, and disappears when the ordinary definition is completed. Not organization but the *kind* of organization effected by adequate methods of tested discovery marks off science. The knowledge of a farmer is systematized in the degree in which he is competent. It is organized on the basis of relation of means to ends—practically organized. Its organization *as* knowledge (that is, in the eulogistic sense of adequately tested and confirmed) is incidental to its organization with reference to securing crops, live-stock, etc. But scientific subject matter is organized with specific reference to the successful conduct of the enterprise of discovery, to knowing as a specialized undertaking.

Reference to the kind of assurance attending science will shed light upon this statement. It is rational assurance,—logical warranty. The ideal of scientific organization is, therefore, that every conception and statement shall be of such a kind as to follow from others and to lead to others. Conceptions and propositions mutually imply and support one another. This double relation of "leading to and confirming" is what is meant by the terms logical and rational. The everyday conception of water is more available for ordinary uses of drinking, washing, irrigation, etc., than the chemist's notion of it. The latter's description of it as H_2O is superior from the standpoint of place and use in inquiry. It states the nature of water in a way which connects it with knowledge of other things, indicating to one who understands it how the knowledge is arrived at and its bearings upon other portions of knowledge of the structure of things. Strictly speaking, it does not indicate the objective relations of water any more than does a statement that water is transparent, fluid, without taste or odor, satisfying to thirst, etc. It is just as true that water has these relations as that it is constituted by two molecules of hydrogen in combination with one of oxygen. But for the *particular purpose* of conducting discovery with a view to ascertainment of fact, the latter relations are fundamental. The more one emphasizes organization as a mark of science, then, the more he is committed to a recognition of the primacy of method in the definition of science. For method defines the kind of organization in virtue of which science is science.

SUBJECT MATTER AS SOCIAL

. . . It remains to say a few words upon subject matter as social, since our prior remarks have been mainly concerned with its intellectual aspect. A difference in breadth and depth exists even in vital knowledge; even in the data and ideas which are relevant to real problems and which are motivated by purposes. For there is a difference in the social scope of purposes and the social importance of problems. With the wide range of possible material to select from, it is important that education (especially in all its phases short of the most specialized) should use a criterion of social worth.

All information and systematized scientific subject matter have been worked out under the conditions of social life and have been transmitted by social means. But this does not prove that all is of equal value for the purposes of forming the disposition and supplying the equipment of members of present society. The scheme of a curriculum must take account of the adaptation of studies to the needs of the existing community life; it must select with the intention of improving the life we live in common so that the future shall be better than the past. Moreover, the curriculum must be planned with reference to placing essentials first, and refinements second. The things which are socially most fundamental, that is, which have to do with the experiences in which the widest groups share, are the essentials. The things which represent the needs of specialized groups and technical pursuits are secondary. There is truth in the saying that education must first be human and only after that professional. But those who utter the saying frequently have in mind in the term human only a highly specialized class: the class of learned men who preserve the classic traditions of the past. They forget that material is humanized in the degree in which it connects with the common interests of men as men.

Democratic society is peculiarly dependent for its maintenance upon the use in forming a course of study of criteria which are broadly human. Democracy cannot flourish where the chief influences in selecting subject matter of instruction are utilitarian ends narrowly conceived for the masses, and, for the higher education of the few, the traditions of a specialized cultivated class. The notion that the "essentials" of elementary education are the three R's mechanically treated, is based upon ignorance of the essentials needed for realization of democratic ideals. Unconsciously it assumes that these ideals are unrealizable; it assumes that in the future, as in the past, getting a livelihood, "making a living," must signify for most men and women doing things which are not significant, freely chosen, and ennobling to those who do them; doing things which serve ends unrecognized by those engaged in them, carried on under the direction of others for the sake of pecuniary reward. For preparation of large numbers for a life of this sort, and only for this purpose, are mechanical efficiency in reading, writing, spelling and figuring, together with attainment of a certain amount of muscular dexterity, "essentials." Such conditions also infect the education called liberal, with illiberality. They imply a somewhat parasitic cultivation bought at the expense of not having the enlightenment and discipline which come from concern with the deepest problems of common humanity. A curriculum which acknowledges the social responsibilities of education must present situations where problems are relevant to the problems of living together, and where observation and information are calculated to develop social insight and interest.

SUMMARY

The subject matter of education consists primarily of the meanings which supply content to existing social life. The continuity of social life means that many of these meanings are contributed to present activity by past collective experience. As social life grows more complex, these factors increase in number and import. There is need of special selection, formulation, and organization in order that they may be adequately transmitted to the new generation. But this very process tends to set up subject matter as something of value just by itself, apart from its function in promoting the realization of the meanings implied in the present experience of the immature. Especially is the educator exposed to the temptation to conceive his task in terms of the pupil's ability to appropriate and reproduce the subject matter in set statements, irrespective of its organization into his activities as a developing social member. The positive principle is maintained when the young begin with active occupations having a social origin and use, and proceed to a scientific insight in the materials and laws involved, through assimilating into their more direct experience the ideas and facts communicated by others who have had a larger experience.

The aims of education

ALFRED NORTH WHITEHEAD

The influence of Alfred North Whitehead's thought has been most strongly felt in the fields of logic, mathematics, and general philosophy; his contributions to these areas have a permanent standing. Whitehead's essays and papers on education, though they have not had such a marked influence, demonstrate the philosopher's serious concern for and profound insight into fundamental areas of modern education.

Although not primarily an educational philosopher, Whitehead cared enough about the implications for education of his general philosophy to develop and clarify their meaning and usefulness in papers presented to various groups. Many of these essays were prepared prior to the development of Whitehead's mature philosophic position. However, a consistency is evident throughout the development of that position and between it and the principles of his educational theory. Keeping in mind that Whitehead's approach to education is determined by the nature of his philosophical objectives (to search out and define the broad configurations of man's nature and experience), we may indeed profit by exploring his conclusions about educational form and function.

Two basic premises shape Whitehead's philosophical formulations and, therefore, his educational theory. The first is that man, by his very nature and under the particular circumstances of his

SOURCE: Alfred North Whitehead, *The Aims of Education and Other Essays* (New York: Macmillan Company, 1967), pp. 1–14, 15–28, 29–41. Copyright 1929 by The Macmillan Company; renewed 1957 by Evelyn Whitehead. Reprinted by permission of The Macmillan Company.

life, will attempt to acquire the "most general and diverse values" possible. Man inherently seeks to explore and to constantly expand his world. Second, man's seeking and exploring proceed cyclically. Each aspect of this seeking and exploring follows the cyclic process leading from what Whitehead terms "romance," to "precision," and, finally, to "generalization." To understand the ways in which these two premises dominate Whitehead's thought on education, and their uses for the educator, we turn to his collected essays, *The Aims of Education and Other Essays,* from which the selections that follow are taken.

In the first essay, "The Aims of Education," Whitehead sets forth in their most general outlines the nature and function of education. To be educated is to have acquired what Whitehead calls the "art of the utilization of knowledge." For Whitehead, the single subject matter of the educational enterprise is the child's experience of life— "life in all its manifestations." To teach the student to utilize knowledge is to provide him with a personal awareness of and feeling for the power, beauty, and structure of ideas. And ideas will be the catalytic agent that, throughout life, both determines and enriches human experience.

For Whitehead, there exists a basic periodicity in human development. The second essay, "The Rhythm of Education," explores the three stages the individual passes through during his lifetime: stages of romance, precision, and generalization. The child is involved in the romantic period from the age of eight until approximately the age of twelve; the second stage, precision, operates through the years from twelve to eighteen; and generalization is the active mode during adulthood. Whitehead's developmental areas are not meant to be mutually exclusive, for although one stage may be dominant, the values and activity of other stages are present in varying degrees. His concern in "The Rhythm of Education" is to relate the developing stages to the *kind* of intellectual dynamic that dominates each one.

The period of romance is one in which learning tends to be spontaneous and undisciplined. It is characterized by the freedom and activity of the imagination. Learning in this stage is usually acquired by direct and immediate apprehension.

During the stage that Whitehead calls precision, the individual begins to learn and master those techniques that will assist him in attaining some of his "romantic" values. Its chief intellectual goal and resource is discipline, especially in the ordering and use of facts. And, crucially, the period of precision is marked by the process in which ends and means come to be directly related in the student's intellectual activity.

The third and lifelong period of generalization sees the individual continually building and expanding his search for values and the means to their realization. Whitehead's generalization is the ever-maturing process of the mind in its analytic search for the meaning of experience and the expansion of aims and goals. It is thus the constant sifting of action and thought, of freedom and necessity, reaching through the modes of imagination and discipline to activate the decisions of growth. This impulse to explore and grow comes into being without effort—provided that the first two periods of development have been ably guided and brought to fruition.

For Whitehead, it is the elementary and secondary school experience that prepares the student for his lifelong process of generalization. The third essay, "Rhythmic Claims of Freedom and Discipline," shows how, even within the stages of romance, precision, and generalization, the alternations between freedom and discipline are essential in the movement toward wisdom. Wisdom, as we call the effect of a successful process of generalization, cannot be a realistic objective without intellectual freedom in the "presence of knowledge." But knowledge is not attained except by the disciplined acquisition of ordered fact. Thus, freedom *and* discipline constitute the essential components of education.

A brief exposition of Whitehead's ideas about some general and particular areas of education, as they are elaborated in the remaining essays of this collection (not reproduced here), should be of help to the reader. They contain striking examples of Whitehead's innovative approach to the field of education. His theories on the nature of "liberality" in education, the function of universities, and the organization of thought are especially pertinent for the light they shed on what we might call Whitehead's insistence on the formal ideal in education. He is convinced that only the awareness of and reaching for that ideal by educators *and* students can infuse the schools with the vitality of ideas and inquiry that brings learning alive. In these essays, Whitehead reasons from the existence to the operation of that ideal.

It is the interdependence of the modes of freedom and discipline that Whitehead is attempting to define in his discussion of "Technical Education and Its Relation to Science and Literature." Whitehead believes that there can be no truly technical education which is not at the same time a liberal education; and, conversely, no education is truly liberal with being an experience at once combining inquiry and fact with their useful application. It is certainly the responsibility of schools to see that the pupil comes to know something well—the emphasis of liberal studies. Equally, the pupil must be able to use well that which he has learned well—the technical aspect of Whitehead's "liberal" art, the utilization of knowledge. Acknowledging the inseparability of knowing and its uses, Whitehead goes on to discuss the kinds of curriculum content his theory would advance.

In "The Place of Classics in Education," Whitehead offers a modified defense of the role of the classics in the curriculum. While this question does not have the immediate concern for American educators that it has for the British, Whitehead's approach to it reveals a major organizing principle in his theoretical construct. Both this essay and "The Mathematical Curriculum" show that a rigorous selection and adaptation of the traditional material must be made according to the particular goal each subject serves. The value of classical studies is primarily historical, bringing the mind of the student to bear upon the freshness of historical perspective, of the values and traditions of other civilizations. Thus those works should be chosen for inclusion in the curriculum which are important to the understanding of a major ancient culture, and which can be read in translation, since the burden of time makes reading in the original impracticable.

Mathematics, too, has a specific function for Whitehead. Its value, apart from its specialized uses for a few individuals, is as training in dealing with certain kinds of abstract reasoning. For example, the mastery of algebra as a formal mathematical system not only is extremely difficult but also is of interest and value to only a few persons. What Whitehead suggests is that algebra should be included in the general curriculum only to the extent that it contributes to training the pupil in the handling of abstract ideas. It is clear from these examples that Whitehead would not attach an a priori value to any subject: particular study must be related to particular ends, in the student's eyes as well as in the teacher's. Only in this way can the process of exploration and expansion in the student be made specific to his own intellect.

Whitehead's essays on "Universities and Their Function" and "The Organization of Thought" bring to the subject of higher education his insistence upon the formal ideal in a new aspect, that of the creative union which can lead to the practice of excellence. Universities do function to educate the young and carry on research, but these activities do not, in Whitehead's eyes, justify their existence. Even the imparting of knowledge is not the universities' primary raison d'être. Universities can be justified only when they continue to connect knowledge and "the zest of life," bringing together the young and the mature "in the imaginative consideration of learning." The imagination of romance is supplied by the young; the discipline of precision is perfected in the faculty. In combination, these forces continuously create the zestful assault on knowledge and experience that is the essence of the generalization process.

At this point, we see that Whitehead's cyclic process of exploration and expansion in the individual is in crucial relation to his treatment of "The Organization of Thought." Each period of development is meant to find realization, finally, in the quality of thought and analysis that will be nurtured through life, granting to the individual the power of determining meanings and re-creating life styles and goals. Again, Whitehead sees the ideal functioning as an imaginative union, this time between logic and observation, the two sides of thoughtful activity. Logic, the rules governing the organization of thought, cannot in and of itself produce thought or advance knowledge. But observation alone, although it contains the seminal power of ideation, cannot be formulated without undergoing conscious organization. Thus, the educational enterprise must not focus exclusively on either logic or observation for the development of the sciences; taught together, they will be the basis in the individual for the maintenance and discipline of his own intellect.

Throughout these essays, Whitehead advocates the need to maintain the "freshness" of knowledge. He means that knowledge is fresh which can at any given moment amplify or vivify the experience of the child. Thus, "fresh knowledge" does not mean recent or new knowledge, but rather any knowledge that can, at a particular time, contribute to the enhancement of experience. The freshness of a subject need not be taken as its relevance in the usual sense—knowledge should indeed be relevant; that is, related to or part of that which is best in the cultural experience. Knowledge which provides the student with insight into the contributions of past experience as they have determined what is best in the present culture is the most relevant knowledge.

In a time of educational change and confusion, Whitehead, like Dewey, offers to the thoughtful educator his rigorous ideals for determining educational goals and aims. Although Whitehead is speaking specifically to the academic situation in England, his concern for the role of the vitality of ideas and the basic humanity of the experience of schooling is universal in spirit. His recommendations for changes and curtailments in the traditional curriculum are most notable for their adherence to a larger ideal. Whether or not the specific reform he advises is applicable to American education, his guiding criteria are profoundly relevant: that changes serve to heighten the child's zest for learning, implant and fashion cultural ideals, and assist the experience of thought, analysis, and decision. Thus the stages of romance, precision, and generalization find their fruition in the individual through his schools, and are carried by him from the schools to the larger society.

THE AIMS OF EDUCATION

Culture is activity of thought, and receptiveness to beauty and humane feeling. Scraps of information have nothing to do with it. A merely well-informed man is the most useless bore on God's earth. What we should aim at producing is men who possess both culture and expert knowledge in some special direction. Their expert knowledge will give them the ground to start from, and their culture will lead them as deep as philosophy and as high as art. We have to remember that the valuable intellectual development is self-development, and that it mostly takes place between the ages of sixteen and thirty. As to training, the most important part is given by mothers before the age of twelve. A saying due to Archbishop Temple illustrates my meaning. Surprise was expressed at the success in after-life of a man, who as a boy at Rugby had been somewhat undistinguished. He answered, "It is not what they are at eighteen, it is what they become afterwards that matters."

In training a child to activity of thought, above all things we must beware of what I will call "inert ideas," that is to say, ideas that are merely received into the mind without being utilised, or tested, or thrown into fresh combinations.

In the history of education, the most striking phenomenon is that schools of learning, which at one epoch are alive with a ferment of genius, in a succeeding generation exhibit merely pedantry and routine. The reason is, that they are overladen with inert ideas. Education with inert ideas is not only useless: it is, above all things, harmful— *Corruptio optimi, pessima.* Except at rare intervals of intellectual ferment, education in the past has been radically infected with inert ideas. That is the reason why uneducated clever women, who have seen much of the world, are in middle life so much the most cultured part of the community. They have been saved from this horrible burden of inert ideas. Every intellectual revolution which has ever stirred humanity into greatness has been a passionate protest against inert ideas. Then, alas, with pathetic ignorance of human psychology, it has proceeded by some educational scheme to bind humanity afresh with inert ideas of its own fashioning.

Let us now ask how in our system of education we are to guard against this mental dryrot. We enunciate two educational commandments, "Do not teach too many subjects," and again, "What you teach, teach thoroughly."

The result of teaching small parts of a large number of subjects is the passive reception of disconnected ideas, not illumined with any spark of vitality. Let the main ideas which are introduced into a child's education be few and important, and let them be thrown into every combination possible. The child should make them his own, and should understand their application here and now in the circumstances of his actual life. From the very beginning of his education, the child should experience the joy of discovery. The discovery which he has to make, is that general ideas give an understanding of that stream of events which pours through his life, which is his life. By understanding I mean more than a mere logical analysis, though that is included. I mean "understanding" in the sense in which it is used in the French proverb, "To understand all, is to forgive all." Pedants sneer at an education which is useful. But if education is not useful, what is it? Is it a talent, to be hidden away in a napkin? Of course, education should be useful, whatever your aim in life. It was useful to Saint Augustine and it was useful to Napoleon. It is useful, because understanding is useful.

I pass lightly over that understanding which should be given by the literary side of education. Nor do I wish to be supposed to pronounce on the relative merits of a classical or a modern curriculum. I would only remark that the understanding which we want is an understanding of an insistent present. The only use of a knowledge of the past is to equip us for the present. No more deadly harm can be done to young minds than by depreciation of the present. The present contains all that there is. It is holy ground; for it is the past, and it is the future. At the same time it must be observed that an age is no less past if it existed two hundred years ago than if it existed two thousand years ago. Do not be deceived by the pedantry of dates. The ages of Shakespeare and of Molière are no less past than are the ages of Sophocles and of Virgil. The communion of saints is a great and inspiring assemblage, but it has only one possible hall of meeting, and that is, the present; and the mere lapse of time through which any particular group of saints must travel to reach that meeting-place, makes very little difference.

Passing now to the scientific and logical side of education, we remember that here also ideas which are not utilised are positively harmful. By utilising an idea, I mean relating it to that stream, compounded of sense perceptions, feelings, hopes, desires, and of mental activities adjusting thought to thought, which forms our life. I can imagine a set of beings which might fortify their souls by passively reviewing disconnected ideas. Humanity is not built that way—except perhaps some editors of newspapers.

In scientific training, the first thing to do with an idea is to prove it. But allow me for one moment to extend the meaning of "prove"; I mean—to prove its worth. Now an idea is not worth much unless the propositions in which it is embodied are true. Accordingly an essential part of the proof of an idea is the proof, either by experiment or by logic, of the truth of the propositions. But it is not essential that this proof of the truth should constitute the first introduction to the idea. After all, its assertion by the authority of respectable teachers is sufficient evidence to begin with. In our first contact with a set of propositions, we commence by appreciating their importance. That is what we all do in after-life. We do not attempt, in the strict sense, to prove or to disprove anything, unless its importance makes it worthy of that honour. These two processes of proof, in the narrow sense, and of appreciation, do not require a rigid separation in time. Both can be proceeded with nearly concurrently. But in so far as either process must have the priority, it should be that of appreciation by use.

Furthermore, we should not endeavour to use propositions in isolation. Emphatically I do not mean, a neat little set of experiments to illustrate Proposition I and then the proof of Proposition I, a neat little set of experiments to illustrate Proposition II and then the proof of Proposition II, and so on to the end of the book. Nothing could be more boring. Interrelated truths are utilised *en bloc,* and the various propositions are employed in any order, and with any reiteration. Choose some important applications of your theoretical subject; and study them concurrently with the systematic theoretical exposition. Keep the theoretical exposition short and simple, but let it be strict and rigid so far as it goes. It should not be too long for it to be easily known with thoroughness and accuracy. The consequences of a plethora of half-digested theoretical knowledge are deplorable. Also the theory should not be muddled up with the practice. The child should have no doubt when it is proving and when it is utilising. My point is that what is proved should be utilised, and that what is utilised should—so far as is practicable—be proved. I am far from asserting that proof and utilisation are the same thing.

At this point of my discourse, I can most directly carry forward my argument in the outward form of a digression. We are only just realising that the art and science of education require a genius and a study of their own; and that this genius and this science are more than a bare knowledge of some branch of science or of literature. This truth was partially perceived in the past generation; and headmasters, somewhat crudely, were apt to supersede learning in their colleagues by requiring left-hand bowling and a taste for football. But culture is more than cricket, and more than football, and more than extent of knowledge.

Education is the acquisition of the art of the utilisation of knowledge. This is an art very difficult to impart. Whenever a text-book is written of real educational worth, you may be quite certain that some reviewer will say that it will be difficult to teach from it. Of course it will be difficult to teach from it. If it were easy, the book ought to be burned; for it cannot be educational. In education, as elsewhere, the broad primrose path leads to a nasty place. This evil path is represented by a book or a set of lectures which will practically enable the student to learn by heart all the questions likely to be asked at the next external examination. And I may say in passing that no educational system is possible unless every question directly asked of a pupil at any examination is either framed or modified by the actual teacher of that pupil in that subject. The external assessor may report on the curriculum or on the performance of the pupils, but never should be allowed to ask the pupil a question which has not been strictly supervised by the actual teacher, or at least inspired by a long conference with him. There are a few exceptions to this rule, but they are exceptions, and could easily be allowed for under the general rule.

We now return to my previous point, that theoretical ideas should always find important applications within the pupil's curriculum. This is not an easy doctrine to apply, but a very hard one. It contains within itself the problem of keeping knowledge alive, of preventing it from becoming inert, which is the central problem of all education.

The best procedure will depend on several factors, none of which can be neglected, namely, the genius of the teacher, the intellectual type of the pupils, their prospects in life, the opportunities offered by the immediate surroundings of the school, and allied factors of this sort. It is for this reason that the uniform external examination is so deadly. We do not denounce it because we are cranks, and like denouncing established things. We are not so childish. Also, of course, such examinations have their use in testing slackness. Our reason of dislike is very definite and very practical. It kills the best part of culture. When you analyse in the light of experience the central task of education, you find that its successful accomplishment depends on a delicate adjustment of many variable factors. The reason is that we are dealing with human minds, and not with dead matter. The evocation of curiosity, of judgment, of the power of mastering a complicated tangle of circumstances, the use of theory in giving foresight in special cases—all these powers are not to be imparted by a set rule embodied in one schedule of examination subjects.

I appeal to you, as practical teachers. With good discipline, it is always possible to pump into the minds of a class a certain quantity of inert knowledge. You take a text-book and make them learn it. So far, so good. The child then knows how to solve a quadratic equation. But what is the point of teaching a child to solve a quadratic equation? There is a traditional answer to this question. It runs thus: The mind is an instrument, you first sharpen it, and then use it; the acquisition of the power of solving a quadratic equation is part of the process of sharpening the mind. Now there is just enough truth in this answer to have made it live through the ages. But for all its half-truth, it embodies a radical error which bids fair to stifle the genius of the modern world. I do not know who was first responsible for this analogy of the mind to a dead instrument. For aught I know, it may have been one of the seven wise men of Greece, or a committee of the whole lot of them. Whoever was the originator, there can be no doubt of the authority which it has acquired by the continuous approval bestowed upon it by eminent persons. But whatever its weight of authority, whatever the high approval which it can quote, I have no hesitation in denouncing it as one of the most fatal, erroneous, and dangerous conceptions ever introduced into the theory of education. The mind is never passive; it is a perpetual activity, delicate, receptive, responsive to stimulus. You cannot postpone its life until you have sharpened it. Whatever interest attaches to your subject-matter must be evoked here and now; whatever powers you are strengthening in the pupil, must be exercised here and now; whatever possibilities of mental life your teaching should impart, must be exhibited here and now. That is the golden rule of education, and a very difficult rule to follow.

The difficulty is just this: the apprehension of general ideas, intellectual habits of mind, and pleasurable interest in mental achievement can be evoked by no form of words, however accurately adjusted. All practical teachers know that education is a patient process of the mastery of details, minute by minute, hour by hour, day by day. There is no royal road to learning through an airy path of brilliant generalisations. There is a proverb about the difficulty of seeing the wood because of the trees. That difficulty is exactly the point which I am enforcing. The problem of education is to make the pupil see the wood by means of the trees.

The solution which I am urging, is to eradicate the fatal disconnection of subjects which kills the vitality of our modern curriculum. There is only one subject-matter for education, and that is Life in all its manifestations. Instead of this single unity, we offer children—Algebra, from which nothing follows; Geometry, from which nothing follows; Science, from which nothing follows; History, from which nothing follows; a Couple of Languages, never mastered; and lastly, most dreary of all, Literature, represented by plays of Shakespeare, with philological notes and short analyses of plot and character to be in substance committed to memory. Can such a list be said to represent Life, as it is known in the midst of the living of it? The best that can be said of it is, that it is a rapid table of contents which a deity might run over in his mind while he was thinking of creating a world, and has not yet determined how to put it together.

Let us now return to quadratic equations. We still have on hand the unanswered question. Why should children be taught their solution? Unless quadratic equations fit into a connected curriculum, of course there is no reason to teach anything about them. Furthermore, extensive as should be the place of mathematics in a complete culture, I am a little doubtful whether for many types of boys algebraic solutions of quadratic equations do not lie on the specialist side of mathematics. I may here remind you that as yet I have not said anything of the psychology or the content of the specialism, which is so necessary a part of an ideal education. But all that is an evasion of our real question, and I merely state it in order to avoid being misunderstood in my answer.

Quadratic equations are part of algebra, and algebra is the intellectual instrument which has been created for rendering clear the quantitative aspects of the world. There is no getting out of it. Through and through the world is infected with quantity. To talk sense, is to talk in quantities. It is no use saying that the nation is large,—How large? It is no use saying that radium is scarce,—How scarce? You cannot evade quantity. You may fly to poetry and to music, and quantity and number will face you in your rhythms and your octaves. Elegant intellects which despise the theory of quantity, are but half developed. They are more to be pitied than blamed. The scraps of gibberish, which in their schooldays were taught to them in the name of algebra, deserve some contempt.

This question of the degeneration of algebra into gibberish, both in word and in fact, affords a pathetic instance of the uselessness of reforming educational schedules without a clear conception of the attributes which you wish to evoke in the living minds of the children. A few years ago there was an outcry that school algebra was in need of reform, but there was a general agreement that graphs would put everything right. So all sorts of things were extruded, and graphs were introduced. So far as I can see, with no sort of idea behind them, but just graphs.

Now every examination paper has one or two questions on graphs. Personally I am an enthusiastic adherent of graphs. But I wonder whether as yet we have gained very much. You cannot put life into any schedule of general education unless you succeed in exhibiting its relation to some essential characteristic of all intelligent or emotional perception. It is a hard saying, but it is true; and I do not see how to make it any easier. In making these little formal alterations you are beaten by the very nature of things. You are pitted against too skilful an adversary, who will see to it that the pea is always under the other thimble.

Reformation must begin at the other end. First, you must make up your mind as to those quantitative aspects of the world which are simple enough to be introduced into general education; then a schedule of algebra should be framed which will about find its exemplification in these applications. We need not fear for our pet graphs, they will be there in plenty when we once begin to treat algebra as a serious means of studying the world. Some of the simplest applications will be found in the quantities which occur in the simplest study of society. The curves of history are more vivid and more informing than the dry catalogues of names and dates which comprise the greater part of that arid school study. What purpose is effected by a catalogue of undistinguished kings and queens? Tom, Dick, or Harry, they are all dead. General resurrections are failures, and are better postponed. The quantitative flux of the forces of modern society is capable of very simple exhibition. Meanwhile, the idea of the variable, of the function, of rate of change, of equations and their solution, of elimination, are being studied as an abstract science for their own sake. Not, of course, in the pompous phrases with which I am alluding to them here, but with that iteration of simple special cases proper to teaching.

If this course be followed, the route from Chaucer to the Black Death, from the Black Death to modern Labour troubles, will connect the tales of the mediæval pilgrims with the abstract science of algebra, both yielding diverse aspects of that single theme, Life. I know what most of you are thinking at this point. It is that the exact course which I have sketched out is not the particular one which you would have chosen, or even see how to work. I quite agree. I am not claiming that I could do it myself. But your objection is the precise reason why a common external examination system is fatal to education. The process of exhibiting the applications of knowledge must, for its success, essentially depend on the character of the pupils and the genius of the teacher. Of course I have left out the easiest applications with which most of us are more at home. I mean the quantitative sides of sciences, such as mechanics and physics.

Again, in the same connection we plot the statistics of social phenomena against the time. We then eliminate the time between suitable pairs. We can speculate how far we have exhibited a real causal connection, or how far a mere temporal coincidence. We notice that we might have plotted against the time one set of statistics for one country and another set for another country, and thus, with suitable choice of subjects, have obtained graphs which certainly exhibited mere coincidence. Also other graphs exhibit obvious causal connections. We wonder how to discriminate. And so are drawn on as far as we will.

But in considering this description, I must beg you to remember what I have been insisting on above. In the first place, one train of thought will not suit all groups of children. For example, I should expect that artisan children will want something more concrete and, in a sense, swifter than I have set down here. Perhaps I am wrong, but that is what I should guess. In the second place, I am not contemplating one beautiful lecture stimulating, once and for all, an admiring class. That is not the way in which education proceeds. No; all the time the pupils are hard at work solving examples, drawing graphs, and making experiments, until they have a thorough hold on the whole subject. I am describing the interspersed explanations, the directions which should be given to their thoughts. The pupils have got to be made to feel that they are studying something, and are not merely executing intellectual minuets.

Finally, if you are teaching pupils for some general examination, the problem of sound teaching is greatly complicated. Have you ever noticed the zig-zag moulding round a Norman arch? The ancient work is beautiful, the modern work is hideous. The reason is, that the modern work is done to exact measure, the ancient work is varied according to the idiosyncrasy of the workman. Here it is crowded, and there it is expanded. Now the essence of getting pupils through examinations is to give equal weight to all parts of the schedule. But mankind is naturally specialist. One man sees a whole subject, where another can find only a few detached examples. I know that it seems contradictory to allow for specialism in a curriculum especially designed for a broad culture. Without contradictions the world would be simpler, and perhaps duller. But I am certain that in education wherever you exclude specialism you destroy life.

We now come to the other great branch of a general mathematical education, namely Geometry. The same principles apply. The theoretical part should be clear-cut, rigid, short, and important. Every proposition not absolutely necessary to exhibit the main connection of ideas should be cut out, but the great fundamental ideas should be all there. No omission of concepts, such as those of Similarity and Proportion. We must remember that, owing to the aid rendered by the visual presence of a figure, Geometry is a field of unequalled excellence for the exercise of the deductive faculties of reasoning. Then, of course, there follows Geometrical Drawing, with its training for the hand and eye.

But, like Algebra, Geometry and Geometrical Drawing must be extended beyond the mere circle of geometrical ideas. In an industrial neighbourhood, machinery and workshop practice form the appropriate extension. For example, in the London Polytechnics this has been achieved with conspicuous success. For many secondary schools I suggest that surveying and maps are the natural applications. In particular, plane-table surveying should lead pupils to a vivid apprehension of the immediate application of geometric truths. Simple drawing apparatus, a surveyor's chain, and a surveyor's compass, should enable the pupils to rise from the survey and mensuration of a field to the construction of the map of a small district. The best education is to be found in gaining the utmost information from the simplest apparatus. The provision of elaborate instruments is greatly to be deprecated. To have constructed the map of a small district, to have considered its roads, its contours, its geology, its climate, its relation to other districts, the effects on the status of its inhabitants, will teach more history and geography than any knowledge of Perkin Warbeck or of Behren's Straits. I mean not a nebulous lecture on the subject, but a serious investigation in which the real facts are definitely ascertained by the aid of accurate theoretical knowledge. A typical mathematical problem should be: Survey such and such a field, draw a plan of it to such and such a scale, and find the area. It would be quite a good procedure to impart the necessary geometrical propositions without their proofs. Then, concurrently in the same term, the proofs of the propositions would be learnt while the survey was being made.

Fortunately, the specialist side of education presents an easier problem than does the provision of a general culture. For this there are many reasons. One is that many of the principles of procedure to be observed are the same in both cases, and it is unnecessary to recapitulate. Another reason is that specialist training takes place—or should take place —at a more advanced stage of the pupil's course, and thus there is easier material to work upon. But undoubtedly the chief reason is that the specialist study is normally a study of peculiar interest to the student. He is studying it because, for some reason, he wants to know it. This makes all the difference. The general culture is designed to foster an activity of mind; the specialist course utilises this activity. But it does not do to lay too much stress on these neat antitheses. As we have already seen, in the general course foci of special interest will arise; and similarly in the special study, the external connections of the subject drag thought outwards.

Again, there is not one course of study which merely gives general culture, and another which gives special knowledge. The subjects pursued for the sake of a general education are special subjects specially studied; and, on the other hand, one of the ways of encouraging general mental activity is to foster a special devotion. You may not divide the seamless coat of learning. What education has to impart is an intimate sense for the power of ideas, for the beauty of ideas, and for the structure of ideas, together with a particular body of knowledge which has peculiar reference to the life of the being possessing it.

The appreciation of the structure of ideas is that side of a cultured mind which can only grow under the influence of a special study. I mean that eye for the whole chess-board, for the bearing of one set of ideas on another. Nothing but a special study can give any appreciation for the exact formulation of general ideas, for their relations when formulated, for their service in the comprehension of life. A mind so disciplined should be both more abstract and more concrete. It has been trained in the comprehension of abstract thought and in the analysis of facts.

Finally, there should grow the most austere of all mental qualities; I mean the sense for style. It is an æsthetic sense, based on admiration for the direct attainment of a foreseen end, simply and without waste. Style in art, style in literature, style in science, style in logic, style in practical execution have fundamentally the same æsthetic qualities, namely, attainment and restraint. The love of a subject in itself and for itself, where it is not the sleepy pleasure of pacing a mental quarter-deck, is the love of style as manifested in that study.

Here we are brought back to the position from which we started, the utility of education. Style, in its finest sense, is the last acquirement of the educated mind; it is also the most useful. It pervades the whole being. The administrator with a sense for style hates waste; the engineer with a sense for style economises his material; the artisan with a sense for style prefers good work. Style is the ultimate morality of mind.

But above style, and above knowledge, there is something, a vague shape like fate above the Greek gods. That something is Power. Style is the fashioning of power, the restraining of power. But, after all, the power of attainment of the desired end is fundamental. The first thing is to get there. Do not bother about your style, but solve your problem, justify the ways of God to man, administer your province, or do whatever else is set before you.

Where, then, does style help? In this, with style the end is attained without side issues, without raising undesirable inflammations. With style you attain your end and nothing but your end. With style the effect of your activity is calculable, and foresight is the last gift of gods to men. With style your power is increased, for your mind is not distracted with irrelevancies, and you are more likely to attain your object. Now style is the exclusive privilege of the expert. Whoever heard of the style of an amateur painter, of the style of an amateur poet? Style is always the product of specialist study, the peculiar contribution of specialism to culture.

English education in its present phase suffers from a lack of definite aim, and from an external machinery which kills its vitality. Hitherto in this address I have been considering the aims which should govern education. In this respect England halts between two opinions. It has not decided whether to produce amateurs or experts. The profound change in the world which the nineteenth century has produced is that the growth of knowledge has given foresight. The amateur is essentially a man with appreciation and with immense versatility in mastering a given routine. But he lacks the foresight which comes from special knowledge. The object of this address is to suggest how to produce the expert without loss of the essential virtues of the amateur. The machinery of our secondary education is rigid where it should be yielding, and lax where it should be rigid. Every school is bound on pain of extinction to train its boys for a small set of definite examinations. No headmaster has a free hand to develop his general education or his specialist studies in accordance with the opportunities of his school, which are created by its staff, its environment, its class of boys, and its endowments. I suggest that no system of external tests which aims primarily at examining individual scholars can result in anything but educational waste.

Primarily it is the schools and not the scholars which should be inspected. Each school should grant its own leaving certificates, based on its own curriculum. The standards of these schools should be sampled and corrected. But the first requisite for educational reform is the school as a unit, with its approved curriculum based on its own needs, and evolved by its own staff. If we fail to secure that, we simply fall from one formalism into another, from one dung-hill of inert ideas into another.

In stating that the school is the true educational unit in any national system for the safeguarding of efficiency, I have conceived the alternative system as being the external examination of the individual scholar. But every Scylla is faced by its Charybdis—or, in more homely language, there is a ditch on both sides of the road. It will be equally fatal to education if we fall into the hands of a supervising department which is under the impression that it can divide all schools into two or three rigid categories, each type being forced to adopt a rigid curriculum. When I say that the school is the educational unit, I mean exactly what I say, no larger unit, no smaller unit. Each school must have the claim to be considered in relation to its special circumstances. The classifying of schools for some purposes is necessary. But no absolutely rigid curriculum, not modified by its own staff, should be permissible. Exactly the same principles apply, with the proper modifications, to universities and to technical colleges.

When one considers in its length and in its breadth the importance of this question of the education of a nation's young, the broken lives, the defeated hopes, the national failures, which result from the frivolous inertia with which it is treated, it is difficult to restrain within oneself a savage rage. In the conditions of modern life the rule is absolute, the race which does not value trained intelligence is doomed. Not all your heroism, not all your social charm, not all your wit, not all your victories on land or at sea, can move back the finger of fate. To-day we maintain ourselves. To-morrow science will have moved forward yet one more step, and there will be no appeal from the judgment which will then be pronounced on the uneducated.

We can be content with no less than the old summary of educational ideal which has been current at any time from the dawn of our civilisation. The essence of education is that it be religious.

Pray, what is religious education?

A religious education is an education which inculcates duty and reverence. Duty arises from our potential control over the course of events. Where attainable knowledge could have changed the issue, ignorance has the guilt of vice. And the foundation of reverence is this perception, that the present holds within itself the complete sum of existence, backwards and forwards, that whole amplitude of time, which is eternity.

THE RHYTHM OF EDUCATION

By the Rhythm of Education I denote a certain principle which in its practical application is well known to everyone with educational experience. Accordingly, when I remember that I am speaking to an audience of some of the leading educationalists in England, I have no expectation that I shall be saying anything that is new to you. I do think, however, that the principle has not been subjected to an adequate discussion taking account of all the factors which should guide its application.

I first seek for the baldest statement of what I mean by the Rhythm of Education, a statement so bald as to exhibit the point of this address in its utter obviousness. The principle is merely this—that different subjects and modes of study should be undertaken by pupils at fitting times when they have reached the proper stage of mental development. You will agree with me that this is a truism, never doubted and known to all. I am really anxious to emphasise the obvious character of the foundational idea of my address; for one reason, because this audience will certainly find it out for itself. But the other reason, the reason why I choose this subject for discourse, is that I do not think that this obvious truth has been handled in educational practice with due attention to the psychology of the pupils.

THE TASKS OF INFANCY

I commence by challenging the adequacy of some principles by which the subjects for study are often classified in order. By this I mean that these principles can only be accepted as correct if they are so explained as to be explained away. Consider first the criterion of difficulty. It is not true that the easier subjects should precede the harder. On the contrary, some of the hardest must come first because nature so dictates, and because they are essential to life. The first intellectual task which confronts an infant is the acquirement of spoken language. What an appalling task, the correlation of meanings with sounds! It requires an analysis of ideas and an analysis of sounds. We all know that the infant does it, and that the miracle of his achievement is explicable. But so are all miracles, and yet to the wise they remain miracles. All I ask is that with this example staring us in the face we should cease talking nonsense about postponing the harder subjects.

What is the next subject in the education of the infant minds? The acquirement of written language; that is to say, the correlation of sounds with shapes. Great heavens! Have our educationists gone mad? They are setting babbling mites of six years old to tasks which might daunt a sage after lifelong toil. Again, the hardest task in mathematics is the study of the elements of algebra, and yet this stage must precede the comparative simplicity of the differential calculus.

I will not elaborate my point further; I merely restate it in the form, that the postponement of difficulty is no safe clue for the maze of educational practice.

The alternative principle of order among subjects is that of necessary antecedence. There we are obviously on firmer ground. It is impossible to read *Hamlet* until you can read; and the study of integers must precede the study of fractions. And yet even this firm principle dissolves under scrutiny. It is certainly true, but it is only true if you give an artificial limitation to the concept of a subject for study. The danger of the principle is that it is accepted in one sense, for which it is almost a necessary truth, and that it is applied in another sense for which it is false. You cannot read Homer before you can read; but many a child, and in ages past many a man, has sailed with Odysseus over the seas of Romance by the help of the spoken word of a mother, or of some wandering bard. The uncritical application of the principle of the necessary antecedence of some subjects to others has, in the hands of dull people with a turn for organisation, produced in education the dryness of the Sahara.

STAGES OF MENTAL GROWTH

The reason for the title which I have chosen for this address, the Rhythm of Education, is derived from yet another criticism of current ideas. The pupil's progress is often conceived as a uniform steady advance undifferentiated by change of type or alteration in pace; for example, a boy may be conceived as starting Latin at ten years of age and by a uniform progression steadily developing into a classical scholar at the age of eighteen or twenty. I hold that this conception of education is based upon a false psychology of the process of mental development which has gravely hindered the effectiveness of our methods. Life is essentially periodic. It comprises daily periods, with their alternations of work and play, of activity and of sleep, and seasonal periods, which dictate our terms and our holidays; and also it is composed of well-marked yearly periods. These are the gross obvious periods which no one can overlook. There are also subtler periods of mental growth, with their cyclic recurrences, yet always different as we pass from cycle to cycle, though the subordinate stages are reproduced in each cycle. That is why I have chosen the term "rhythmic," as meaning essentially the conveyance of difference within a framework of repetition. Lack of attention to the rhythm and character of mental growth is a main source of wooden futility in education. I think that Hegel was right when he analysed progress into three stages, which he called Thesis, Antithesis, and Synthesis; though for the purpose of the application of his idea to educational theory I do not think that the names he gave are very happily suggestive. In relation to intellectual progress I would term them, the stage of romance, the stage of precision, and the stage of generalisation.

THE STAGE OF ROMANCE

The stage of romance is the stage of first apprehension. The subject-matter has the vividness of novelty; it holds within itself unexplored connexions with possibilities half-disclosed by glimpses and half-concealed by the wealth of material. In this stage knowledge is not dominated by systematic procedure. Such system as there must be is created piecemeal *ad hoc*. We are in the presence of immediate cognisance of fact, only intermittently subjecting fact to systematic dissection. Romantic emotion is essentially the excitement consequent on the transition from the bare facts to the first realisations of the import of their unexplored relationships. For example, Crusoe was a mere man, the sand was mere sand, the footprint was a mere footprint, and the island a mere island, and Europe was the busy world of men. But the sudden perception of the half-disclosed and half-hidden possibilities relating Crusoe and the sand and the footprint and the lonely island secluded from Europe constitutes romance. I have had to take an extreme case for illustration in order to make my meaning perfectly plain. But construe it as an allegory representing the first stage in a cycle of progress. Education must essentially be a setting in order of a ferment already stirring in the mind: you cannot educate mind in *vacuo*. In our conception of education we tend to confine it to the second stage of the cycle; namely, to the stage of precision. But we cannot so limit our task without misconceiving the whole problem. We are concerned alike with the ferment, with the acquirement of precision, and with the subsequent fruition.

THE STAGE OF PRECISION

The stage of precision also represents an addition to knowledge. In this stage, width of relationship is subordinated to exactness of formulation. It is the stage of grammar, the grammar of language and the grammar of science. It proceeds by forcing on the students' acceptance a given way of analysing the facts, bit by bit. New facts are added, but they are the facts which fit into the analysis.

It is evident that a stage of precision is barren without a previous stage of romance: unless there are facts which have already been vaguely apprehended in their broad generality, the previous analysis is an analysis of nothing. It is simply a series of meaningless statements about bare facts, produced artificially and without any further relevance. I repeat that in this stage we do not merely remain within the circle of the facts elicited in the romantic epoch. The facts of romance have disclosed ideas with possibilities of wide significance, and in the stage of precise progress we acquire other facts in a systematic order, which thereby form both a disclosure and an analysis of the general subject-matter of the romance.

THE STAGE OF GENERALISATION

The final stage of generalisation is Hegel's synthesis. It is a return to romanticism with added advantage of classified ideas and relevant technique. It is the fruition which has been the goal of the precise training. It is the final success. I am afraid that I have had to give a dry analysis of somewhat obvious ideas. It has been necessary to do so because my subsequent remarks presuppose that we have clearly in our minds the essential character of this threefold cycle.

THE CYCLIC PROCESSES

Education should consist in a continual repetition of such cycles. Each lesson in its minor way should form an eddy cycle issuing in its own subordinate process. Longer periods should issue in definite attainments, which then form the starting-grounds for fresh cycles. We should banish the idea of a mythical, far-off end of education. The pupils must be continually enjoying some fruition and starting afresh—if the teacher is stimulating in exact proportion to his success in satisfying the rhythmic cravings of his pupils.

An infant's first romance is its awakening to the apprehension of objects and to the appreciation of their connexions. Its growth in mentality takes the exterior form of occupying itself in the co-ordination of its perceptions with its bodily activities. Its first stage of precision is mastering spoken language as an instrument for classifying its contemplation of objects and for strengthening its apprehension of emotional relations with other beings. Its first stage of generalisation is the use of language for a classified and enlarged enjoyment of objects.

This first cycle of intellectual progress from the achievement of perception to the acquirement of language, and from the acquirement of language to classified thought and keener perception, will bear more careful study. It is the only cycle of progress which we can observe in its purely natural state. The later cycles are necessarily tinged by the procedure of the current mode of education. There is a characteristic of it which is often sadly lacking in subsequent education; I mean, that it achieves complete success. At the end of it the child *can* speak, its ideas *are* classified, and its perceptions *are* sharpened. The cycle achieves its object. This is a great deal more than can be said for most systems of education as applied to most pupils. But why should this be so? Certainly, a new-born baby looks a most unpromising subject for intellectual progress when we remember the difficulty of the task before it. I suppose it is because nature, in the form of surrounding circumstances, sets it a task for which the normal development of its brain is exactly fitted. I do not think that there is any particular mystery about the fact of a child learning to speak and in consequence thinking all the better; but it does offer food for reflection.

In the subsequent education we have not sought for cyclic processes which in a finite time run their course and within their own limited sphere achieve a complete success. This completion is one outstanding character in the natural cycle for infants. Later on we start a child on some subject, say Latin, at the age of ten, and hope by a uniform system of formal training to achieve success at the age of twenty. The natural result is failure, both in interest and in acquirement. When I speak of failure, I am comparing our results with the brilliant success of the first natural cycle. I do not think that it is because our tasks are intrinsically too hard, when I remember that the infant's cycle is the hardest of all. It is because our tasks are set in an unnatural way, without rhythm and without the stimulus of intermediate successes and without concentration.

I have not yet spoken of this character of concentration which so conspicuously attaches to the infant's progress. The whole being of the infant is absorbed in the practice of its cycle. It has nothing else to divert its mental development. In this respect there is a striking difference between this natural cycle and the subsequent history of the student's development. It is perfectly obvious that life is very various and that the mind and brain naturally develop so as to adapt themselves to the many-hued world in which their lot is cast. Still, after making allowance for this consideration, we will be wise to preserve some measure of concentration for each of the subsequent cycles. In particular, we should avoid a competition of diverse subjects in the same stage of their cycles. The fault of the older education was unrhythmic concentration on a single undifferentiated subject. Our modern system, with its insistence on a preliminary general education, and with its easy toleration of the analysis of knowledge into distinct subjects, is an equally unrhythmic collection of distracting scraps. I am pleading that we shall endeavour to weave in the learner's mind a harmony of patterns, by co-ordinating the various elements of instruction into subordinate cycles each of intrinsic worth for the immediate apprehension of the pupil. We must garner our crops each in its due season.

THE ROMANCE OF ADOLESCENCE

We will now pass to some concrete applications of the ideas which have been developed in the former part of my address.

The first cycle of infancy is succeeded by the cycle of adolescence, which opens with by far the greatest stage of romance which we ever experience. It is in this stage that the lines of character are graven. How the child emerges from the romantic stage of adolescence is how the subsequent life will be moulded by ideals and coloured by imagination. It rapidly follows on the generalisation of capacity produced by the acquirement of spoken language and of reading. The stage of generalisation belonging to the infantile cycle is comparatively short because the romantic material of infancy is so scanty. The initial knowledge of the world in any developed sense of the word "knowledge" really commences after the achievement of the first cycle, and thus issues in the tremendous age of romance. Ideas, facts, relationships, stories, histories, possibilities, artistry in words, in sounds, in form and in colour, crowd into the child's life, stir his feelings, excite his appreciation, and incite his impulses to kindred activities. It is a saddening thought that on this golden age there falls so often the shadow of the crammer. I am thinking of a period of about four years of the child's life, roughly, in ordinary cases, falling between the ages of eight and twelve or thirteen. It is the first great period of the utilisation of the native language, and of developed powers of observation and of manipulation. The infant cannot manipulate, the child can; the infant cannot observe, the child can; the infant cannot retain thoughts by the recollection of words, the child can. The child thus enters upon a new world.

Of course, the stage of precision prolongs itself as recurring in minor cycles which form eddies in the great romance. The perfecting of writing, of spelling, of the elements of arithmetic, and of lists of simple facts, such as the Kings of England, are all elements of precision, very necessary both as training in concentration and as useful acquirements. However, these are essentially fragmentary in character, whereas the great romance is the flood which bears on the child towards the life of the spirit.

The success of the Montessori system is due to its recognition of the dominance of romance at this period of growth. If this be the explanation, it also points to the limitations in the usefulness of that method. It is the system which in some measure is essential for every romantic stage. Its essence is browsing and the encouragement of vivid freshness. But it lacks the restraint which is necessary for the great stages of precision.

THE MASTERY OF LANGUAGE

As he nears the end of the great romance the cyclic course of growth is swinging the child over towards an aptitude for exact knowledge. Language is now the natural subject-matter for concentrated attack. It is the mode of expression with which he is thoroughly familiar. He is acquainted with stories, histories, and poems illustrating the lives of other people and of other civilisations. Accordingly, from the age of eleven onwards there is wanted a gradually increasing concentration towards precise knowledge of language. Finally, the three years from twelve to fifteen should be dominated by a mass attack upon language, so planned that a definite result, in itself worth having, is thereby achieved. I should guess that within these limits of time, and given adequate concentration, we might ask that at the end of that period the children should have command of English, should be able to read fluently fairly simple French, and should have completed the elementary stage of Latin; I mean, a precise knowledge of the more straightforward parts of Latin grammar, the knowledge of the construction of Latin sentences, and the reading of some parts of appropriate Latin authors, perhaps simplified and largely supplemented by the aid of the best literary translations so that their reading of the original, plus translation, gives them a grip of the book as a literary whole. I conceive that such a measure of attainment in these three languages is well within the reach of the ordinary child, provided that he has not been distracted by the effort at precision in a multiplicity of other subjects. Also some more gifted children could go further. The Latin would come to them easily, so that it would be possible to start Greek before the end of the period, always provided that their bent is literary and that they mean later to pursue that study at least for some years. Other subjects will occupy a subordinate place in the time-table and will be undertaken in a different spirit. In the first place, it must be remembered that the semi-literary subjects, such as history, will largely have been provided in the study of the languages. It will be hardly possible to read some English, French, and Latin literature without imparting some knowledge of European history. I do not mean that all special history teaching should be abandoned. I do, however, suggest that the subject should be exhibited in what I have termed the romantic spirit, and that the pupils should not be subjected to the test of precise recollection of details on any large systematic scale.

At this period of growth science should be in its stage of romance. The pupils should see for themselves, and experiment for themselves, with only fragmentary precision of thought. The essence of the importance of science, both for interest in theory or for technological purposes, lies in its application to concrete detail, and every such application evokes a novel problem for research. Accordingly, all training in science should begin as well as end in research, and in getting hold of the subject-matter as it occurs in nature. The exact form of guidance suitable to this age and the exact limitations of experiment are matters depending on experience. But I plead that this period is the true age for the romance of science.

CONCENTRATION ON SCIENCE

Towards the age of fifteen the age of precision in language and of romance in science draws to its close, to be succeeded by a period of generalisation in language and of precision in science. This should be a short period, but one of vital importance. I am thinking of about one year's work, and I suggest that it would be well decisively to alter the balance of the preceding curriculum. There should be a concentration on science and a decided diminution of the linguistic work. A year's work on science, coming on the top of the previous romantic study, should make everyone understand the main principles which govern the development of mechanics, physics, chemistry, algebra and geometry. Understand that they are not beginning these subjects, but they are putting together a previous discursive study by an exact formulation of their main ideas. For example, take algebra and geometry, which I single out as being subjects with which I have some slight familiarity. In the previous three years there has been work on the applications of the simplest algebraic formulæ and geometrical propositions to problems of surveying, or of some other scientific work involving calculations. In this way arithmetic has been carefully strengthened by the insistence on definite numerical results, and familiarity with the ideas of literal formulæ and of geometrical properties has been gained; also some minor methods of manipulation have been inculcated. There is thus no long time to be wasted in getting used to the ideas of the sciences. The pupils are ready for the small body of algebraic and geometrical truths which they ought to know thoroughly. Furthermore, in the previous period some boys will have shown an aptitude for mathematics and will have pushed on a little more, besides in the final year somewhat emphasising their mathematics at the expense of some of the other subjects. I am simply taking mathematics as an illustration.

Meanwhile, the cycle of language is in its stage of generalisation. In this stage the precise study of grammar and composition is discontinued, and the language study is confined to reading the literature with emphasised attention to its ideas and to the general history in which it is embedded; also the time allotted to history will pass into the precise study of a short definite period, chosen to illustrate exactly what does happen at an important epoch and also to show how to pass the simpler types of judgments on men and policies.

I have now sketched in outline the course of education from babyhood to about sixteen and a half, arranged with some attention to the rhythmic pulses of life. In some such way a general education is possible in which the pupil throughout has the advantage of concentration and of freshness. Thus precision will always illustrate subject-matter already apprehended and crying out for drastic treatment. Every pupil will have concentrated in turn on a variety of different subjects, and will know where his strong points lie. Finally—and this of all the objects to be attained is the most dear to my heart—the science students will have obtained both an invaluable literary education and also at the most impressionable age an early initiation into habits of thinking for themselves in the region of science.

After the age of sixteen new problems arise. For literary students science passes into the stage of generalisation, largely in the form of lectures on its main results and general ideas. New cycles of linguistic, literary, and historical study commence. But further detail is now unnecessary. For the scientists the preceding stage of precision maintains itself to the close of the school period with an increasing apprehension of wider general ideas.

However, at this period of education the problem is too individual, or at least breaks up into too many cases, to be susceptible of broad general treatment. I do suggest, nevertheless, that all scientists should now keep up their French, and initiate the study of German if they have not already acquired it.

UNIVERSITY EDUCATION

I should now like, if you will bear with me, to make some remarks respecting the import of these ideas for a University education.

The whole period of growth from infancy to manhood forms one grand cycle. Its stage of romance stretches across the first dozen years of life, its stage of precision comprises the whole school period of secondary education, and its stage of generalisation is the period of entrance into manhood. For those whose formal education is prolonged beyond the school age, the University course or its equivalent is the great period of generalisation. The spirit of generalisation should dominate a University. The lectures should be addressed to those to whom details and procedure are familiar; that is to say, familiar at least in the sense of being so congruous to pre-existing training as to be easily acquirable. During the school period the student has been mentally bending over his desk; at the University he should stand up and look around. For this reason it is fatal if the first year at the University be frittered away in going over the old work in the old spirit. At school the boy painfully rises from the particular towards glimpses at general ideas;

at the University he should start from general ideas and study their applications to concrete cases. A well-planned University course is a study of the wide sweep of generality. I do not mean that it should be abstract in the sense of divorce from concrete fact, but that concrete fact should be studied as illustrating the scope of general ideas.

CULTIVATION OF MENTAL POWER

This is the aspect of University training in which theoretical interest and practical utility coincide. Whatever be the detail with which you cram your student, the chance of his meeting in after-life exactly that detail is almost infinitesimal; and if he does meet it, he will probably have forgotten what you taught him about it. The really useful training yields a comprehension of a few general principles with a thorough grounding in the way they apply to a variety of concrete details. In subsequent practice the men will have forgotten your particular details; but they will remember by an unconscious common sense how to apply principles to immediate circumstances. Your learning is useless to you till you have lost your text-books, burnt your lecture notes, and forgotten the minutiæ which you learnt by heart for the examination. What, in the way of detail, you continually require will stick in your memory as obvious facts like the sun and moon; and what you casually require can be looked up in any work of reference. The function of a University is to enable you to shed details in favour of principles. When I speak of principles I am hardly even thinking of verbal formulations. A principle which has thoroughly soaked into you is rather a mental habit than a formal statement. It becomes the way the mind reacts to the appropriate stimulus in the form of illustrative circumstances. Nobody goes about with his knowledge clearly and consciously before him. Mental cultivation is nothing else than the satisfactory way in which the mind will function when it is poked up into activity. Learning is often spoken of as if we are watching the open pages of all the books which we have ever read, and then, when occasion arises, we select the right page to read aloud to the universe.

Luckily, the truth is far otherwise from this crude idea; and for this reason the antagonism between the claims of pure knowledge and professional acquirement should be much less acute than a faulty view of education would lead us to anticipate. I can put my point otherwise by saying that the ideal of a University is not so much knowledge, as power. Its business is to convert the knowledge of a boy into the power of a man.

THE RHYTHMIC CHARACTER OF GROWTH

I will conclude with two remarks which I wish to make by way of caution in the interpretation of my meaning. The point of this address is the rhythmic character of growth. The interior spiritual life of man is a web of many strands. They do not all grow together by uniform extension. I have tried to illustrate this truth by considering the normal unfolding of the capacities of a child in somewhat favourable circumstances but otherwise with fair average capacities. Perhaps I have misconstrued the usual phenomena. It is very likely that I have so failed, for the evidence is complex and difficult. But do not let any failure in this respect prejudice the main point which I am here to enforce. It is that the development of mentality exhibits itself as a rhythm involving an interweaving of cycles, the whole process being dominated by a greater cycle of the same general character as its minor eddies. Furthermore, this rhythm exhibits certain ascertainable general laws which are valid for most pupils, and the quality of our teaching should be so adapted as to suit the stage in the rhythm to which our pupils have advanced. The problem of a curriculum is not so much the succession of subjects; for all subjects should in essence be begun with the dawn of mentality. The truly important order is the order of quality which the educational procedure should assume.

My second caution is to ask you not to exaggerate into sharpness the distinction between the three stages of a cycle. I strongly suspect that many of you, when you heard me detail the three stages in each cycle, said to yourselves—How like a mathematician to make such formal divisions! I assure you that it is not mathematics but literary incompetence that may have led me into the error against which I am warning you. Of course, I mean throughout a distinction of emphasis, of pervasive quality—romance, precision, generalisation, are all present throughout. But there is an alternation of dominance, and it is this alternation which constitutes the cycles.

THE RHYTHMIC CLAIMS OF FREEDOM AND DISCIPLINE

The fading of ideals is sad evidence of the defeat of human endeavour. In the schools of antiquity philosophers aspired to impart wisdom, in modern colleges our humbler aim is to teach subjects. The drop from the divine wisdom, which was the goal of the ancients, to text-book knowledge of subjects, which is achieved by the moderns, marks an educational failure, sustained through the ages. I am not maintaining that in the practice of education the ancient were more successful than ourselves. You have only to read Lucian, and to note his satiric dramatizations of the pretentious claims of philosophers, to see that in this respect the ancients can boast over us no superiority. My point is that, at the dawn of our European civilisation, men started with the full ideals which should inspire education, and that gradually our ideals have sunk to square with our practice.

But when ideals have sunk to the level of practice, the result is stagnation. In particular, so long as we conceive intellectual education as merely consisting in the acquirement of mechanical mental aptitudes, and of formulated statements of useful truths, there can be no progress; though there will be much activity, amid aimless re-arrangement of syllabuses, in the fruitless endeavour to dodge the inevitable lack of time. We must take it as an unavoidable fact, that God has so made the world that there are more topics desirable for knowledge than any one person can possibly acquire. It is hopeless to approach the problem by the way of the enumeration of subjects which every one ought to have mastered. There are too many of them, all with excellent title-deeds. Perhaps, after all, this plethora of material is fortunate; for the world is made interesting by a delightful ignorance of important truths. What I am anxious to impress on you is that though knowledge is one chief aim of intellectual education, there is another ingredient, vaguer but greater, and more dominating in its importance. The ancients called it "wisdom." You cannot be wise without some basis of knowledge; but you may easily acquire knowledge and remain bare of wisdom.

Now wisdom is the way in which knowledge is held. It concerns the handling of knowledge, its selection for the determination of relevant issues, its employment to add value to our immediate experience. This mastery of knowledge, which is wisdom, is the most intimate freedom obtainable. The ancients saw clearly—more clearly than we do—the necessity for dominating knowledge by wisdom. But, in the pursuit of wisdom in the region of practical education, they erred sadly. To put the matter simply, their popular practice assumed that wisdom could be imparted to the young by procuring philosophers to spout at them. Hence the crop of shady philosophers in the schools of the ancient world. The only avenue towards wisdom is by freedom in the presence of knowledge. But the only avenue towards knowledge is by discipline in the acquirement of ordered fact. Freedom and discipline are the two essentials of education, and hence the title of my discourse to-day, "The Rhythmic Claims of Freedom and Discipline."

The antithesis in education between freedom and discipline is not so sharp as a logical analysis of the meanings of the terms might lead us to imagine. The pupil's mind is a growing organism. On the one hand, it is not a box to be ruthlessly packed with alien ideas: and, on the other hand, the ordered acquirement of knowledge is the natural food for a developing intelligence. Accordingly, it should be the aim of an ideally constructed education that the discipline should be the voluntary issue of free choice, and that the freedom should gain an enrichment of possibility as the issue of discipline. The two principles, freedom and discipline, are not antagonists, but should be so adjusted in the child's life that they correspond to a natural sway, to and fro, of the developing personality. It is this adaptation of freedom and discipline to the natural sway of development that I have elsewhere called The Rhythm of Education. I am convinced that much disappointing failure in the past has been due to neglect of attention to the importance of this rhythm. My main position is that the dominant note of education at its beginning and at its end is freedom, but that there is an intermediate stage of discipline with freedom in subordination: Furthermore, that there is not one unique threefold cycle of freedom, discipline, and freedom; but that all mental development is composed of such cycles, and of cycles of such cycles. Such a cycle is a unit cell, or brick; and the complete stage of growth is an organic structure of such cells. In analysing any one such cell, I call the first period of freedom the "stage of Romance," the intermediate period of discipline I call the "stage of Precision," and the final period of freedom is the "stage of Generalisation."

Let me now explain myself in more detail. There can be no mental development without interest. Interest is the *sine qua non* for attention and apprehension. You may endeavour to excite interest by means of birch rods, or you may coax it by the incitement of pleasurable activity. But without interest there will be no progress. Now the natural mode by which living organisms are excited towards suitable self-development is enjoyment. The infant is lured to adapt itself to its environment by its love of its mother and its nurse; we eat because we like a good dinner: we subdue the forces of nature because we have been lured to discovery by an insatiable curiosity: we enjoy exercise: and we enjoy the unchristian passion of hating our dangerous enemies. Undoubtedly pain is one subordinate means of arousing an organism to action. But it only supervenes on the failure of pleasure. Joy is the normal healthy spur for the *élan vital*. I am not maintaining that we can safely abandon ourselves to the allurement of the greater immediate joys. What I do mean is that we should seek to arrange the development of character along a path of natural activity, in itself pleasurable. The subordinate stiffening of discipline must be directed to secure some long-time good; although an adequate object must not be too far below the horizon, if the necessary interest is to be retained.

The second preliminary point which I wish to make, is the unimportance—indeed the evil—of barren knowledge. The importance of knowledge lies in its use, in our active mastery of it—that is to say, it lies in wisdom. It is a convention to speak of mere knowledge, apart from wisdom, as of itself imparting a peculiar dignity to its possessor. I do not share in this reverence for knowledge as such. It all depends on who has the knowledge and what he does with it. That knowledge which adds greatness to character is knowledge so handled as to transform every phase of immediate experience. It is in respect to the activity of knowledge that an over-vigorous discipline in education is so harmful. The habit of active thought, with freshness, can only be generated by adequate freedom. Undiscriminating discipline defeats its own object by dulling the mind. If you have much to do with the young as they emerge from school and from the university, you soon note the dulled minds of those whose education has consisted in the acquirement of inert knowledge. Also the deplorable tone of English society in respect to learning is a tribute to our educational failure. Furthermore, this overhaste to impart mere knowledge defeats itself. The human mind rejects knowledge imparted in this way. The craving for expansion, for activity, inherent in youth is disgusted by a dry imposition of disciplined knowledge. The discipline, when it comes, should satisfy a natural craving for the wisdom which adds value to bare experience.

But let us now examine more closely the rhythm of these natural cravings of the human intelligence. The first procedure of the mind in a new environment is a somewhat discursive activity amid a welter of ideas and experience. It is a process of discovery, a process of becoming used to curious thoughts, of shaping questions, of seeking for answers, of devising new experiences, of noticing what happens as the result of new ventures. This general process is both natural and of absorbing interest. We must often have noticed children between the ages of eight and thirteen absorbed in its ferment. It is dominated by wonder, and cursed be the dullard who destroys wonder. Now undoubtedly this stage of development requires help, and even discipline. The environment within which the mind is working must be carefully selected. It must, of course, be chosen to suit the child's stage of growth, and must be adapted to individual needs. In a sense it is an imposition from without; but in a deeper sense it answers to the call of life within the child. In the teacher's consciousness the child has been sent to his telescope to look at the stars, in the child's consciousness he has been given free access to the glory of the heavens. Unless, working somewhere, however obscurely, even in the dullest child, there is this transfiguration of imposed routine, the child's nature will refuse to assimilate the alien material. It must never be forgotten that education is not a process of packing articles in a trunk. Such a simile is entirely inapplicable. It is, of course, a process completely of its own peculiar genus. Its nearest analogue is the assimilation of food by a living organism: and we all know how necessary to health is palatable food under suitable conditions. When you have put your boots in a trunk, they will stay there till you take them out again; but this is not at all the case if you feed a child with the wrong food.

This initial stage of romance requires guidance in another way. After all the child is the heir to long ages of civilisation, and it is absurd to let him wander in the intellectual maze of men in the Glacial Epoch. Accordingly, a certain pointing out of important facts, and of simplifying ideas, and of usual names, really strengthens the natural impetus of the pupil. In no part of education can you do without discipline or can you do without freedom; but in the stage of romance the emphasis must always be on freedom, to allow the child to see for itself and to act for itself. My point is that a block in the assimilation of ideas inevitably arises when a discipline of precision is imposed before a stage of romance has run its course in the growing mind. There is no comprehension apart from romance. It is my strong belief that the cause of so much failure in the past has been due to the lack of careful study of the due place of romance. Without the adventure of romance, at the best you get inert knowledge without initiative, and at the worst you get contempt of ideas—without knowledge.

But when this stage of romance has been properly guided another craving grows. The freshness of inexperience has worn off; there is general knowledge of the groundwork of fact and theory: and, above all, there has been plenty of independent browsing amid first-hand experiences, involving adventures of thought and of action. The enlightenment which comes from precise knowledge can now be understood. It corresponds to the obvious requirements of common sense, and deals with familiar material. Now is the time for pushing on, for knowing the subject exactly, and for retaining in the memory its salient features. This is the stage of precision. This stage is the sole stage of learning in the traditional scheme of education, either at school or university. You had to learn your subject, and there was nothing more to be said on the topic of education. The result of such an undue extension of a most necessary period of development was the production of a plentiful array of dunces, and of a few scholars whose natural interest had survived the car of Juggernaut. There is, indeed, always the temptation to teach pupils a little more of fact and of precise theory than at that stage they are fitted to assimilate. If only they could, it would be so useful. We—I am talking of schoolmasters and of university dons—are apt to forget that we are only subordinate elements in the education of a grown man; and that, in their own good time, in later life our pupils will learn for themselves. The phenomena of growth cannot be hurried beyond certain very narrow limits. But an unskilful practitioner can easily damage a sensitive organism. Yet, when all has been said in the way of caution, there is such a thing as pushing on, of getting to know the fundamental details and the main exact generalisations, and of acquiring an easy mastery of technique. There is no getting away from the fact that things have been found out, and that to be effective in the modern world you must have a store of definite acquirement of the best practice. To write poetry you must study metre; and to build bridges you must be learned in the strength of material. Even the Hebrew prophets had learned to write, probably in those days requiring no mean effort. The untutored art of genius is—in the words of the Prayer Book—a vain thing, fondly invented.

During the stage of precision, romance is the background. The stage is dominated by the inescapable fact that there are right ways and wrong ways, and definite truths to be known. But romance is not dead, and it is the art of teaching to foster it amidst definite application to appointed task. It must be fostered for one reason, because romance is after all a necessary ingredient of that balanced wisdom which is the goal to be attained. But there is another reason: The organism will not absorb the fruits of the task unless its powers of apprehension are kept fresh by romance. The real point is to discover in practice that exact balance between freedom and discipline which will give the greatest rate of progress over the things to be known. I do not believe that there is any abstract formula which will give information applicable to all subjects, to all types of pupils, or to each individual pupil; except indeed the formula of rhythmic sway which I have been insisting on, namely, that in the earlier stage the progress requires that the emphasis be laid on freedom, and that in the later middle stage the emphasis be laid on the definite acquirement of allotted tasks. I freely admit that if the stage of romance has been properly managed, the discipline of the second stage is much less apparent, that the children know how to go about their work, want to make a good job of it, and can be safely trusted with the details. Furthermore, I hold that the only discipline, important for its own sake, is self-discipline, and that this can only be acquired by a wide use of freedom. But yet—so many are the delicate points to be considered in education—it is necessary in life to have acquired the habit of cheerfully undertaking imposed tasks. The conditions can be satisfied if the tasks correspond to the natural cravings of the pupil at his stage of progress, if they keep his powers at full stretch, and if they attain an obviously sensible result, and if reasonable freedom is allowed in the mode of execution.

The difficulty of speaking about the way a skilful teacher will keep romance alive in his pupils arises from the fact that what takes a long time to describe, takes a short time to do. The beauty of a passage of Virgil may be rendered by insisting on beauty of verbal enunciation, taking no longer than prosy utterance. The emphasis on the beauty of a mathematical argument, in its marshalling of general considerations to unravel complex fact, is the speediest mode of procedure. The responsibility of the teacher at this stage is immense. To speak the truth, except in the rare case of genius in the teacher, I do not think that it is possible to take a whole class very far along the road of precision without some dulling of the interest. It is the unfortunate dilemma that initiative and training are both necessary, and that training is apt to kill initiative.

But this admission is not to condone a brutal ignorance of methods of mitigating this untoward fact. It is not a theoretical necessity, but arises because perfect tact is unattainable in the treatment of each individual case. In the past the methods employed assassinated interest; we are discussing how to reduce the evil to its smallest dimensions. I merely utter the warning that education is a difficult problem, to be solved by no one simple formula.

In this connection there is, however, one practical consideration which is largely neglected. The territory of romantic interest is large, ill-defined, and not to be controlled by any explicit boundary. It depends on the chance flashes of insight. But the area of precise knowledge, as exacted in any general educational system, can be, and should be, definitely determined. If you make it too wide you will kill interest and defeat your own object: if you make it too narrow your pupils will lack effective grip. Surely, in every subject in each type of curriculum, the precise knowledge required should be determined after the most anxious inquiry. This does not now seem to be the case in any effective way. For example, in the classical studies of boys destined for a scientific career—a class of pupils in whom I am greatly interested— What is the Latin vocabulary which they ought definitely to know? Also what are the grammatical rules and constructions which they ought to have mastered? Why not determine these once and for all, and then bend every exercise to impress just these on the memory, and to understand their derivatives, both in Latin and also in French and English. Then, as to other constructions and words which occur in the reading of texts, supply full information in the easiest manner. A certain ruthless definiteness is essential in education. I am sure that one secret of a successful teacher is that he has formulated quite clearly in his mind what the pupil has got to know in precise fashion. He will then cease from half-hearted attempts to worry his pupils with memorising a lot of irrelevant stuff of inferior importance. The secret of success is pace, and the secret of pace is concentration. But, in respect to precise knowledge, the watchword is pace, pace, pace. Get your knowledge quickly, and then use it. If you can use it, you will retain it.

We have now come to the third stage of the rhythmic cycle, the stage of generalisation. There is here a reaction towards romance. Something definite is now known; aptitudes have been acquired; and general rules and laws are clearly apprehended both in their formulation and their detailed exemplification. The pupil now wants to use his new weapons. He is an effective individual, and it is effects that he wants to produce. He relapses into the discursive adventures of the romantic stage, with the advantage that his mind is now a disciplined regiment instead of a rabble. In this sense, education should begin in research and end in research. After all, the whole affair is merely a preparation for battling with the immediate experiences of life, a preparation by which to qualify each immediate moment with relevant ideas and appropriate actions. An education which does not begin by evoking initiative and end by encouraging it must be wrong. For its whole aim is the production of active wisdom.

In my own work at universities I have been much struck by the paralysis of thought induced in pupils by the aimless accumulation of precise knowledge, inert and unutilised. It should be the chief aim of a university professor to exhibit himself in his own true character—that is, as an ignorant man thinking, actively utilising his small share of knowledge. In a sense, knowledge shrinks as wisdom grows: for details are swallowed up in principles. The details of knowledge which are important will be picked up *ad hoc* in each avocation of life, but the habit of the active utilisation of well-understood principles is the final possession of wisdom. The stage of precision is the stage of growing into the apprehension of principles by the acquisition of a precise knowledge of details. The stage of generalisations is the stage of shedding details in favour of the active application of principles, the details retreating into subconscious habits. We don't go about explicitly retaining in our own minds that two and two make four, though once we had to learn it by heart. We trust to habit for our elementary arithmetic. But the essence of this stage is the emergence from the comparative passivity of being trained into the active freedom of application. Of course, during this stage, precise knowledge will grow, and more actively than ever before, because the mind has experienced the power of definiteness, and responds to the acquisition of general truth, and of richness of illustration. But the growth of knowledge becomes progressively unconscious, as being an incident derived from some active adventure of thought.

So much for the three stages of the rhythmic unit of development. In a general way the whole period of education is dominated by this threefold rhythm. Till the age of thirteen or fourteen there is the romantic stage, from fourteen to eighteen the stage of precision, and from eighteen to two and twenty the stage of generalisation. But these are only average characters, tinging the mode of development as a whole. I do not think that any pupil completes his stages simultaneously in all subjects. For example, I should plead that while language is initiating its stage of precision in the way of acquisition of vocabulary and of grammar, science should be in its full romantic stage. The romantic stage of language begins in infancy with the acquisition of speech, so that it passes early towards a stage of precision; while science is a late comer. Accordingly a precise inculcation of science at an early age wipes out initiative and interest, and destroys any chance of the topic having any richness of content in the child's apprehension. Thus, the romantic stage of science should persist for years after the precise study of language has commenced.

There are minor eddies, each in itself a threefold cycle, running its course in each day, in each week, and in each term. There is the general apprehension of some topic in its vague possibilities, the mastery of the relevant details, and finally the putting of the whole subject together in the light of the relevant knowledge. Unless the pupils are continually sustained by the evocation of interest, the acquirement of technique, and the excitement of success, they can never make progress, and will certainly lose heart. Speaking generally, during the last thirty years the schools of England have been sending up to the universities a disheartened crowd of young folk, inoculated against any outbreak of intellectual zeal. The universities have seconded the efforts of the schools and emphasised the failure. Accordingly, the cheerful gaiety of the young turns to other topics, and thus educated England is not hospitable to ideas. When we can point to some great achievement of our nation—let us hope that it may be something other than a war— which has been won in the class-room of our schools, and not in their playing-fields, then we may feel content with our modes of education.

So far I have been discussing intellectual education, and my argument has been cramped on too narrow a basis. After all, our pupils are alive, and cannot be chopped into separate bits, like the pieces of a jig-saw puzzle. In the production of a mechanism the constructive energy lies outside it, and adds discrete parts to discrete parts. The case is far different for a living organism which grows by its own impulse towards self-development. This impulse can be stimulated and guided from outside the organism, and it can also be killed. But for all your stimulation and guidance the creative impulse towards growth comes from within, and is intensely characteristic of the individual. Education is the guidance of the individual towards a comprehension of the art of life; and by the art of life I mean the most complete achievement of varied activity expressing the potentialities of that living creature in the face of its actual environment. This completeness of achievement involves an artistic sense, subordinating the lower to the higher possibilities of the indivisible personality. Science, art, religion, morality, take their rise from this sense of values within the structure of being. Each individual embodies an adventure of existence. The art of life is the guidance of this adventure. The great religions of civilisation include among their original elements revolts against the inculcation of morals as a set of isolated prohibitions. Morality, in the petty negative sense of the term, is the deadly enemy of religion. Paul denounces the Law, and the Gospels are vehement against the Pharisees. Every outbreak of religion exhibits the same intensity of antagonism—an antagonism diminishing as religion fades. No part of education has more to gain from attention to the rhythmic law of growth than has moral and religious education. Whatever be the right way to formulate religious truths, it is death to religion to insist on a premature stage of precision. The vitality of religion is shown by the way in which the religious spirit has survived the ordeal of religious education.

The problem of religion in education is too large to be discussed at this stage of my address. I have referred to it to guard against the suspicion that the principles here advocated are to be conceived in a narrow sense. We are analysing the general law of rhythmic progress in the higher stages of life, embodying the initial awakening, the discipline, and the fruition on the higher plane. What I am now insisting is that the principle of progress is from within: the discovery is made by ourselves, the discipline is self-discipline, and the fruition is the outcome of our own initiative. The teacher has a double function. It is for him to elicit the enthusiasm by resonance from his own personality, and to create the environment of a larger knowledge and a firmer purpose. He is there to avoid the waste, which in the lower stages of existence is nature's way of evolution. The ultimate motive power, alike in science, in morality, and in religion, is the sense of value, the sense of importance. It takes the various forms of wonder, of curiosity, of reverence, or worship, of tumultuous desire for merging personality in something beyond itself. This sense of value imposes on life incredible labours, and apart from it life sinks back into the passivity of its lower types. The most penetrating exhibition of this force is the sense of beauty, the æsthetic sense of realised perfection. This thought leads me to ask, whether in our modern education we emphasise sufficiently the functions of art.

The typical education of our public schools was devised for boys from well-to-do cultivated homes. They travelled in Italy, in Greece, and in France, and often their own homes were set amid beauty. None of these circumstances hold for modern national education in primary or secondary schools, or even for the majority of boys and girls in our enlarged system of public schools. You cannot, without loss, ignore in the life of the spirit so great a factor as art. Our æsthetic emotions provide us with vivid apprehensions of value. If you maim these, you weaken the force of the whole system of spiritual apprehensions. The claim for freedom in education carries with it the corollary that the development of the whole personality must be attended to. You must not arbitrarily refuse its urgent demands. In these days of economy, we hear much of the futility of our educational efforts and of the possibility of curtailing them. The endeavour to develop a bare intellectuality is bound to issue in a large crop of failure. This is just what we have done in our national schools. We do just enough to excite and not enough to satisfy. History shows us that an efflorescence of art is the first activity of nations on the road to civilisation. Yet, in the face of this plain fact, we practically shut out art from the masses of the population. Can we wonder that such an education, evoking and defeating cravings, leads to failure and discontent? The stupidity of the whole procedure is, that art in simple popular forms is just what we can give to the nation without undue strain on our resources. You may, perhaps, by some great reforms, obviate the worse kind of sweated labour and the insecurity of employment. But you can never greatly increase average incomes. On that side all hope of Utopia is closed to you. It would, however, require no very great effort to use our schools to produce a population with some love of music, some enjoyment of drama, and some joy in beauty of form and colour. We could also provide means for the satisfaction of these emotions in the general life of the population. If you think of the simplest ways, you will see that the strain on material resources would be negligible; and when you have done that, and when your population widely appreciates what art can give—its joys and its terrors—do you not think that your prophets and your clergy and your statesmen will be in a stronger position when they speak to the population of the love of God, of the inexorableness of duty, and of the call of patriotism?

Shakespeare wrote his plays for English people reared in the beauty of the country, amid the pageant of life as the Middle Age merged into the Renaissance, and with a new world across the ocean to make vivid the call of romance. To-day we deal with herded town populations, reared in a scientific age. I have no doubt that unless we can meet the new age with new methods, to sustain for our populations the life of the spirit, sooner or later, amid some savage outbreak of defeated longings, the fate of Russia will be the fate of England. Historians will write as her epitaph that her fall issued from the spiritual blindness of her governing classes, from their dull materialism, and from their Pharisaic attachment to petty formulæ of statesmanship.

Compulsory mis-education

PAUL GOODMAN

As previously indicated in the introduction to John Holt's *How Children Fail,* Paul Goodman along with Holt is considered one of the leading educational radicals. However, whereas Holt tends to direct most of his comments toward the schools, Goodman also wages war on society. Holt, in *How Children Fail,* writes with the guise of presumed objectivity, Goodman, to the contrary, is more candid and willing to admit his biases. For example, he admits in the opening sentence of *Compulsory Mis-Education* that he has no intention to be "generous or fair" about his "remarks on the schools." Both authors are polemists who possess extraordinary verbal abilities, but Holt's *How Children Fail* appears as a cool, detached commentary, whereas Goodman's writing in *Compulsory Mis-Education* is sometimes emotional and idealistic and is influenced by the classical and utopian ideas of Western civilization. Both authors see little, if any, hope for reforming schools under present conditions. The difference is that Holt points to the teachers and school administrators as the major villains, whereas Goodman contends that the larger society is at fault, and before the schools can be improved society needs to be rectified and reconstructed.

In the book as a whole, Goodman maintains that ours is a sick society—corrupt, dehumanizing, and repressive; full of materialistic and spurious values—that has produced the same type of sick school: corrupt, dehumanizing, and repressive. Although school is

SOURCE: Paul Goodman, *Compulsory Mis-Education* (New York: Horizon Press, 1964), pp. 19–23, 26–42, 66–74, 76–77, 127, 129–135, 150–158, 172–178, 180–182. Copyright © 1964. Reprinted by permission of Paul Goodman and Horizon Press.

supposed to help the individual fulfill his human potential, it actually molds and manipulates him. It is part of a threefold interlocking system—also comprising big business and mass media —that processes the populace. Almost everyone perceives in the same way, the American way. (In light of the current overt dissonance, and polarization between blacks and whites, youth and adults, one might argue such a view is now dated, though it was very evident when Goodman wrote his book.) There is no need for dialogue. Even "competing" newspapers and political parties agree on the major issues. The whole situation adds up to brainwashing: a uniform world view, the programming of consumers into revolving cash accounts, the absence of viable alternatives, confusion about one's identity, and a chronic anxiety so that one clings to the homogenized system as the only security.

In this connection, Goodman points out in this selection that it might be better if many of us did not know how to read; it would be harder to brainwash us, to keep us "informed," to regiment us into the rat race and into buying nonessential consumer goods. With less stress on literacy, there would be greater folk culture, less suffering of inferiority, and fewer unnecessary standards. Given the present system, schools are unable to teach "authentic literacy"—reading as a means of enjoyment, liberation, and cultivation.

The emphasis in society, according to Goodman, is on production, making money, and overkill rather than on moral virtue, human beauty, and the pleasure of life. Our mores and values lead to urban blight, suburban anomie, and rural waste; needless wars, racism, and poverty among the affluent; increased destruction of community life and man's environment; increased psychosomatic and mental illness; the powerless man in a powerful society; an era of dropout, drug-addicted, violent youth culture and pill-gorging, gin-guzzling, bed-hopping adult culture.

The emphasis in school is on tests, grades, and credits; it extinguishes the spirit and spontaneity of youth and turns them into mass-producing workers and consumers. It is docility, dullness, and conformity that is rewarded in school; it is freedom, creativity, and individuality that is frowned upon in school. In the excerpts here, Goodman refers to school as a jail, an arm of the police, and to schooling as a device to keep youth off the streets by putting

them into concentration camps called schools. The public welcomes
and supports schools (though they are stingy at times) because
youth are useless, nonproductive, and in the way under the present
system. Since we no longer depend on them, we keep them out of
our way in school and put them through useless and obsolete
training. The longer the student remains, the greater is his
mis-education. He does not really learn; he prepares himself for a
job. Those who drop out of school are often doing the best thing.
Going to school, for these youth, is not the best use of most of
their time and energy. In any event, society is not genuinely interested in them but mainly concerned about them because they
are a nuisance and, in large numbers, perhaps even a threat to the
existing social order.

We also read that education today is geared toward economic
advancement. Schools are, according to Goodman, "petty-bourgeois,
bureaucratic, time-serving, . . . and *nouveau riche* climbing" institutions. The middle class know no other way of succeeding in the
system than by obtaining the right diplomas, and the poor and
minorities have been "conned" into believing that school will lead
to upward mobility. (Again, one might question whether Goodman's
analysis of socioeconomic mobility is still true. Some educators
and social scientists contend that we have passed the "exhibit"
stage.)

School fits people into the economic system; it serves as an
enormous weeding-out and selecting agent for the few large corporations. The giant firms, at least in prosperous times, swoop down
on the college campuses and gobble up the talented. Even the large
department stores require that their sales people have a high school
diploma, for it is supposed to guarantee the "right" character—
honesty, docility, punctuality, neatness—which it does not really do.
Thus the diploma is used as a tool for screening out and selecting
people for the system. Those who have a high school diploma
usually fit into the assembly line and enter at the lower end of
the scale in terms of money and status. Those who graduate from
college have been molded to fit more easily into the system as
organization men and at a higher level on the scale of money and
status. No matter where the individual fits into the system, the
fact that he is a part of the system means he is a member of
the rat race, buys the right brands, votes Democratic or Republican,

and for the greater part lives a bland existence—unable to enjoy esthetic, artistic, intellectual, and human endeavors.

We read further that even the colleges practice mis-education. Many professors and students are corrupted by money, the professors seeking research grants and higher salaries and the students jobs with IBM, Xerox, and AT&T. Colleges produce an elite of disillusioned and cynical bureaucrats and executives.

According to Goodman, the compulsory and monolithic system of schooling is a universal trap. Consequently, he would make school voluntary and diminish the monopoly of the school system; the latter would be achieved by offering viable alternatives, for no single institution can fit the needs and interests of every youngster up to age sixteen and beyond. The alternatives include little theaters, store-front schools, club houses, work camps, the city as a school, and decentralized urban schools. He would encourage experimental schools and payment of money to students for any feasible, self-chosen educational goal or school—somewhat similar to today's voucher idea.

Goodman would also break the lockstep approach to education by allowing students to quit periodically and easily return to school. Thus, the young should have a moratorium on their life-career opportunity, find themselves if necessary, and study when they are ready. In this vein, he believes students need life experiences in the social sciences and humanities to relate to and make the most of their college education. Others could benefit from work-study programs similar to the ones at Reed and Antioch colleges. Still others need to find themselves through purposeful travel, by performing community and social service or farm work, and the like.

Many of the above alternatives outlined by Goodman seemed radical when he wrote *Compulsory Mis-Education;* however, many of his ideas were eventually adopted. Similarly, his idea about quitting and returning to school is now accepted by most educators, and many colleges are granting credit for life experiences, field work, and travel. In the spirit of Paul Goodman, one can appreciate his ideal school: it would be noncompulsory; there would be no police stationed in the hallways, no blackboard jungle; it would encourage spontaneity, imagination, independent thought, esthetic and artistic activities, manual skills, and continuity with emotional and attitudinal experiences; it would reject all tests, grades, credits, and competition; it would have individualized programs; and there would be opportunity to drop out and come back.

PRIMARY GRADES

THE UNIVERSAL TRAP

A conference of experts on school drop-outs will discuss the background of poverty, cultural deprivation, race prejudice, family and emotional troubles, neighborhood uprooting, urban mobility. It will explore ingenious expedients to counteract these conditions, though it will not much look to remedying them—that is not its business. And it will suggest propaganda—e.g. no school, no job—to get the youngsters back in school. It is axiomatic that they ought to be in school.

After a year, it proves necessary to call another conference to cope with the alarming fact that more than 75 percent of the drop-outs who have been cajoled into returning have dropped out again. They persist in failing; they still are not sufficiently motivated. What curricular changes must there be? how can the teachers learn the life-style of the underprivileged?

Curiously muffled in these conferences is the question that puts the burden of proof the other way: What are they drop-outs from? Is the schooling really good for them, or much good for anybody? Since, for many, there are such difficulties with the present arrangements, might not some better arrangements be invented? Or bluntly, since schooling undertakes to be compulsory, must it not continually review its claim to be useful? Is it the only means of education? Isn't it unlikely that *any* single type of social institution could fit almost every youngster up to age 16 and beyond? . . .

But conferences on drop-outs are summoned by school professionals, so perhaps we cannot hope that such elementary questions will be raised. Yet neither are they raised by laymen. There is a mass superstition, underwritten by additional billions every year, that adolescents must continue going to school. The middle-class *know* that no professional competence—i.e. status and salary—can be attained without many diplomas; and poor people have allowed themselves to be convinced that the primary remedy for their increasing deprivation is to agitate for better schooling. Nevertheless, I doubt that, *at present or with any reforms that are conceivable under present school adminis-tration,* going to school is the best use for the time of life of the majority of youth.

Education is a natural community function and occurs inevitably, since the young grow up on the old, toward their activities, and into (or against) their institutions; and the old foster, teach, train, exploit, and abuse the young. Even neglect of the young, except physical neglect has an educational effect—not the worst possible.

Formal schooling is a reasonable auxiliary of the inevitable process, whenever an activity is best learned by singling it out for special at-tention with a special person to teach it. Yet it by no means follows that the complicated artifact of a school system has much to do with education, and certainly not with good education.

Let us bear in mind the way in which a big school system might have nothing to do with education at all. The New York system turns over $700 millions annually, not including capital improvements. There are 750 schools, with perhaps 15 annually being replaced at an extra cost of $2 to $5 millions each. There are 40,000 paid employees. This is a vast vested interest, and it is very probable that—like much of our economy and almost all of our political structure, of which the public schools are a part—it goes on for its own sake, keeping more than a million people busy, wasting wealth, and pre-empting time and space in which something else could be going on. It is a gigantic market for textbook manufacturers, building contractors, and graduate-schools of Education.

The fundamental design of such a system is ancient, yet it has not been altered although the present operation is altogether different in scale from what it was, and therefore it must have a different meaning. For example, in 1900, 6 percent of the 17-year-olds graduated from high school, and less than ½ percent went to college; whereas in 1963, 65 percent graduated from high school and 35 percent went on to something called college. Likewise, there is a vast difference between schooling intermitted in life on a farm or in a city with plenty of small jobs, and schooling that is a child's only "serious" occupation and often his only adult contact. Thus, a perhaps outmoded institution has be-come almost the only allowable way of growing up. And with this pre-empting, there is an increasing intensification of the one narrow experience, e.g. in the shaping of the curriculum and testing according to the increasing requirements of graduate schools far off in time and place. Just as our American society as a whole is more and more tightly organized, so its school system is more and more regimented as part of that organization.

In the organizational plan, the schools play a non-educational and an educational role. The non-educational role is very important. In the tender grades, the schools are a baby-sitting service during a period of collapse of the old-type family and during a time of extreme urbanization and urban mobility. In the junior and senior high school grades, they are an arm of the police, providing cops and concentration camps paid for in the budget under the heading "Board of Education." The educational role is, by and large, to provide—at public and parents' expense—apprentice-training for corporations, government, and the teaching profession itself, and also to train the young, as New York's Commissioner of Education has said (in the Worley case), "to handle constructively their problems of adjustment to authority."

The public schools of America have indeed been a powerful, and beneficent, force for the democratizing of a great mixed population. But we must be careful to keep reassessing them when, with changing conditions, they become a universal trap and democracy begins to look like regimentation.

• • • • •

It is said that our schools are geared to "middle-class values," but this is a false and misleading use of terms. The schools less and less represent *any* human values, but simply adjustment to a mechanical system.

Because of the increasing failure of the schools with the poor urban mass, there has developed a line of criticism—e.g. Oscar Lewis, Patricia Sexton, Frank Riessman, and even Edgar Friedenberg—asserting that there is a "culture of poverty" which the "middle-class" schools do not fit, but which has its own virtues of spontaneity, sociality, animality. The implication is that the "middle class," for all its virtues, is obsessional, prejudiced, prudish.

Pedagogically, this insight is indispensable. A teacher must try to reach each child in terms of what he brings, his background, his habits, the language he understands. But if taken to be more than technical, it is a disastrous conception. The philosophic aim of education must be to get each one out of his isolated class and into the one humanity. Prudence and responsibility are not middle class virtues but human virtues; and spontaneity and sexuality are not powers of the simple but of human health. One has the impression that our social-psychologists are looking not to a human community but to a future in which the obsessionals will take care of the impulsives!

In fact, some of the most important strengths that have historically belonged to the middle class are flouted by the schools: independence, initiative, scrupulous honesty, earnestness, utility, respect for thorough scholarship. Rather than bourgeois, our schools have become petty-bourgeois, bureaucratic, time-serving, gradgrind-practical, timid, and *nouveau riche* climbing. In the upper grades and colleges, they often exude a cynicism that belongs to rotten aristocrats.

Naturally, however, the youth of the poor and of the middle class respond differently to the petty bourgeois atmosphere. For many poor children, school is orderly and has food, compared to chaotic and hungry homes, and it might even be interesting compared to total deprivation of toys and books. Besides, the wish to improve a child's lot, which on the part of a middle class parent might be frantic status-seeking and pressuring, on the part of a poor parent is a loving aspiration. There is here a gloomy irony. The school that for a poor Negro child might be a great joy and opportunity is likely to be dreadful; whereas the middle class child might be better off *not* in the "good" suburban school he has.

Other poor youth, herded into a situation that does not fit their disposition, for which they are unprepared by their background, and which does not interest them, simply develop a reactive stupidity very different from their behavior on the street or ball field. They fall behind, play truant, and as soon as possible drop out. If the school situation is immediately useless and damaging to them, their response must be said to be life-preservative. They thereby somewhat diminish their chances of a decent living, but we shall see that the usual propaganda—that schooling is a road to high salaries—is for most poor youth a lie; and the increase in security is arguably not worth the torture involved.

The reasonable social policy would be not to have these youth in school, certainly not in high school, but to educate them otherwise and provide opportunity for a decent future in some other way. How? I shall venture some suggestions later; in my opinion, the wise thing would be to have our conferences on *this* issue, and omit the idea of drop-out altogether. But the brute fact is that our society isn't really interested; the concern for the drop-outs is mainly because they are a nuisance and a threat and can't be socialized by the existing machinery.

Numerically far more important than these overt drop-outs at 16, however, are the children who conform to schooling between the ages of 6 to 16 or 20, but who drop out internally and day-dream, their days wasted, their liberty caged and scheduled. And there are many such in the middle class, from backgrounds with plenty of food and some books and art, where the youth is seduced by the prospect of money and status, but even more where he is terrified to jeopardize the only pattern of life he knows.

It is in the schools and from the mass media, rather than at home or from their friends, that the mass of our citizens in all classes learn that life is inevitably routine, depersonalized, venally graded; that it is best to toe the mark and shut up; that there is no place for spontaneity, open sexuality, free spirit. Trained in the schools, they go on to the same quality of jobs, culture, politics. This *is* education, mis-education, socializing to the national norms and regimenting to the national "needs."

John Dewey used to hope, naively, that the schools could be a community somewhat better than society and serve as a lever for social change. In fact, our schools reflect our society closely, except that they *emphasize* many of its worst features, as well as having the characteristic defects of academic institutions of all times and places.

Let us examine realistically half a dozen aspects of the school that is dropped out *from*.

(a) There is widespread anxiety about the children not learning to read, and hot and defensive argument about the methods of teaching reading. Indeed, reading deficiency is an accumulating scholastic disadvantage that results in painful feeling of inferiority, truancy, and drop-out. Reading is crucial for school success—all subjects depend on it—and therefore for the status-success that the diploma is about. Yet in all the anxiety and argument, there is no longer any mention of the freedom and human cultivation that literacy is supposed to stand for.

In my opinion, there is something phony here. For a change, let us look at this "reading" coldly and ask if it is really such a big deal except precisely in the school that is supposed to teach it and is sometimes failing to do so.

With the movies, TV, and radio that the illiterate also share, there is certainly no lack of "communications." We cannot say that as humanities or science, the reading-matter of the great majority is in any way superior to the content of these other media. And in the present stage of technology and economy, it is probably *less* true than it was in the late nineteenth century—the time of the great push to universal literacy and arithmetic—that the mass-teaching of reading is indispensable to operate the production and clerical system. It is rather our kind of urbanism, politics, and buying and selling that require literacy. These are not excellent.

Perhaps in the present dispensation we should be as well off if it were socially acceptable for large numbers not to read. It would be harder to regiment people if they were not so well "informed"; as Norbert Wiener used to point out, every repetition of a cliché only increases the noise and *prevents* communication. With less literacy, there would be more folk culture. Much suffering of inferiority would be avoided if youngsters did not have to meet a perhaps unnecessary standard. Serious letters could only benefit if society were less swamped by trash, lies, and bland verbiage. Most important of all, *more* people might become genuinely literate if it were understood that reading is not a matter-of-course but a *special useful art with a proper subject-matter, imagination and truth,* rather than a means of communicating top-down decisions and advertising. . . .

(b) Given their present motives, the schools are not competent to teach authentic literacy, reading as a means of liberation and cultivation. And I doubt that most of us who seriously read and write the English language ever learned it by the route of "Run, Spot, Run" to *Silas Marner*. Rather, having picked up the rudiments either in cultured homes or in the first two grades, we really learned to read by our own will and free exploration, following our bent, generally among books that are considered inappropriate by school librarians!

. . . Now what do our schools do? We use tricks of mechanical conditioning. These do positive damage to spontaneous speech, meant expression, earnest understanding. Inevitably, they create *in the majority* the wooden attitude toward "writing," as entirely different from speech, that college-teachers later try to cope with in Freshman Composition. And reading inevitably becomes a manipulation of signs, e.g. for test-passing, that has no relation to experience.

• • • • •

(c) The young rightly resist animal constraint. But, at least in New York where I have been a school-board Visitor, most teachers—and the principals who supervise their classes—operate as if progressive education had not proved the case for noise and freedom of bodily motion. (Dewey stresses the salutary alternation of boisterousness and tranquility.) The seats are no longer bolted to the floor, but they still face front. Of course, the classes are too large to cope with without "discipline." Then make them smaller, or don't wonder if children escape out of the cage, either into truancy or baffled daydream. . . .

• • • • •

(d) Terrible damage is done to children simply by the size and standardization of the big system. Suppose a class size of 20 is good for average purposes; it does *not* follow that 35 is better than nothing. Rather, it is likely to be positively harmful, because the children have ceased to be persons and the teacher is destroyed as a teacher. . . .

. . . We are so mesmerized by the operation of a system with the appropriate name, for instance "Education," that we assume that it *must* be working somewhat, though admittedly not perfectly, when perhaps it has ceased to fulfill its function altogether and might even be preventing the function, for instance education.

• • • • •

(e) . . . What is the moral for our purposes? Can it be denied that in some respects the drop-outs make a wiser choice than many who go to school, not to get real goods but to get money? Their choice of the "immediate"—their notorious "inability to tolerate delay"—is not altogether impulsive and neurotic. The bother is that in our present culture, which puts its entire emphasis on the consumption of expensive commodities, they are so nagged by inferiority, exclusion, and despair of the future that they cannot enjoy their leisure with a good conscience. Because they know little, they are deprived of many profound simple satisfactions and they never know what to do with themselves. Being afraid of exposing themselves to awkwardness and ridicule, they just hang around. And our urban social arrangements—e.g. high rent— have made it impossible for anybody to be decently poor on a "low" standard. One is either in the rat-race or has dropped out of society altogether.

• • • • •

What then? The compulsory system has become a universal trap, and it is no good. Very many of the youth, both poor and middle class, might be better off if the system simply did not exist, even if they then had no formal schooling at all. (I am extremely curious for a philosophic study of Prince Edward County in Virginia, where for some years schooling did not exist for Negro children.)

But what would become of these children? For very many, both poor and middle class, their homes are worse than the schools, and the city streets are worse in another way. Our urban and suburban environments are precisely not cities or communities where adults naturally attend to the young and educate to a viable life. Also, perhaps especially in the case of the overt drop-outs, the state of their body and soul is such that we must give them refuge and remedy, whether it be called school, settlement house, youth worker, or work camp.

There are thinkable alternatives. Throughout this little book, as occasion arises, I shall offer alternative proposals that I as a single individual have heard of or thought up. Here are half a dozen directly relevant to the subject we have been discussing, the system as compulsory trap. In principle, when a law begins to do more harm than good, the best policy is to alleviate it or try doing without it.

i. Have "no school at all" for a few classes. These children should be selected from tolerable, though not necessarily cultured, homes. They should be neighbors and numerous enough to be a society for one another and so that they do not feel merely "different." Will they learn the rudiments anyway? This experiment cannot do the children any academic harm, since there is good evidence that normal children will make up the first seven years school-work with four to seven months of good teaching.

ii. Dispense with the school building for a few classes; provide teachers and use the city itself as the school—its streets, cafeterias, stores, movies, museums, parks, and factories. Where feasible, it certainly makes more sense to teach using the real subject-matter than to bring an abstraction of the subject-matter into the school-building as "curriculum." Such a class should probably not exceed 10 children for one pedagogue. The idea—it is the model of Athenian education—is not dissimilar to Youth gang work, but not applied to delinquents and not playing to the gang ideology.

iii. Along the same lines, but both outside and inside the school building, use appropriate *unlicensed* adults of the community—the druggist, the storekeeper, the mechanic—as the proper educators of the young into the grown-up world. By this means we can try to overcome the separation of the young from the grown-up world so characteristic in modern urban life, and to diminish the omnivorous authority of the professional school-people. Certainly it would be a useful and animating experience for the adults. (There is the beginning of such a volunteer program in the New York and some other systems.)

iv. Make class attendance not compulsory, in the manner of A. S. Neill's Summerhill. If the teachers are good, absence would tend to be eliminated; if they are bad, let them know it. The compulsory law is useful to get the children away from the parents, but it must not result in trapping the children. A fine modification of this suggestion is the rule used by Frank Brown in Florida: he permits the children to be absent for a week or a month to engage in any worthwhile enterprise or visit any new environment.

v. Decentralize an urban school (or do not build a new big building) into small units, 20 to 50, in available store-fronts or clubhouses. These tiny schools, equipped with record-player and pin-ball machine, could combine play, socializing, discussion, and formal teaching. For special events, the small units can be brought together into a common auditorium or gymnasium, so as to give the sense of the greater community. Correspondingly, I think it would be worthwhile to give the Little Red Schoolhouse a spin under modern urban conditions, and see how it works out: that is, to combine all the ages in a little room for 25 to 30, rather than to grade by age.

vi. Use a pro rata part of the school money to send children to economically marginal farms for a couple of months of the year, perhaps 6 children from mixed backgrounds to a farmer. The only requirement is that the farmer feed them and not beat them; best, of course, if they take part in the farm-work. This will give the farmer cash, as part of the generally desirable program to redress the urban-rural ratio to something nearer to 70 percent to 30 percent. (At present, less than 8 percent of families are rural.) Conceivably, some of the urban children will take to the other way of life, and we might generate a new kind of rural culture.

I frequently suggest these and similar proposals at teachers colleges, and I am looked at with an eerie look—do I really mean to *diminish* the state-aid grant for each student-day? But mostly the objection is that such proposals entail intolerable administrative difficulties.

Above all, we must apply these or any other proposals to particular individuals and small groups, without the obligation of uniformity. There is a case for uniform standards of achievement, lodged in the Regents, but they *cannot* be reached by uniform techniques. The claim that standardization of procedure is more efficient, less costly, or alone administratively practical, is often false. Particular inventiveness requires thought, but thought does not cost money.

HIGH SCHOOL

A PROPOSAL TO EXTEND COMPULSORY SCHOOLING

· · · · ·

It is claimed that society needs more people who are technically trained. But informed labor people tell me that, for a job requiring skill but no great genius, a worker can be found at once, or quickly trained, to fill it. For instance, the average job in General Motors' most automated plant requires three weeks of training for those who have no education whatever. It used to require six weeks; for such jobs, automation has diminished rather than increased the need for training. In the Army and Navy, fairly complicated skills, e.g. radar operation and repair, are taught in a year *on the job,* often to practical illiterates.

Naturally, if diplomas are pre-requisite to hiring a youngster, the correlation of schooling and employment is self-proving. Because of this fad, there is a fantastic amount of mis-hiring, hiring young people far too school-trained for the routine jobs they get. I was struck by a recent report in the *Wall Street Journal* of firms philanthropically deciding to hire *only* drop-outs for certain categories of jobs, since the diploma made no difference in performance.

Twist it and turn it how you will, there is no logic to the proposal to extend compulsory schooling *except* as a device to keep the unemployed off the streets by putting them into concentration camps called schools. . . .

As an academic, I am appalled by this motivation for schooling. As a citizen and human being, I am appalled by this waste of youthful vitality. It is time that we stopped using the word "education" honorifically. We must ask, education how? where? for what? and under whose administration? Certainly every youth should get the best possible education, but, in my opinion, the present kind of compulsory schooling under the present administrators, far from being extended, should be sharply curtailed.

As I have been saying, by and large primary schooling is, and should be, mainly baby-sitting. It has the great mission of democratic socialization—it certainly must not be segregated by race and income; apart from this, it should be happy, interesting, not damaging. The noise about stepping-up the primary curriculum is quite uncalled for; I have seen no convincing evidence—not by progressive educators either—that early schooling makes much academic difference in the long run. But in the secondary schools, after puberty, the tone of the baby-sitting must necessarily turn to regimentation and policing, and it is at peril that we require schooling; it fits some, it hurts others. A recent study by Edgar Friedenberg concludes that spirit-breaking is the *principal* function of typical lower middle-class schools.

. . . The legal justifications for compulsory schooling have been to protect children from exploitation by parents and employers, and to ensure the basic literacy and civics necessary for a democratic electorate. It is quite a different matter to deprive adolescents of their freedom in order to alleviate the difficulties of a faulty economic and political system. Is this constitutional?

• • • • •

In his speech [on February 24, 1964, former Secretary of Labor Willard Wirtz] referred to the admirable extension of free education from 1850 to, say, 1930. But this is again entirely misleading with regard to our present situation. To repeat, that opening of opportunity took place in an open economy, with an expanding market for skills and cultural learning. Young people took advantage of it *of their own volition;* therefore there were no blackboard jungles and endemic problems of discipline. Teachers taught those who wanted to learn; therefore there was no especial emphasis on grading. What is the present situation? The frantic competitive testing and grading means that the market for skills and learning is *not* open, it is tight. There are relatively few employers for those who score high; and almost none of the high-scorers become independent enterprisers. This means, in effect, that a few great corporations are getting the benefit of an enormous weeding-out and selective process—all children are fed into the mill and everybody pays for it.

If our present high schools, junior colleges, and colleges reflected the desire, freedom, and future of opportunity of the young, there would be no grading, no testing except as a teaching method, and no blackboard jungles. In fact, we are getting lockstep scheduling and grading to the point of torture. The senior year of high school is sacrificed to batteries of national tests, and policemen are going to stand in the corridors. Even an élite school such as Bronx Science—singled out by Dr. Conant as the best school in the country—is run as if for delinquents, with corridor passes and a ban on leaving the building. The conclusion is inevitable: The scholastically bright are not following their aspirations but are being pressured and bribed; the majority—those who are bright but not scholastic, and those who are not especially bright but have other kinds of vitality—are being subdued.

. . . As one observes the sprawling expansion of the universities and colleges, eating up their neighborhoods, dislocating the poor, dictating to the lower schools, battening on Federal billions for research and development, and billions for buildings, and billions through the National Defense Education Act, and billions from foundations and endowments—one suddenly realizes that here again is the Dead Hand of the medieval church, that inherits and inherits and never dies. The University, which should be dissident and poor, has become the Establishment. The streets are full of its monks.

. . . We must remember that, whatever the motive, *pouring money into the school-and-college system and into the academic social-work way of coping with problems, is strictly class legislation that confirms the inequitable structure of the economy.* I have mentioned how the professor-ridden Peace Corps needs $15,000 to get a single youngster in the field for a year, whereas the dedicated Quakers achieve almost the same end for $3,500. Again, when $13 millions are allotted for a local Mobilization for Youth program, it is soon found that nearly $12 millions have gone for sociologists doing "research," diplomated social workers, the New York school system, and administrators, but only one million to field workers and the youths themselves. . . .

Fundamentally, there is no right education except growing up into a worthwhile world. Indeed, our excessive concern with problems of education at present simply means that the grown-ups do not have such a world. The poor youth of America will *not* become equal by rising through the middle class, going to middle-class schools. By plain social justice, the Negroes and other minorities have the right to, and must get, equal opportunity for schooling with the rest, but the exaggerated expectation from the schooling is a chimera—and, I fear, will be shockingly disappointing. But also the middle-class youth will not escape their increasing exploitation and *anomie* in such schools. A decent education aims at, prepares for, a more worthwhile future, with a different community spirit, different occupations, and more real utility than attaining status and salary.

· · · · ·

On the whole, the education must be voluntary rather than compulsory, for no growth to freedom occurs except by intrinsic motivation. Therefore the educational opportunities must be various and variously administered. We must diminish rather than expand the present monolithic school system. I would suggest that, on the model of the GI-Bill, we experiment, giving the school money directly to the high-school age adolescents, for any plausible self-chosen educational proposals, such as purposeful travel or individual enterprise. This would also, of course, lead to the proliferation of experimental schools.

Unlike the present inflexible lockstep, our educational policy must allow for periodic quitting and easy return to the scholastic ladder, so that the young have time to find themselves and to study when they are themselves ready. This is Erik Erickson's valuable notion of the need for *moratoria* in the life-career; and the anthropological insistence of Stanley Diamond and others, that our society neglects the crises of growing up.

Education must foster independent thought and expression, rather than conformity. For example, to countervail the mass communications, we have an imperative social need, indeed a constitutional need to protect liberty, for many thousands of independent media: local newspapers, independent broadcasters, little magazines, little theaters; and these, under professional guidance, could provide remarkable occasions for the employment and education of adolescents of brains and talent. (I have elsewhere proposed a graduated tax on the audience-size of mass-media, to provide a Fund to underwrite such new independent ventures for a period, so that they can try to make their way.)

Finally, contemporary education must inevitably be heavily weighted toward the sciences. But this does not necessarily call for school-training of a relatively few technicians, or rare creative scientists (if such can indeed be trained in schools). Our aim must be to make a great number of citizens at home in a technological environment, not alienated from the machines we use, not ignorant as consumers, who can somewhat judge governmental scientific policy, who can enjoy the humanistic beauty of the sciences, and, above all, who can understand the morality of a scientific way of life. . . .

COLLEGE

"I DON'T WANT TO WORK—WHY SHOULD I?"

At 17 and 18, nearly half go off to something called college, and the others go to work, if there are jobs. We shall see that college is not a very educative environment, but by and large the world of work is even less so.

• • • • •

There is an evident and sickening disproportion between the money that people work hard for, whether as dish-washer, hospital orderly, stenographer, schoolteacher, or artist, and the "soft" money that comes from expense accounts, tax-dodge foundations, having "made it" as a personality. I have referred to the disproportionate cut of the pie that falls to the academic monks in any welfare operation. Then why should those who are not going to be in the Establishment *work* for money, rather than look for an angle or wait for luck? And it does not help when kids see an immense part of their parents' hard-earned money go on usurious installment payments for high-priced hardware, and rent swallowing up more than a quarter of income.

My guess is that many poor kids are in the cruel dilemma of feeling guilty about not working, and yet uneasy among their peers and even in their own better judgment if they do try to get jobs—especially when trying to get a job has its own degrading humiliations, of confronting prejudice, bureaucratic callousness, and gouging agencies, and often when the young are frustrated by sheer ignorance of how to look for a job at all.

And there is another philosophical aspect, usually overlooked, that is obviously important for these young. I have mentioned it before. So far as they can see—and they see clearly—the absorbing satisfactions of life do *not* require all this work and rat-race. In societies where it is possible to be decently poor, persons of superior education and talent often choose to be poor rather than hustle for money.

In the inflationary American economy, however, decent poverty is almost impossible. To be secure at all, one has to engage in the competition and try to rise; and the so-called "education" is geared to economic advancement. Thus, a common-sensible youth—and especially a poor one whose opportunities for advancement are limited and whose cultural background is unacademic—might reasonably judge that games, sex, and the gang are *preferable* to school and work, but he will then get not independence but misery. He will be so out of things that he will have nothing to occupy his mind. He is disqualified for marriage. He is inferior, out-caste.

As it is, the only ones who can afford the absorbing and simple satisfactions that do not cost much money are those who have succeeded economically and are by then likely unfit to enjoy anything. From this point of view, the chief blessing that our copious society could bestow on us would be a kind of subsistence work that allowed spirited people to be decently poor without frantic insecurity and long drudgery.

If we turn to the deeper human and religious answers to the question "Why should I work?"—for example, work as fulfillment of one's potentialities, work as the vocation that gives justification—our present economy has little to offer to poor youth.

Unskilled and semi-skilled jobs are parts of elaborate enterprises rationalized for their own operation and not to fulfill the lives of workmen. Work processes are rarely interesting. Workmen are not taught the rationale of the whole. The products are often humanly pretty worthless, so there is no pride of achievement or utility. Craft and style are built into the machines, lost to the workmen. Labor unions have improved the conditions and dignity of the job, but they have also become bureaucratized and do not give the sense of solidarity.

It is only in the higher job brackets, beyond most poor youth, that there begins to be a place for inventiveness and art; and independent initiative belongs only to top management and expert advisors. There are fewer small shops. Neighborhood stores give way to centralized supermarkets where the employees have no say. There is a great increase in social services, but these require official licenses and are not open to those otherwise qualified who wish to work in them.

The total background of poor youth, including the inadequacies of the schools, conduces to dropping out; but the simplest worthwhile jobs require diplomas.

• • • • •

Some of the human deficiencies in the jobs can be ameliorated—at least until automation makes the whole matter nugatory by vanishing the jobs. For example, with elementary thoughtfulness, a big plant that has many positions can allow a prospective employee to visit and try out various stations, rather than making an arbitrary assignment. Work processes can be efficiently designed on psychological grounds; for instance, a small group assembling a big lathe from beginning to end, so they have something to show for their day, as the crane carries the product away. In a form of "collective contract" or gang-system used in Coventry, England, fifty workers contract with the firm on a piece-work basis, and then settle among themselves the particular assignments, personnel, schedule, and many of the processes; there must be many industries where this humanizing procedure is feasible. With technical education paid for by industry in cooperation with the schools, we could have more understanding workmen.

The important point is that job-worthiness, the educative value of the job, must be recognized by managers and labor-unions as a specific good.

But of course this is part of the much larger need, to make our whole environment more educative, rather than rigidly restricting the concept of education to what happens in schools.

Socially useful work is probably an indispensable element in the education of most adolescents. It provides an objective structure, a bridge of norms and values, in the transition from being in the family to being oneself. This is the rationale of a good Youth Work Camp, as I described it in *Utopian Essays;* a community of youth democratically directing itself, and controlling itself, to do a job. Many colleges have adopted the Antioch plan of alternating academic periods with periods of work in the economy, which are then made the subject of further academic criticism. But what a pity that precisely the poor youth, who *have* to go to work, get no value from the jobs they work at!

• • • • •

Certainly the current proposals to make the school the employment agency are reasonable; the school is at least familiar, even if the kid hates it and has dropped out.

Our classical ideology is that the job should be looked for with resolution and ambition. But how are these possible on the basis of ignorance and alienation? Here as elsewhere, our problem is lapse of community. Our society has less and less community between its adults and its youth. Traditional and family crafts and trades no longer exist, and a youth has few chances to form himself on model workmen in his neighborhood and learn the ropes and opportunities. The difficulties of getting into a union seem, and often are, insuperable. Middle class academic youth in their colleges have at least some contact with the adults who belong to the ultimate job-world, and placement is pretty good. But poor urban youth in schools whose culture is quite alien to them and whose aims fit neither their desires nor their capacities, are among jailers, not models.

These remarks are not optimistic toward solving the problems of employment, and unemployment, of youth. By and large, I think those problems are insoluble, and *should* be insoluble, until our affluent society becomes worthier to work in, more honorable in its functions, and more careful of its human resources.

• • • • •

TWO SIMPLE PROPOSALS

• • • • •

Let me repeat the facts. From early childhood, the young are subjected to a lockstep increasingly tightly geared to the extra-mural demands. There is little attention to individual pace, rhythm, or choice, and none whatever to the discovery of identity or devotion to intellectual goals. The aptitude and achievement testing and the fierce competition for high grades are a race up the ladder to high-salaried jobs in the businesses of the world, including the schooling business. In this race, time is literally money. Middle class youngsters—or their parents—realistically opt for Advanced Placement and hasten to volunteer for the National Merit examinations. Negro parents want the same for their children, although the children have less tendency to cooperate.

Disappointingly, but not surprisingly, the colleges and universities go along with this spiritual destruction, and indeed devise the tests and the curricula to pass the tests. Thereby they connive at their own spiritual destruction; yet it is not surprising, for that is where the money and the grandeur are. I do not expect for a moment that they will, in the foreseeable future, recall their primary duties: to pass on the tradition of disinterested learning, to provide a critical standard, to educate the free young (*liberi*) to be free citizens and independent professionals.

The question is, *could* the colleges and universities act otherwise, even if they wished to? Of course they could. Most of them are autonomous corporations. Let me here suggest two modest changes, that are feasible almost immediately, that would entail no risk whatever, and yet would immensely improve these academic communities and importantly liberate them in relation to society.

First, suppose that half a dozen of the most prestigious liberal arts colleges—say Amherst, Swarthmore, Connecticut, Wesleyan, Carleton, etc.—would announce that . . . they required for admission a two-year period, after high school, spent in some maturing activity. These colleges are at present five times oversubscribed; they would not want for applicants on *any* conditions that they set; and they are explicitly committed to limiting their expansion.

By "maturing activity" could be meant: working for a living, especially if the jobs are gotten without too heavy reliance on connections; community service, such as the Northern Student Movement, volunteer service in hospital or settlement house, domestic Peace Corps; the army—though I am a pacifist and would urge a youngster to keep out of the army; a course of purposeful travel that met required standards; independent enterprise in art, business, or science, away from home, with something to show for the time spent.

The purpose of this proposal is twofold: to get students with enough life-experience to be educable on the college level, especially in the social sciences and humanities; and to break the lockstep of twelve years of doing assigned lessons for grades, so that the student may approach his college studies with some intrinsic motivation, and therefore perhaps assimilate something that might change him. Many teachers remember with nostalgia the maturer students who came under the GI-bill, though to be sure a large number of them were pretty shell-shocked.

A subsidiary advantage of the plan would be to relieve the colleges of the doomed, and hypocritical, effort to serve *in loco parentis* on matters of morality. If young persons have been out working for a living, or have traveled in foreign parts, or have been in the army, a college can assume that they can take care of themselves.

. . . It *is* possible to teach mathematics and physics to boys and girls, especially boys. These abstract subjects suit their alert and schematizing minds, the more so if the teaching treats science as the solution of puzzles. But it is not possible to teach sociology, anthropology, world literature to boys and girls, for they have no experience and judgment. When it is done, the message is merely verbal. The harsh facts and the relativity of morals are bound to be embarrassing and shocking. Regarded as "assignments"—as high school graduates must regard them —the voluminous readings are indigestible straw and are annotated by rote; more mature students might be able to take them as books. In brief, whiz-bang youngsters who have found their identity as mathematicians, chemists, or electronic technicians might well speed on to M.I.T. at age 15. The liberal arts colleges, that are essentially concerned with educating citizens and statesmen, social scientists and social professionals, scholars and men-of-letters, require more maturity to begin with. If the average age of entrance were higher, these colleges would also serve as the next step for the many disappointed science-students, who can hardly be expected to backtrack among the seventeens. (A very numerous group switch from the physical sciences to the social sciences and humanities.)

Throughout our educational system there is a desperate need for institutional variety and interims in which a youth can find himself. If we are going to require as much schooling as we do, we must arrange for breaks and return-points, otherwise the schooling inevitably becomes spirit-breaking and regimentation. In my opinion, however, a much more reasonable over-all pattern is to structure all of society and the whole environment as educative, with the schools playing the much more particular and traditional role of giving intensive training when it is needed and sought, or of being havens for those scholarly by disposition.

My other proposal is even simpler, and not at all novel. Let half a dozen of the prestigious Universities—Chicago, Stanford, the Ivy League—abolish grading, and use testing only and entirely for pedagogic purposes as teachers see fit.

Anyone who knows the frantic temper of the present schools will understand the transvaluation of values that would be effected by this modest innovation. For most of the students, the competitive grade has come to be the essence. The naive teacher points to the beauty of the subject and the ingenuity of the research; the shrewd student asks if he is responsible for that on the final exam.

Let me at once dispose of an objection whose unanimity is quite fascinating. I think that the great majority of professors agree that grading hinders teaching and creates a bad spirit, going as far as cheating and plagiarizing. I have before me the collection of essays, *Examining in Harvard College,* and this is the consensus. It is uniformly asserted, however, that the grading is inevitable; for how else will the graduate schools, the foundations, the corporations *know* whom to accept, reward, hire? How will the talent scouts know whom to tap?

By testing the applicants, of course, according to the specific task-requirements of the inducting institution, just as applicants for the Civil Service or for licenses in medicine, law, and architecture are tested. Why should Harvard professors do the testing *for* corporations and graduate-schools?

The objection is ludicrous. Dean Whitla, of the Harvard Office of Tests, points out that the scholastic-aptitude and achievement tests used for *admission* to Harvard are a super-excellent index for all-around Harvard performance, better than high-school grades or particular Harvard course-grades. Presumably, these college-entrance tests are tailored for what Harvard and similar institutions want. By the same logic, would not an employer do far better to apply his own job-aptitude test rather than to rely on the vagaries of Harvard sectionmen. Indeed, I doubt that many employers bother to look at such grades; they are more likely to be interested merely in the fact of a Harvard diploma, whatever that connotes to them. . . .

· · · · ·

A miserable effect of grading is to nullify the various uses of testing. Testing, for both student and teacher, is a means of structuring, and also of finding out what is blank or wrong and what has been assimilated and can be taken for granted. Review—including high-pressure review—is a means of bringing together the fragments, so that there are flashes of synoptic insight.

There are several good reasons for testing, and kinds of test. But if the aim is to discover weakness, what is the point of down-grading and punishing it, and thereby inviting the student to conceal his weakness, by faking and bulling, if not cheating? The natural conclusion of synthesis is the insight itself, not a grade for having had it. For the important purpose of placement, if one can establish in the student the belief that one is testing *not* to grade and make invidious comparisons but for his own advantage, the student should normally seek his own level, where he is challenged and yet capable, rather than trying to get by. If the student dares to accept himself as he is, a teacher's grade is a crude instrument compared with a student's self-awareness. But it is rare in our universities that students are encouraged to notice objectively their vast confusion. Unlike Socrates, our teachers rely on power-drives rather than shame and ingenuous idealism.

• • • • •

A USUAL CASE—NOTHING FANCY

• • • • •

The argument of this book is that every child must be educated to the fullest extent, brought up to be useful to society and to fulfill his own best powers. . . .

• • • • •

In my opinion, there *is* no single institution, like the monolithic school-system programmed by a few graduate universities and the curriculum reformers of the National Science Foundation, that can prepare everybody for an open future of a great society.

Thus at present, facing a confusing future of automated technology, excessive urbanization, and entirely new patterns of work and leisure, the best educational brains ought to be devoting themselves to devising *various* means of educating and paths of growing up, appropriate to various talents, conditions, and careers. We should be experimenting with different kinds of school, no school at all, the real city as school, farm schools, practical apprenticeships, guided travel, work camps, little theaters and local newspapers, community service. Many others, that other people can think of. Probably more than anything, we need a community, and community spirit, in which many adults who know something, and not only professional teachers, will pay attention to the young.

· · · · ·

Like any mass belief, the superstition that schooling is the only path to success is self-proving. There are now no professions, whether labor-statesman, architect, or trainer in gymnastics, that do not require college diplomas. Standards of licensing are set by Boards of Regents that talk only school language. For business or hotel-management it is wise to have a Master's. Access to the billions for Research and Development is by the Ph.D. in physical sciences, and prudent parents push their children accordingly; only a few are going to get this loot, but all must compete for it. And so we go down to the diplomas and certificates required for sales-girls and typists. If you are Personnel, you need a piece of paper to apply, and almost everybody is Personnel. Thus, effectively, a youth *has* no future if he quits, or falls off, the school ladder. Farm youth can still drop out without too much clatter, but the rural population is now 8 percent and rapidly diminishing.

If, in this climate of opinion, I demur, I am accused of being against the National Goals and against suburbia. So I am. But on the other hand, I have been accused of being a racist-élitist who thinks that some people are "not good enough" to go to school. But I am not an élitist and I do not think that some people are not good enough. The scholastic disposition is a beautiful and useful one; we are lucky that a minority of people are so inclined. But I do not think it is the moon and the stars.

To understand our present situation, let us review the history of schooling in this century.

By 1900, our present school system was established in its main outlines, including the liberal arts colleges and the German-imitating Universities. At that time there was almost universal primary schooling in a great variety of local arrangements, yet—we saw—only 6 percent of the 17-year-olds graduated from high school. Maybe another 10 percent would have graduated if they could have afforded it. (Recently, Dr. Conant has estimated that 15 percent are academically talented.) We may assume that that 6 percent or 16 percent would be in school because they wanted to be there; not only would there be no startling problems of discipline, but they could be taught a curriculum, whether traditional or vocational, that was interesting and valuable for itself. They were not conscripted soldiers, being chased up a ladder.

Now the 94 percent who did not graduate obviously were not "dropouts." They were everybody: future farmer, shopkeeper, millionaire, politician, inventor, journalist. . . .

• • • • •

As the decades passed, higher schooling began to be a mass phenomenon. In 1930, 30 percent graduated from high school and 11 percent went to college. By 1963, we see that 65 percent have graduated, of whom more than half go to college.

Who now are the other 35 percent? They are the Dropouts, mostly urban-underprivileged or rural. From this group we do not much expect splendid careers, in architecture, politics, or literature. They are not allowed to get jobs before 16; they find it hard to get jobs after 16; they might drop out of society altogether, because there is now no other track than going to school.

• • • • •

Suddenly, since the Korean war and hysterically since Sputnik, there has developed a disastrous overestimation of schools and scholarship. . . .

• • • • •

We are witnessing an educational calamity. Every kind of youth is hurt. The bright but unacademic can, as we have seen, perform; but the performance is inauthentic and there is a pitiful loss of what they *could* be doing with intelligence, grace, and force. The average are anxious. The slow are humiliated. But also the authentically scholarly are ruined. Bribed and pampered, they forget the meaning of their gifts. As I have put it before, they "do" high school in order to "make" Harvard, and then they "do" Harvard.

I doubt that any of this rat-race is useful. Given quiet, and food and lodging, young scholars would study anyway, without grades. The drill and competitiveness are bad for their powers, and they mistake themselves and become snobbish craft-idiots. There is no evidence that highly creative youngsters in the sciences, arts, or professions, especially thrive on formal schooling at all, rather than by exploring and gradually gravitating to the right work and environment. For some, schooling no doubt saves time; for others it is interruptive and depressing. And on lower levels of performance, do the technical and clerical tasks of automated production really require so many years of boning and test-passing as is claimed? We have seen that the evidence is otherwise.

For urban poor kids who are cajoled not to drop out, the mis-education is a cruel hoax. They are told that the high school diploma is worth money, but we have seen that this is not necessarily so.

Of course, there is no real choice for any of them. Poor people must picket for better schools that will not suit most of their children and won't pay off. Farm youth must ride to central schools that are a waste of time for most of them, while they lose the remarkable competence they have. Middle-class youth must doggedly compete and be tested to death to get into colleges where most of them will doggedly (or cynically) serve time. It is ironical. With all the money spent on Research and Development, for hardware, computers, and tranquilizers, America can think up only one institution for its young human resources. Apparently the schooling that we have already had has brainwashed everybody.

Childhood and society

ERIK H. ERIKSON

Erik H. Erikson's work in the formulation and application of psychoanalytic theory is widely studied and respected in American scholarly communities. One of his major achievements in the field was the publication in 1950 of *Childhood and Society,* a probing study of the pervasive influence of cultural institutions and mores on childhood growth and development. It is Erikson's purpose in *Childhood and Society* to explore the ways in which the child-rearing practices of a given society are used to develop in the child the cultural norms valued by that society. His basic premise is that a parent society must seek its continued life and stability in its young. From infancy, the parent society pursues that end through the inculcation and then the exploitation of infantile anxiety, bringing to the child and adult the certainty that his inner meaning and identity find their fulfillment in societal roles and institutions.

If there is a single theme in *Childhood and Society,* it is the analysis of the growth process from psychoanalytic, social, and anthropological points of view. And though Erikson is at every step in his book developing this theme, we have chosen to reproduce from *Childhood and Society* the chapter entitled "Eight Ages of Man," Erikson's description of the critical periods of the human life cycle and the ego qualities that must emerge during those periods for a successful integration of the individual's needs and

SOURCE: Erik H. Erikson, *Childhood and Society,* 2d ed. (New York: W. W. Norton and Company, 1963), pp. 247-274. Copyright 1950, © 1963 by W. W. Norton and Company, Inc. Reprinted by permission of W. W. Norton and Company, Inc.

experience with the cultural demands of his society. "Eight Ages of Man" may thus be viewed as *Childhood and Society*'s central chapter, being Erikson's primary statement of conclusions reached about the nature of human development after studying it, as this book does, in both its normal and abnormal manifestations.

But before discussing in detail this central chapter, a brief review of Erikson's larger design in *Childhood and Society* should assist the reader in placing "Eight Ages of Man" in a proper and helpful perspective.

Childhood and Society has four major divisions, the first three of which are an effort to discover, among the varied patterns and pressures of child training, some general information about the kinds of adult roles that surround us. (The fourth part provides application of these discoveries through the study of the legends of individuals such as Adolph Hitler and Maxim Gorky.) Erikson is a clinician, and his method is largely clinical; he uses the case history to illustrate some child-training techniques and their relative success or failure in the individual child. Naturally, since he deals with the pathological consequences of those techniques in his work, Erikson's case histories involve the reader in instances of failure. But he believes that from these instances, which are examples of the stress and anxiety of the organism in the face of societal demands, we may deduce the general principles of development that have in some way gone awry in the individual child.

The first part of *Childhood and Society* is devoted to the study of several of these case histories, of the impact of human anxiety on psychological and social growth. Erikson's description is usually of a temporary interruption in the normal process of the child's gradual recognition and acceptance of himself *in relation to* the other; that is, of his identity as a social being. It is from these histories that Erikson abstracts what he considers to be the nature of such ego failure. Then, in a discussion of infantile sexuality and socially integrative training, the points of weakness which may lead to breakdown in the child's development are traced to the subtle but crucial pressures on the infant's behavior by his mother, at this stage his only experience of the "other."

Part I of the book thus identifies the basis of social behavior in the child in his infantile and early childhood experiences. Its major implication for our later discussion of "Eight Ages of Man" is its definition of the infant-mother relationship as one of *mutuality*, in which two human beings interact with and profoundly affect one another, thus beginning for the infant the process of knowing the self through the experience of the other.

In Part II of *Childhood and Society*, Erikson, to broaden the scope of his study of child development, turns to two American Indian nations, the Sioux and the Yurok, testing their patterns of child training and contrasting the societal norms and values produced by those patterns with the dominant American experience. This section is most useful for its illustration of the relation between childhood and national character. It is an inquiry into the ways in which social communities create in their young lasting identification with the parent culture, thus ensuring the re-creation of that culture. Again, mutuality is the informing mode: the child is carefully nurtured in the societal myth and ritual so that he will be able to find his meaningful role within the social structures at hand. Thus he becomes himself a bearer of the parent tradition and an assurance of societal stability, an important step in personal integration, discussed by Erikson in "Eight Ages of Man."

It is the third part of *Childhood and Society*, Erikson's study of the processes of the human ego, that focuses most profoundly on psychosocial growth, culminating in the chapter that is reprinted here. This section deals with the child's gradually increasing social experience, especially through his play world, and his success or failure as a developing member of the parent culture. This discussion concerns ego growth from its "formless beginning to the formulated consciousness of its self."

Erikson begins with the classical definitions of id and superego as the excesses, respectively, of self-gratification and self-regimentation. Between these the ego must function as healthful regulator, balancing the extremes of the other two. Erikson defines the ego as an "inner institution" evolved to safeguard that order within individuals on which all internal order depends.

In the child, play activity maintains a key ego function, to attempt to bring bodily and social processes into alignment with his sense of selfhood. During play, the child emphasizes his need to master differing areas of his experience, but especially those roles in which he feels he is failing. The child uses play to understand and control the outer world he is gradually entering, containing

in the gestures and movements of his games the fears and apprehensions he feels.

But perhaps the most important aspect of play activity is its
social import. Play provides the increasingly wide social contact
and experience that is crucial to the child's social development, a
development that hinges on a varied involvement with the persons
and objects in his world. This increasing involvement is the hall-
mark of growth, and, for the child, play is its major source.

Play is a means of mastering experience; the individual *way*
this mastery is accomplished is determined by the particular sense
of self as it develops in the child. Erikson's concern for this developing sense finds its ultimate expression in "Eight Ages of Man."
His subject, as we have said, is the qualities of the ego that are
vital developments in the life cycle of the individual, and that
bring his cycle to personal and cultural fulfillment.

1. *Basic trust vs. basic mistrust.* His initial and continuing sen-
suous experiences are, for the infant, havens of familiarity and
feelings of inner goodness. The mother, having become a certain
and predictable presence, may be out of his sight without causing
undue anxiety in the infant—his first social achievement. Inner
and outer consistency, continuity, and sameness of experience provide a rudimentary sense of ego-identity. As the infant chooses to
trust in that consistency of experience when he becomes anxious,
his ego is performing its first task in the solution of conflict.

2. *Autonomy vs. shame and doubt.* This is the period of muscular
maturation, of the "holding on" and "letting go" decisions of early
childhood. The child now needs the gradual and well-guided experience of the autonomy of free choice. Outer control must be
firmly reassuring to protect him against the potential anarchy of
his as yet undiscriminating senses. If he loses self-control and is
subject to outside overcontrol, the child may develop a lasting
doubt of his own decision-making powers.

3. *Initiative vs. guilt.* This stage is that specifically human crisis
during which the child must turn from an exclusive, pregenital
attachment to the parents to the slow process of becoming a
parent, a carrier of tradition. At this stage he is eager and able
to make things cooperatively and to combine with other children
to construct and plan. He is willing to profit from teachers and
emulate ideal prototypes. He requires insight into the institutions,

functions, and roles that will permit his responsible participation, for he is now beginning to move from the infantile to the parental value-set.

4. *Industry vs. inferiority.* In this stage, the child learns to win recognition by producing things and by adjusting himself to the inorganic laws of the tool world. The fundamentals of technology are developed. Inferiority may develop if he despairs of his skills or status among his tool partners. The wider society now becomes significant in its ways of admitting the child to a meaningful role in its technology through a sense of differential opportunity.

5. *Identity vs. role confusion.* Childhood proper is now at an end; genital maturity is accomplished at a time when body growth is equal to that of early childhood. At this stage, the sense of ego-identity is the accrued confidence that the sameness and continuity of the self in the past will be justified by its acceptance in the wider society, in the tangible promise of a career. Role confusion is a result of strong doubt as to one's sexual identity, which may lead to delinquency and neurosis. Where confusion exists, many adolescents try the remedy of submitting to apparent loss of identity in cliques and identifications. The adolescent mind is essentially a mind of the moratorium between the learned morality of the child and the ethics to be developed by the adult.

6. *Intimacy vs. isolation.* Emerging from the search for and the insistence on identity, the young adult is willing to fuse his identity with that of others. Intimacy is the capacity to commit oneself to concrete affiliations and partnerships, and to withstand those significant sacrifices and compromises that must be made. The healthy individual at this point is able to face the fear of ego loss in situations that call for self-abandonment—solidarity, orgasm, physical combat. Orgasm is the supreme experience of mutual regulation of two beings begun in infancy with breast feeding. The danger of this stage is that intimacy and competition are experienced with and against the same people in the areas of competition and sexuality. But as the competitive encounter and the sexual embrace become differentiated, they become subject to that ethical sense which is the mark of the adult.

7. *Generativity vs. stagnation.* The term generativity encompasses the evolutionary development which has made man the teaching and instituting animal as well as the learning animal. It involves

the adult's concern in establishing and guiding the next generation. The ability to lose oneself in the meeting of bodies and minds
leads to a gradual expansion of ego interests and to a libidinal
investment in that which is being generated. When the enrichment
of generative experience fails, a regression to an obsessive need
for pseudo-intimacy takes place, often shown in early invalidism,
physical or psychological, as the vehicle of self-concern.

8. *Ego integrity vs. despair.* Ego integrity is the fruit of these
seven stages. The sense of ego integrity is the ego's accrued assurance of its proclivity for order and meaning. It is the acceptance of one's one and only life cycle in coincidence with but one
segment of history. Despair is the lack of this accrued ego integration, and it is signified by fear of death. The time is now felt
to be too short for the attempt to discover alternative roads to
integrity, which is the ego's goal throughout the life cycle.

To become a mature adult, each individual must develop all the
ego qualities named to a sufficient degree. But each cultural entity
develops the particular style of integrity suggested by its historical
place and utilizes a particular combination of these conflicts, along
with specific provocations and prohibitions of infantile sexuality.
Infantile conflicts become creative only if sustained by the firm
support of cultural institutions.

The central concept of *Childhood and Society* is the forceful link
between the practices of child training and their exploitation by
the parent society for the purpose of its continuing life and culture.
The child's growth and development derive their meanings from
those cultural norms and horizons that society supplies. The child
will absorb his meaning from the set of values, pressures, and
demands that emanate from the parents, who are society's sym-
bolic presence. Erikson, though he is at pains to show society's
exploitative treatment of latent infantile anxieties, is always convinced that the paradigmatic relationship between child training and
cultural valuation is the ultimate form of mutuality toward which
the human experience strives. He is further convinced that such
mutuality, in its most successful form, is a life-giving process on
which the health of the individual and the dominant culture depend.

"Eight Ages of Man" traces the human life cycle from birth to
death as a series of strivings toward mutuality in the individual
through societal (other) forms of mother, play, and love. The developing sense of identity in the child evinces his growing mastery

of the parent culture's norms and meanings. Making these his own, that is, integrating them with his personal experiences, is the assurance of the culture's extension in himself. Thus the accruing sense of the ego's rightness and health in the parent culture is that culture's strength; and the experience of childhood is crucial to the successful integration of the child's, and later the adult's, sense of selfhood in its relation to the dominant society. So Erikson has traced the stages of mutuality through which the child progresses to reach mature acceptance of the other as the true consciousness of the self.

EIGHT AGES OF MAN

1. BASIC TRUST VS. BASIC MISTRUST

The first demonstration of social trust in the baby is the ease of his feeding, the depth of his sleep, the relaxation of his bowels. The experience of a mutual regulation of his increasingly receptive capacities with the maternal techniques of provision gradually helps him to balance the discomfort caused by the immaturity of homeostasis with which he was born. In his gradually increasing waking hours he finds that more and more adventures of the senses arouse a feeling of familiarity, of having coincided with a feeling of inner goodness. Forms of comfort, and people associated with them, become as familiar as the gnawing discomfort of the bowels. The infant's first social achievement, then, is his willingness to let the mother out of sight without undue anxiety or rage, because she has become an inner certainty as well as an outer predictability. Such consistency, continuity, and sameness of experience provide a rudimentary sense of ego identity which depends, I think, on the recognition that there is an inner population of remembered and anticipated sensations and images which are firmly correlated with the outer population of familiar and predictable things and people.

What we here call trust coincides with what Therese Benedek has called confidence. If I prefer the word "trust," it is because there is more naïveté and more mutuality in it: an infant can be said to be trusting where it would go too far to say that he has confidence. The general state of trust, furthermore, implies not only that one has learned to rely on the sameness and continuity of the outer providers, but also that one may trust oneself and the capacity of one's own organs to cope with urges; and that one is able to consider oneself trustworthy enough so that the providers will not need to be on guard lest they be nipped.

The constant tasting and testing of the relationship between inside and outside meets its crucial test during the rages of the biting stage, when the teeth cause pain from within and when outer friends either prove of no avail or withdraw from the only action which promises relief: biting. Not that teething itself seems to cause all the dire consequences sometimes ascribed to it. As outlined earlier, the infant now is driven to "grasp" more, but he is apt to find desired presences elusive: nipple and breast, and the mother's focused attention and care. Teething seems to have a prototypal significance and may well be the model for the masochistic tendency to assure cruel comfort by enjoying one's hurt whenever one is unable to prevent a significant loss.

In psychopathology the absence of basic trust can best be studied in infantile schizophrenia, while lifelong underlying weakness of such trust is apparent in adult personalities in whom withdrawal into schizoid and depressive states is habitual. The re-establishment of a state of trust has been found to be the basic requirement for therapy in these cases. For no matter what conditions may have caused a psychotic break, the bizarreness and withdrawal in the behavior of many very sick individuals hides an attempt to recover social mutuality by a testing of the border-lines between senses and physical reality, between words and social meanings.

Psychoanalysis assumes the early process of differentiation between inside and outside to be the origin of projection and introjection which remain some of our deepest and most dangerous defense mechanisms. In introjection we feel and act as if an outer goodness had become an inner certainty. In projection, we experience an inner harm as an outer one: we endow significant people with the evil which actually is in us. These two mechanisms, then, projection and introjection, are assumed to be modeled after whatever goes on in infants when they would like to externalize pain and internalize pleasure, an intent which must yield to the testimony of the maturing senses and ultimately of reason. These mechanisms are, more or less normally, reinstated in acute crises of love, trust, and faith in adulthood and can characterize irrational attitudes toward adversaries and enemies in masses of "mature" individuals.

The firm establishment of enduring patterns for the solution of the nuclear conflict of basic trust versus basic mistrust in mere existence is the first task of the ego, and thus first of all a task for maternal care. But let it be said here that the amount of trust derived from earliest infantile experience does not seem to depend on absolute quantities of food or demonstrations of love, but rather on the quality of the maternal relationship. Mothers create a sense of trust in their children by that kind of administration which in its quality combines sensitive care of the baby's individual needs and a firm sense of personal trustworthiness within the trusted framework of their culture's life style. This forms the basis in the child for a sense of identity which will later combine a sense of being "all right," of being oneself, and of becoming what other people trust one will become. There are, therefore (within certain limits previously defined as the "musts" of child care), few frustrations in either this or the following stages which the growing child cannot endure if the frustration leads to the ever-renewed experience of greater sameness and stronger continuity of development, toward a final integration of the individual life cycle with some meaningful wider belongingness. Parents must not only have certain ways of guiding by prohibition and permission; they must also be able to represent to the child a deep, an almost somatic conviction that there is a meaning to what they are doing. Ultimately, children become neurotic not from frustrations, but from the lack or loss of societal meaning in these frustrations.

But even under the most favorable circumstances, this stage seems to introduce into psychic life (and become prototypical for) a sense of inner division and universal nostalgia for a paradise forfeited. It is against this powerful combination of a sense of having been deprived, of having been divided, and of having been abandoned—that basic trust must maintain itself throughout life.

Each successive stage and crisis has a special relation to one of the basic elements of society, and this for the simple reason that the human life cycle and man's institutions have evolved together. In this chapter we can do little more than mention, after the description of each stage, what basic element of social organization is related to it. This relation is twofold: man brings to these institutions the remnants of his infantile mentality and his youthful fervor, and he receives from them— as long as they manage to maintain their actuality—a reinforcement of his infantile gains.

The parental faith which supports the trust emerging in the newborn, has throughout history sought its institutional safeguard (and, on occasion, found its greatest enemy) in organized religion. Trust born of care is, in fact, the touchstone of the *actuality* of a given religion. All religions have in common the periodical childlike surrender to a Provider or providers who dispense earthly fortune as well as spiritual health; some demonstration of man's smallness by way of reduced posture and humble gesture; the admission in prayer and song of misdeeds, of misthoughts, and of evil intentions; fervent appeal for inner unification by divine guidance; and finally, the insight that individual trust must become a common faith, individual mistrust a commonly formulated evil, while the individual's restoration must become part of the ritual practice of many, and must become a sign of trustworthiness in the community.* We have illustrated how tribes dealing with one segment of nature develop a collective magic which seems to treat the Supernatural Providers of food and fortune as if they were angry and must be appeased by prayer and self-torture. Primitive religions, the most primitive layer in all religions, and the religious layer in each individual, abound with efforts at atonement which try to make up for vague deeds against a maternal matrix and try to restore faith in the goodness of one's strivings and in the kindness of the powers of the universe.

Each society and each age must find the institutionalized form of reverence which derives vitality from its world-image—from predestination to indeterminacy. The clinician can only observe that many are proud to be without religion whose children cannot afford their being without it. On the other hand, there are many who seem to derive a vital faith from social action or scientific pursuit. And again, there are many who profess faith, yet in practice breathe mistrust both of life and man.

2. AUTONOMY VS. SHAME AND DOUBT

In describing the growth and the crises of the human person as a series of alternative basic attitudes such as trust vs. mistrust, we take recourse to the term a "sense of," although, like a "sense of health," or a "sense of being unwell," such "senses" pervade surface and depth,

---

* This is the communal and psychosocial side of religion. Its often paradoxical relation to the spirituality of the individual is a matter not to be treated briefly and in passing (see *Young Man Luther*). (E.H.E.)

consciousness and the unconscious. They are, then, at the same time, ways of *experiencing* accessible to introspection; ways of *behaving,* observable by others; and unconscious *inner states* determinable by test and analysis. It is important to keep these three dimensions in mind, as we proceed.

Muscular maturation sets the stage for experimentation with two simultaneous sets of social modalities: holding on and letting go. As is the case with all of these modalities, their basic conflicts can lead in the end to either hostile or benign expectations and attitudes. Thus, to hold can become a destructive and cruel retaining or restraining, and it can become a pattern of care: to have and to hold. To let go, too, can turn into an inimical letting loose of destructive forces, or it can become a relaxed "to let pass" and "to let be."

Outer control at this stage, therefore, must be firmly reassuring. The infant must come to feel that the basic faith in existence, which is the lasting treasure saved from the rages of the oral stage, will not be jeopardized by this about-face of his, this sudden violent wish to have a choice, to appropriate demandingly, and to eliminate stubbornly. Firmness must protect him against the potential anarchy of his as yet untrained sense of discrimination, his inability to hold on and to let go with discretion. As his environment encourages him to "stand on his own feet," it must protect him against meaningless and arbitrary experiences of shame and of early doubt.

The latter danger is the one best known to us. For if denied the gradual and well-guided experience of the autonomy of free choice (or if, indeed, weakened by an initial loss of trust) the child will turn against himself all his urge to discriminate and to manipulate. He will overmanipulate himself, he will develop a precocious conscience. Instead of taking possession of things in order to test them by purposeful repetition, he will become obsessed by his own repetitiveness. By such obsessiveness, of course, he then learns to repossess the environment and to gain power by stubborn and minute control, where he could not find large-scale mutual regulation. Such hollow victory is the infantile model for a compulsion neurosis. It is also the infantile source of later attempts in adult life to govern by the letter, rather than by the spirit.

Shame is an emotion insufficiently studied, because in our civilization it is so early and easily absorbed by guilt. Shame supposes that one is completely exposed and conscious of being looked at: in one word, self-conscious. One is visible and not ready to be visible; which is why we dream of shame as a situation in which we are stared at in a condition of incomplete dress, in night attire, "with one's pants down." Shame is early expressed in an impulse to bury one's face, or to sink, right then and there, into the ground. But this, I think, is essentially rage turned against the self. He who is ashamed would like to force the world not to look at him, not to notice his exposure. He would like to destroy the eyes of the world. Instead he must wish for his own invisibility. This potentiality is abundantly used in the educational method of "shaming" used so exclusively by some primitive peoples. Visual shame precedes auditory guilt, which is a sense of badness to be had all by oneself when nobody watches and when everything is quiet—except the voice of the superego. Such shaming exploits an increasing sense of being small, which can develop only as the child stands up and as his awareness permits him to note the relative measures of size and power.

Too much shaming does not lead to genuine propriety but to a secret determination to try to get away with things, unseen—if, indeed, it does not result in defiant shamelessness. There is. an impressive American ballad in which a murderer to be hanged on the gallows before the eyes of the community, instead of feeling duly chastened, begins to berate the onlookers, ending every salvo of defiance with the words, "God damn your eyes." Many a small child, shamed beyond endurance, may be in a chronic mood (although not in possession of either the courage or the words) to express defiance in similar terms. What I mean by this sinister reference is that there is a limit to a child's and an adult's endurance in the face of demands to consider himself, his body, and his wishes as evil and dirty, and to his belief in the infallibility of those who pass such judgment. He may be apt to turn things around, and to consider as evil only the fact that they exist: his chance will come when they are gone, or when he will go from them.

Doubt is the brother of shame. Where shame is dependent on the consciousness of being upright and exposed, doubt, so clinical observation leads me to believe, has much to do with a consciousness of having a front and a back—and especially a "behind." For this reverse area of the body, with its aggressive and libidinal focus in the sphincters and in the buttocks, cannot be seen by the child, and yet it can be dominated by the will of others. The "behind" is the small being's dark continent, an area of the body which can be magically dominated and effectively invaded by those who would attack one's power of autonomy and who would designate as evil those products of the bowels which were felt to be all right when they were being passed. This basic sense of doubt in whatever one has left behind forms a substratum for later and more verbal forms of compulsive doubting; this finds its adult expression in paranoiac fears concerning hidden persecutors and secret persecutions threatening from behind (and from within the behind).

This stage, therefore, becomes decisive for the ratio of love and hate, cooperation and willfulness, freedom of self-expression and its suppression. From a sense of self-control without loss of self-esteem comes a lasting sense of good will and pride; from a sense of loss of self-control and of foreign overcontrol comes a lasting propensity for doubt and shame.

If, to some reader, the "negative" potentialities of our stages seem overstated throughout, we must remind him that this is not only the result of a preoccupation with clinical data. Adults, and seemingly mature and unneurotic ones, display a sensitivity concerning a possible shameful "loss of face" and fear of being attacked "from behind" which is not only highly irrational and in contrast to the knowledge available to them, but can be of fateful import if related sentiments influence, for example, interracial and international policies.

We have related basic trust to the institution of religion. The lasting need of the individual to have his will reaffirmed and delineated within an adult order of things which at the same time reaffirms and delineates the will of others has an institutional safeguard in the *principle of law and order*. In daily life as well as in the high courts of law—domestic and international—this principle apportions to each his privileges and his limitations, his obligations and his rights. A sense of rightful dignity and lawful independence on the part of adults around him gives to the child of good will the confident expectation that the kind of autonomy fostered in childhood will not lead to undue doubt or shame in later life. Thus the sense of autonomy fostered in the child and modified as life progresses, serves (and is served by) the preservation in economic and political life of a sense of justice.

3. INITIATIVE VS. GUILT

There is in every child at every stage a new miracle of vigorous unfolding, which constitutes a new hope and a new responsibility for all.

Such is the sense and the pervading quality of initiative. The criteria for all these senses and qualities are the same: a crisis, more or less beset with fumbling and fear, is resolved, in that the child suddenly seems to "grow together" both in his person and in his body. He appears "more himself," more loving, relaxed and brighter in his judgment, more activated and activating. He is in free possession of a surplus of energy which permits him to forget failures quickly and to approach what seems desirable (even if it also seems uncertain and even dangerous) with undiminished and more accurate direction. Initiative adds to autonomy the quality of undertaking, planning and "attacking" a task for the sake of being active and on the move, where before self-will, more often than not, inspired acts of defiance or, at any rate, protested independence.

I know that the very word "initiative," to many, has an American and industrial connotation. Yet, initiative is a necessary part of every act, and man needs a sense of initiative for whatever he learns and does, from fruit-gathering to a system of enterprise.

The ambulatory stage and that of infantile genitality add to the inventory of basic social modalities that of "making," first in the sense of "being on the make." There is no simpler, stronger word for it; it suggests pleasure in attack and conquest. In the boy, the emphasis remains on phallic-intrusive modes; in the girl it turns to modes of "catching" in more aggressive forms of snatching or in the milder form of making oneself attractive and endearing.

The danger of this stage is a sense of guilt over the goals contemplated and the acts initiated in one's exuberant enjoyment of new locomotor and mental power: acts of aggressive manipulation and coercion which soon go far beyond the executive capacity of organism and mind and therefore call for an energetic halt on one's contemplated initiative. While autonomy concentrates on keeping potential rivals out, and therefore can lead to jealous rage most often directed against encroachments by younger siblings, initiative brings with it anticipatory rivalry with those who have been there first and may, therefore, occupy with their superior equipment the field toward which one's initiative is directed. Infantile jealousy and rivalry, those often embittered and yet essentially futile attempts at demarcating a sphere of unquestioned privilege, now come to a climax in a final contest for a favored position with the mother; the usual failure leads to resignation, guilt, and anxiety. The child indulges in fantasies of being a giant and a tiger, but in his dreams he runs in terror for dear life. This, then, is the stage of the "castration complex," the intensified fear of finding the (now energetically erotized) genitals harmed as a punishment for the fantasies attached to their excitement.

Infantile sexuality and incest taboo, castration complex and superego all unite here to bring about that specifically human crisis during which the child must turn from an exclusive, pregenital attachment to his parents to the slow process of becoming a parent, a carrier of tradition. Here the most fateful split and transformation in the emotional power-house occurs, a split between potential human glory and potential total destruction. For here the child becomes forever divided in himself. The instinct fragments which before had enhanced the growth of his infantile body and mind now become divided into an infantile set which perpetuates the exuberance of growth potentials, and a parental set which supports and increases self-observation, self-guidance, and self-punishment.

The problem, again, is one of mutual regulation. Where the child, now so ready to overmanipulate himself, can gradually develop a sense of moral responsibility, where he can gain some insight into the institutions, functions, and roles which will permit his responsible participation, he will find pleasurable accomplishment in wielding tools and weapons, in manipulating meaningful toys—and in caring for younger children.

Naturally, the parental set is at first infantile in nature: the fact that human conscience remains partially infantile throughout life is the core of human tragedy. For the superego of the child can be primitive, cruel, and uncompromising, as may be observed in instances where children overcontrol and overconstrict themselves to the point of self-obliteration; where they develop an over-obedience more literal than the one the parent has wished to exact; or where they develop deep regressions and lasting resentments because the parents themselves do not seem to live up to the new conscience. One of the deepest conflicts in life is the hate for a parent who served as the model and the executor of the superego, but who (in some form) was found trying to get away with the very transgressions which the child can no longer tolerate in himself. The suspiciousness and evasiveness which is thus mixed in with the all-or-nothing quality of the superego, this organ of moral tradition, makes moral (in the sense of moralistic) man a great potential danger to his own ego—and to that of his fellow men.

In adult pathology, the residual conflict over initiative is expressed either in hysterical denial, which causes the repression of the wish or the abrogation of its executive organ by paralysis, inhibition, or impotence; or in overcompensatory showing off, in which the scared individual, so eager to "duck," instead "sticks his neck out." Then also a plunge into psychosomatic disease is now common. It is as if the culture had made a man over-advertise himself and so identify with his own advertisement that only disease can offer him escape.

But here, again, we must not think only of individual psychopathology, but of the inner powerhouse of rage which must be submerged at this stage, as some of the fondest hopes and the wildest phantasies are repressed and inhibited. The resulting self-righteousness —often the principal reward for goodness—can later be most intolerantly turned against others in the form of persistent moralistic surveillance, so that the prohibition rather than the guidance of initiative becomes the dominant endeavor. On the other hand, even moral man's initiative is apt to burst the boundaries of self-restriction, permitting him to do to others, in his or in other lands, what he would neither do nor tolerate being done in his own home.

In view of the dangerous potentials of man's long childhood, it is well to look back at the blueprint of the life-stages and to the possibilities of guiding the young of the race while they are young. And here we note that according to the wisdom of the ground plan the child is at no time more ready to learn quickly and avidly, to become bigger in the sense of sharing obligation and performance than during this period of his development. He is eager and able to make things cooperatively, to combine with other children for the purpose of constructing and planning, and he is willing to profit from teachers and to emulate ideal prototypes. He remains, of course, identified with the parent of the same sex, but for the present he looks for opportunities where work-identification seems to promise a field of initiative without too much infantile conflict or oedipal guilt and a more realistic identification based on a spirit of equality experienced in doing things together. At any rate, the "oedipal" stage results not only in the oppressive establishment of a moral sense restricting the horizon of the permissible; it also sets the direction toward the possible and the tangible which permits the dreams of early childhood to be attached to the goals of an active adult life. Social institutions, therefore, offer children of this age an *economic ethos,* in the form of ideal adults recognizable by their uniforms and their functions, and fascinating enough to replace, the heroes of picture book and fairy tale.

4. INDUSTRY VS. INFERIORITY

Thus the inner stage seems all set for "entrance into life," except that life must first be school life, whether school is field or jungle or classroom. The child must forget past hopes and wishes, while his exuberant imagination is tamed and harnessed to the laws of impersonal things— even the three R's. For before the child, psychologically already a rudimentary parent, can become a biological parent, he must begin to be a worker and potential provider. With the oncoming latency period, the normally advanced child forgets, or rather sublimates, the necessity to "make" people by direct attack or to become papa and mama in a hurry: he now learns to win recognition by producing things. He has mastered the ambulatory field and the organ modes. He has experienced a sense of finality regarding the fact that there is no workable future within the womb of his family, and thus becomes ready to apply himself to given skills and tasks, which go far beyond the mere playful expression of his organ modes or the pleasure in the function of his limbs. He develops a sense of industry—i.e., he adjusts himself to the inorganic laws of the tool world. He can become an eager and absorbed unit of a productive situation. To bring a productive situation to completion is an aim which gradually supersedes the whims and wishes of play. His ego boundaries include his tools and skills: the work principle (Ives Hendrick) teaches him the pleasure of work completion by steady attention and persevering diligence. In all cultures, at this stage, children receive some *systematic instruction,* although . . . it is by no means always in the kind of school which literate people must organize around special teachers who have learned how to teach literacy. In preliterate people and in nonliterate pursuits much is learned from adults who become teachers by dint of gift and inclination rather than by appointment, and perhaps the greatest amount is learned from older children. Thus the *fundamentals of technology* are developed, as the child becomes ready to handle the utensils, the tools, and the weapons used by the big people. Literate people, with more specialized careers, must prepare the child by teaching him things which first of all make him literate, the widest possible basic education for the greatest number of possible careers. The more confusing specialization becomes, however, the more indistinct are the eventual goals of initiative; and the more complicated social reality, the vaguer are the father's and mother's role in it. School seems to be a culture all by itself, with its own goals and limits, its achievements and disappointments.

The child's danger, at this stage, lies in a sense of inadequacy and inferiority. If he despairs of his tools and skills or of his status among his tool partners, he may be discouraged from identification with them and with a section of the tool world. To lose the hope of such "industrial" association may pull him back to the more isolated, less tool-conscious familial rivalry of the oedipal time. The child despairs of his equipment in the tool world and in anatomy, and considers himself doomed to mediocrity or inadequacy. It is at this point that wider society becomes significant in its ways of admitting the child to an understanding of meaningful roles in its technology and economy. Many a child's development is disrupted when family life has failed to prepare him for school life, or when school life fails to sustain the promises of earlier stages.

Regarding the period of a developing sense of industry, I have referred to *outer and inner hindrances* in the use of new capacities but not to aggravations of new human drives, nor to submerged rages resulting from their frustration. This stage differs from the earlier ones in that it is not a swing from an inner upheaval to a new mastery. Freud calls it the latency stage because violent drives are normally dormant. But it is only a lull before the storm of puberty, when all the earlier drives reemerge in a new combination, to be brought under the dominance of genitality.

On the other hand, this is socially a most decisive stage: since industry involves doing things beside and with others, a first sense of division of labor and of differential opportunity, that is, a sense of the *technological ethos* of a culture, develops at this time. We have pointed in the last section to the danger threatening individual and society where the schoolchild begins to feel that the color of his skin, the background of his parents, or the fashion of his clothes rather than his wish and his will to learn will decide his worth as an apprentice, and thus his sense of *identity*—to which we must now turn. But there is another, more fundamental danger, namely man's restriction of himself and constriction of his horizons to include only his work to which, so the Book says, he has been sentenced after his expulsion from paradise. If he accepts work as his only obligation, and "what works" as his only criterion of worthwhileness, he may become the conformist and thoughtless slave of his technology and of those who are in a position to exploit it.

5. IDENTITY VS. ROLE CONFUSION

With the establishment of a good initial relationship to the world of skills and tools, and with the advent of puberty, childhood proper comes to an end. Youth begins. But in puberty and adolescence all samenesses and continuities relied on earlier are more or less questioned again, because of a rapidity of body growth which equals that of early childhood and because of the new addition of genital maturity. The growing and developing youths, faced with this physiological revolution within them, and with tangible adult tasks ahead of them are now primarily concerned with what they appear to be in the eyes of others as compared with what they feel they are, and with the question of how to connect the roles and skills cultivated earlier with the occupational prototypes of the day. In their search for a new sense of continuity and sameness, adolescents have to refight many of the battles of earlier years, even though to do so they must artificially appoint perfectly well-meaning people to play the roles of adversaries; and they are ever ready to install lasting idols and ideals as guardians of a final identity.

The integration now taking place in the form of ego identity is, as pointed out, more than the sum of the childhood identifications. It is the accrued experience of the ego's ability to integrate all identifications with the vicissitudes of the libido, with the aptitudes developed out of endowment, and with the opportunities offered in social roles. The sense of ego identity, then, is the accrued confidence that the inner sameness and continuity prepared in the past are matched by the sameness and continuity of one's meaning for others, as evidenced in the tangible promise of a "career."

The danger of this stage is role confusion.* Where this is based on a strong previous doubt as to one's sexual identity, delinquent and outright psychotic episodes are not uncommon. If diagnosed and treated correctly, these incidents do not have the same fatal significance which

* See "The Problem of Ego-Identity," *J. Amer. Psa. Assoc.,* 4:56–121.

they have at other ages. In most instances, however, it is the inability to settle on an occupational identity which disturbs individual young people. To keep themselves together they temporarily overidentify, to the point of apparent complete loss of identity, with the heroes of cliques and crowds. This initiates the stage of "falling in love," which is by no means entirely, or even primarily, a sexual matter—except where the mores demand it. To a considerable extent adolescent love is an attempt to arrive at a definition of one's identity by projecting one's diffused ego image on another and by seeing it thus reflected and gradually clarified. This is why so much of young love is conversation.

Young people can also be remarkably clannish, and cruel in their exclusion of all those who are "different," in skin color or cultural background, in tastes and gifts, and often in such petty aspects of dress and gesture as have been temporarily selected as *the* signs of an in-grouper or out-grouper. It is important to understand (which does not mean condone or participate in) such intolerance as a defense against a sense of identity confusion. For adolescents not only help one another temporarily through much discomfort by forming cliques and by stereotyping themselves, their ideals, and their enemies; they also perversely test each other's capacity to pledge fidelity. The readiness for such testing also explains the appeal which simple and cruel totalitarian doctrines have on the minds of the youth of such countries and classes as have lost or are losing their group identities (feudal, agrarian, tribal, national) and face world-wide industrialization, emancipation, and wider communication.

The adolescent mind is essentially a mind of the *moratorium,* a psychosocial stage between childhood and adulthood, and between the morality learned by the child, and the ethics to be developed by the adult. It is an ideological mind—and, indeed, it is the ideological outlook of a society that speaks most clearly to the adolescent who is eager to be affirmed by his peers, and is ready to be confirmed by rituals, creeds, and programs which at the same time define what is evil, uncanny, and inimical. In searching for the social values which guide identity, one therefore confronts the problems of *ideology* and *aristocracy,* both in their widest possible sense which connotes that within a defined world image and a predestined course of history, the best people will come to rule and rule develops the best in people. In order not to become cynically or apathetically lost, young people must somehow be able to convince themselves that those who succeed in their anticipated adult world thereby shoulder the obligation of being the best. We will discuss later the dangers which emanate from human ideals harnessed to the management of super-machines, be they guided by nationalistic or international, communist or capitalist ideologies. In the last part of this book we shall discuss the way in which the revolutions of our day attempt to solve and also to exploit the deep need of youth to redefine its identity in an industrialized world.

6. INTIMACY VS. ISOLATION

The strength acquired at any stage is tested by the necessity to transcend it in such a way that the individual can take chances in the next stage with what was most vulnerably precious in the previous one. Thus, the young adult, emerging from the search for and the insistence on identity, is eager and willing to fuse his identity with that of others. He is ready for intimacy, that is, the capacity to commit himself to concrete affiliations and partnerships and to develop the ethical strength to abide by such commitments even though they may call for significant sacrifices and compromises. Body and ego must now be masters of the organ modes and of the nuclear conflicts; in order to be able to face the fear of ego loss in situations which call for self-abandon: in the solidarity of close affiliations, in orgasms and sexual unions, in close friendships and in physical combat, in experiences of inspiration by teachers and of intuition from the recesses of the self. The avoidance of such experiences because of a fear of ego loss may lead to a deep sense of isolation and consequent self-absorption.

The counterpart of intimacy is distantiation: the readiness to isolate and, if necessary, to destroy those forces and people whose essence seems dangerous to one's own, and whose "territory" seems to encroach on the extent of one's intimate relations. Prejudices thus developed (and utilized and exploited in politics and in war) are a more mature outgrowth of the blinder repudiations which during the struggle for identity differentiate sharply and cruelly between the familiar and the foreign. The danger of this stage is that intimate, competitive, and combative relations are experienced with and against the selfsame people. But as the areas of adult duty are delineated, and as the competitive encounter, and the sexual embrace, are differentiated, they eventually become subject to that *ethical sense* which is the mark of the adult.

Strictly speaking, it is only now that *true genitality* can fully develop; for much of the sex life preceding these commitments is of the identity-searching kind, or is dominated by phallic or vaginal strivings which make of sex-life a kind of genital combat. On the other hand, genitality is all too often described as a permanent state of reciprocal sexual bliss. This then, may be the place to complete our discussion of genitality.

For a basic orientation in the matter I shall quote what has come to me as Freud's shortest saying. It has often been claimed, and bad habits of conversation seem to sustain the claim, that psychoanalysis as a treatment attempts to convince the patient that before God and man he has only one obligation: to have good orgasms, with a fitting "object," and that regularly. This, of course, is not true. Freud was once asked what he thought a normal person should be able to do well. The questioner probably expected a complicated answer. But Freud, in the curt way of his old days, is reported to have said: *"Lieben und arbeiten"* (to love and to work). It pays to ponder on this simple formula; it gets deeper as you think about it. For when Freud said "love" he meant *genital* love, and genital *love;* when he said love *and* work, he meant a general work-productiveness which would not preoccupy the individual to the extent that he loses his right or capacity to be a genital and a loving being. Thus we may ponder, but we cannot improve on "the professor's" formula.

Genitality, then, consists in the unobstructed capacity to develop an orgastic potency so free of pregenital interferences that genital libido (not just the sex products discharged in Kinsey's "outlets") is expressed in heterosexual mutuality, with full sensitivity of both penis and vagina, and with a convulsion-like discharge of tension from the whole body. This is a rather concrete way of saying something about a process which we really do not understand. To put it more situationally: the total fact of finding, via the climactic turmoil of the orgasm, a supreme experience of the mutual regulation of two beings in some way takes the edge off the hostilities and potential rages caused by the oppositeness of male and female, of fact and fancy, of love and hate. Satisfactory sex relations thus make sex less obsessive, overcompensation less necessary, sadistic controls superfluous.

Preoccupied as it was with curative aspects, psychoanalysis often failed to formulate the matter of genitality in a way significant for the processes of society in all classes, nations, and levels of culture. The kind of mutuality in orgasm which psychoanalysis has in mind is apparently easily obtained in classes and cultures which happen to make a leisurely institution of it. In more complex societies this mutuality is interfered with by so many factors of health, of tradition, of opportunity, and of temperament, that the proper formulation of sexual health would be rather this: A human being should be potentially able to accomplish mutuality of genital orgasm, but he should also be so constituted as to bear a certain amount of frustration in the matter without undue regression wherever emotional preference or considerations of duty and loyalty call for it.

While psychoanalysis has on occasion gone too far in its emphasis on genitality as a universal cure for society and has thus provided a new addiction and a new commodity for many who wished to so interpret its teachings, it has not always indicated all the goals that genitality actually should and must imply. In order to be of lasting social significance, the utopia of genitality should include:

1. mutuality of orgasm
2. with a loved partner
3. of the other sex
4. with whom one is able and willing to share a mutual trust
5. and with whom one is able and willing to regulate the cycles of
   a. work
   b. procreation
   c. recreation
6. so as to secure to the offspring, too, all the stages of a satisfactory development.

It is apparent that such utopian accomplishment on a large scale cannot be an individual or, indeed, a therapeutic task. Nor is it a purely sexual matter by any means. It is integral to a culture's style of sexual selection, cooperation, and competition.

The danger of this stage is isolation, that is the avoidance of contacts which commit to intimacy. In psychopathology, this disturbance can lead to severe "character-problems." On the other hand, there are partnerships which amount to an isolation à deux, protecting both partners from the necessity to face the next critical development—that of generativity.

7. GENERATIVITY VS. STAGNATION

In this book the emphasis is on the childhood stages, otherwise the section on generativity would of necessity be the central one, for this term encompasses the evolutionary development which has made man the teaching and instituting as well as the learning animal. The fashionable insistence on dramatizing the dependence of children on adults often blinds us to the dependence of the older generation on the younger one. Mature man needs to be needed, and maturity needs guidance as well as encouragement from what has been produced and must be taken care of.

Generativity, then, is primarily the concern in establishing and guiding the next generation, although there are individuals who, through misfortune or because of special and genuine gifts in other directions, do not apply this drive to their own offspring. And indeed, the concept generativity is meant to include such more popular synonyms as *productivity* and *creativity,* which, however, cannot replace it.

It has taken psychoanalysis some time to realize that the ability to lose oneself in the meeting of bodies and minds leads to a gradual expansion of ego-interests and to a libidinal investment in that which is being generated. Generativity thus is an essential stage on the psychosexual as well as on the psychosocial schedule. Where such enrichment fails altogether, regression to an obsessive need for pseudo-intimacy takes place, often with a pervading sense of stagnation and personal impoverishment. Individuals, then, often begin to indulge themselves as if they were their own—or one another's—one and only child; and where conditions favor it, early invalidism, physical or psychological, becomes the vehicle of self-concern. The mere fact of having or even wanting children, however, does not "achieve" generativity. In fact, some young parents suffer, it seems, from the retardation of the ability to develop this stage. The reasons are often to be found in early childhood impressions; in excessive self-love based on a too strenuously self-made personality; and finally (and here we return to the beginnings) in the lack of some faith, some "belief in the species," which would make a child appear to be a welcome trust of the community.

As to the institutions which safeguard and reinforce generativity, one can only say that all institutions codify the ethics of generative succession. Even where philosophical and spiritual tradition suggests the renunciation of the right to procreate or to produce, such early turn to "ultimate concerns," wherever instituted in monastic movements, strives to settle at the same time the matter of its relationship to the Care for the creatures of this world and to the Charity which is felt to transcend it.

If this were a book on adulthood, it would be indispensable and profitable at this point to compare economic and psychological theories (beginning with the strange convergencies and divergencies of Marx and Freud) and to proceed to a discussion of man's relationship to his production as well as to his progeny.

8. EGO INTEGRITY VS. DESPAIR

Only in him who in some way has taken care of things and people and has adapted himself to the triumphs and disappointments adherent to being, the originator of others or the generator of products and ideas—only in him may gradually ripen the fruit of these seven stages. I know no better word for it than ego integrity. Lacking a clear definition, I shall point to a few constituents of this state of mind. It is the ego's accrued assurance of its proclivity for order and meaning. It is a post-narcissistic love of the human ego—not of the self—as an experience which conveys some world order and spiritual sense, no matter how dearly paid for. It is the acceptance of one's one and only life cycle as something that had to be and that, by necessity, permitted of no substitutions: it thus means a new, a different love of one's parents. It is a comradeship with the ordering ways of distant times and different pursuits, as expressed in the simple products and sayings of such times and pursuits. Although aware of the relativity of all the various life styles which have given meaning to human striving, the possessor of integrity is ready to defend the dignity of his own life style against all physical and economic threats. For he knows that an individual life is the accidental coincidence of but one life cycle with but one segment of history; and that for him all human integrity stands or falls with the one style of integrity of which he partakes. The style of integrity developed by his culture or civilization thus becomes the "patrimony of his soul," the seal of his moral paternity of himself (". . . *pero el honor/Es patrimonio del alma*": Calderón). In such final consolidation, death loses its sting.

The lack or loss of this accrued ego integration is signified by fear of death: the one and only life cycle is not accepted as the ultimate of life. Despair expresses the feeling that the time is now short, too short for the attempt to start another life and to try out alternate roads to integrity. Disgust hides despair, if often only in the form of "a thousand little disgusts" which do not add up to one big remorse: *"mille petits dégôuts de soi, dont le total ne fait pas un remords, mais un gêne obscure."* (Rostand)

Each individual, to become a mature adult, must to a sufficient degree develop all the ego qualities mentioned, so that a wise Indian, a true gentleman, and a mature peasant share and recognize in one another the final stage of integrity. But each cultural entity, to develop the particular style of integrity suggested by its historical place, utilizes a particular combination of these conflicts, along with specific provocations and prohibitions of infantile sexuality. Infantile conflicts become creative only if sustained by the firm support of cultural institutions and of the special leader classes representing them. In order to approach or experience integrity, the individual must know how to be a follower of image bearers in religion and in politics, in the economic order and in technology, in aristocratic living and in the arts and sciences. Ego integrity, therefore, implies an emotional integration which permits participation by followership as well as acceptance of the responsibility of leadership.

Webster's Dictionary is kind enough to help us complete this outline in a circular fashion. Trust (the first of our ego values) is here defined as "the assured reliance on another's integrity," the last of our values. I suspect that Webster had business in mind rather than babies, credit rather than faith. But the formulation stands. And it seems possible to further paraphrase the relation of adult integrity and infantile trust by saying that healthy children will not fear life if their elders have integrity enough not to fear death.

9. AN EPIGENETIC CHART

In this book the emphasis is on the childhood stages. The foregoing conception of the life cycle, however, awaits systematic treatment. To prepare this, I shall conclude this chapter with a diagram. In this, as in the diagram of pregenital zones and modes, the diagonal represents the normative sequence of psychosocial gains made as at each stage one more nuclear conflict adds a new ego quality, a new criterion of accruing human strength. Below the diagonal there is space for the precursors of each of these solutions, all of which begin with the beginning; above the diagonal there is space for the designation of the derivatives of these gains and their transformations in the maturing and the mature personality.

The underlying assumptions for such charting are (1) that the human personality in principle develops according to steps predetermined in the growing person's readiness to be driven toward, to be aware of, and to interact with, a widening social radius; and (2) that society, in principle, tends to be so constituted as to meet and invite this succession of potentialities for interaction' and attempts to safeguard and to encourage the proper rate and the proper sequence of their enfolding. This is the "maintenance of the human world."

But a chart is only a tool to think with, and cannot aspire to be a prescription to abide by, whether in the practice of childtraining, in psychotherapy, or in the methodology of child study. In the presentation of the psychosocial stages in the form of an *epigenetic chart, . . .* we have definite and delimited methodological steps in mind. It is one purpose of this work to facilitate the comparison of the stages first discerned by Freud as sexual to other schedules of development (physical, cognitive). But any one chart delimits one schedule only, and it must not be imputed that our outline of the psychosocial schedule is intended to imply obscure generalities concerning other aspects of development—or, indeed, of existence. If the chart, for example, lists a series of conflicts or crises, we do not consider all development a series of crises: we claim only that psychosocial development proceeds by critical steps—"critical" being a characteristic of turning points, of moments of decision between progress and regression, integration and retardation.

It may be useful at this point to spell out the methodological implications of an epigenetic matrix. The more heavily-lined squares of the diagonal signify both a sequence of stages and a gradual development of component parts: in other words, the chart formalizes a progression through time of a differentiation of parts. This indicates (1) that each critical item of psychosocial strength discussed here is systematically related to all others, and that they all depend on the proper development in the proper sequence of each item; and (2) that each item exists in some form before its critical time normally arrives.

If I say, for example, that a favorable ratio of basic trust over basic mistrust is the first step in psychosocial adaptation, a favorable ratio of autonomous will over shame and doubt, the second, the corresponding diagrammatic statement expresses a number of fundamental relations that exist between the two steps, as well as some facts fundamental to each. Each comes to its ascendance, meets its crisis, and finds its lasting solution during the stage indicated. But they all must exist from the beginning in some form, for every act calls for an integration of all. Also, an infant may show something like "autonomy" from the beginning in the particular way in which he angrily tries to wriggle himself free when tightly held. However, under normal conditions, it is not until the second year that he begins to experience the whole *critical opposition of being an autonomous creature and being a dependent one;* and it is not until then that he is ready for a decisive encounter with his environment, an environment which, in turn, feels called upon to convey to him its particular ideas and concepts of autonomy and coercion in ways decisively contributing to the character and the health of his personality in his culture. It is this encounter, together with the resulting crisis, that we have tentatively described for each stage. As to the progression from one stage to the next, the diagonal indicates the sequence to be followed. However, it also makes room for variations in tempo and intensity. An individual, or a culture, may linger excessively over trust and proceed from I 1 over I 2 to II 2, or an accelerated progression may move from I 1 over II 1 to II 2. Each such acceleration or (relative) retardation, however, is assumed to have a modifying influence on all later stages.

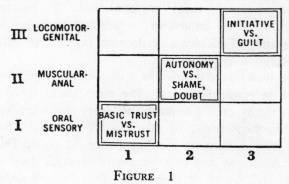

FIGURE 1

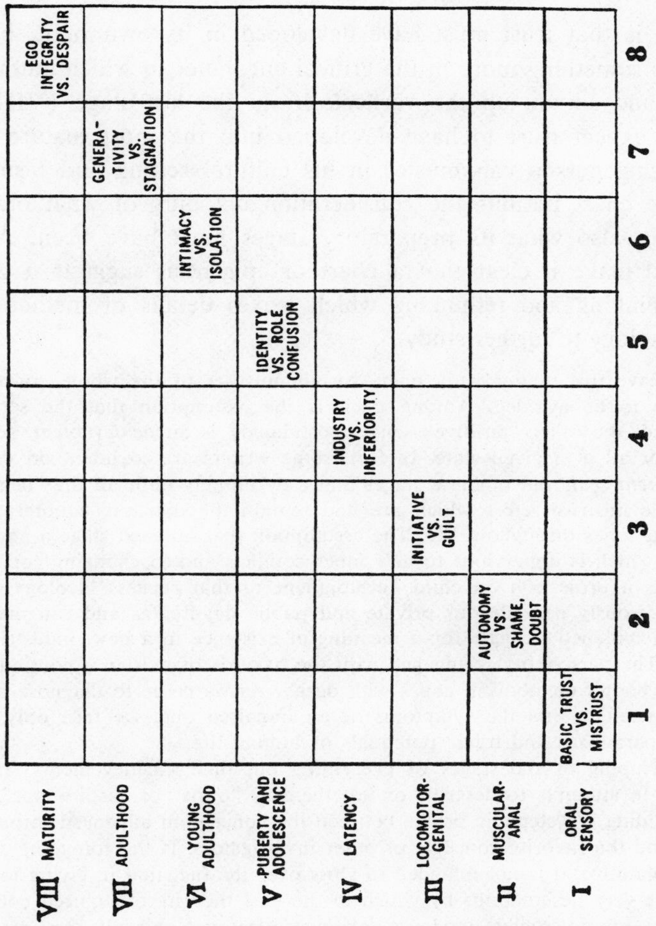

	1	2	3	4	5	6	7	8
VIII MATURITY								EGO INTEGRITY VS. DESPAIR
VII ADULTHOOD							GENERATIVITY VS. STAGNATION	
VI YOUNG ADULTHOOD						INTIMACY VS. ISOLATION		
V PUBERTY AND ADOLESCENCE					IDENTITY VS. ROLE CONFUSION			
IV LATENCY				INDUSTRY VS. INFERIORITY				
III LOCOMOTOR-GENITAL			INITIATIVE VS. GUILT					
II MUSCULAR-ANAL		AUTONOMY VS. SHAME, DOUBT						
I ORAL SENSORY	BASIC TRUST VS. MISTRUST							

FIGURE 2

An epigenetic diagram thus lists a system of stages dependent on each other; and while individual stages may have been explored more or less thoroughly or named more or less fittingly, the diagram suggests that their study be pursued always with the total configuration of stages in mind. The diagram invites, then, a thinking through of all its empty boxes: if we have entered Basic Trust in I 1 and Integrity in VIII 8, we leave the question open, as to what trust might have become in a stage dominated by the need for integrity even as we have left open what it may look like and, indeed, be called in the stage dominated by a striving for autonomy (II 1). All we mean to emphasize is that trust must have developed in its own right, before it becomes something more in the critical encounter in which autonomy develops—and so on, up the vertical. If, in the last stage (VIII 1), we would expect trust to have developed into the most mature *faith* that an aging person can muster in his cultural setting and historical period, the chart permits the consideration not only of what old age can be, but also what its preparatory stages must have been. All of this should make it clear that a chart of epigenesis suggests a global form of thinking and rethinking which leaves details of methodology and terminology to further study.*

* To leave this matter truly open, certain misuses of the whole conception would have to be avoided. Among them is the assumption that the sense of trust (and all the other "positive" senses postulated) is an *achievement,* secured once and for all at a given state. In fact, some writers are so intent on making an *achievement scale* out of these stages that they blithely omit all the "negative" senses (basic mistrust, etc.) which are and remain the dynamic counterpart of the "positive" ones throughout life. The assumption that on each stage a goodness is achieved which is impervious to new inner conflicts and to changing conditions is, I believe, a projection on child development of that success ideology which can so dangerously pervade our private and public daydreams and can make us inept in a heightened struggle for a meaningful existence in a new, industrial era of history. The personality is engaged with the hazards of existence continuously, even as the body's metabolism copes with decay. As we come to diagnose a state of relative strength and the symptoms of an impaired one, we face only more clearly the paradoxes and tragic potentials of human life.

The stripping of the stages of everything but their "achievements" has its counterpart in attempts to describe or test them as "traits" or "aspirations" without first building a systematic bridge between the conception advanced throughout this book and the favorite concepts of other investigators. If the foregoing sounds somewhat plaintive, it is not intended to gloss over the fact that in giving to these strengths the very designations by which in the past they have acquired countless connotations of superficial goodness, affected niceness, and all too strenuous virtue, I invited misunderstandings and misuses. However, I believe, that there is an intrinsic relationship between ego and language and that despite passing vicissitudes certain basic words retain essential meanings.

I have since attempted to formulate for Julian Huxley's *Humanist Frame* (Allen and Unwin, 1961; Harper and Brothers, 1962) a blueprint of essential strengths which evolution has built both into the ground plan of the life stages and into that of man's institutions. While I cannot discuss here the methodological problems involved (and aggravated by my use of the term "basic virtues"), I should append the list of these strengths because they are really the lasting out-come of the "favorable ratios" mentioned at every step of the chapter on psychosocial stages. Here they are:

> Basic Trust vs. Basic Mistrust: Drive and *Hope*
> Autonomy vs. Shame and Doubt: Self-Control and *Willpower*
> Initiative vs. Guilt: Direction and *Purpose*
> Industry vs. Inferiority: Method and *Competence*
> Identity vs. Role Confusion: Devotion and *Fidelity*

Intimacy vs. Isolation: Affiliation and *Love*
Generativity vs. Stagnation: Production and *Care*
Ego Integrity vs. Despair: Renunciation and *Wisdom*

The italicized words are called *basic* virtues because without them, and their re-emergence from generation to generation, all other and more changeable systems of human values lose their spirit and their relevance. Of this list, I have been able so far to give a more detailed account only for Fidelity (see *Youth, Change and Challenge,* E. H. Erikson, editor, Basic Books, 1963). But here again, the list represents a total conception within which there is much room for a discussion of terminology and methodology. (E.H.E.)

On becoming a person

CARL R. ROGERS

Education is again experiencing the development of a number of educational movements and fads. These movements range from an extreme form of behaviorism, represented most recently by performance contractors, to an extreme form of child-centered activity exhibited in some forms of the so-called open classroom. One defense against educational movements becoming mere fads is to make explicit the basic assumptions concerning the nature of man and learning that are implicit in the movements.

Carl Rogers is a psychologist commonly associated with what has come to be called "humanistic" or "third force" psychology. He is the one member of this group, which includes such men as Abraham Maslow and Rollo May, who has written directly on the topic of education. Humanistic psychology represents a movement within psychology which is basically in opposition to the operant conditioning and rigid behaviorism schools. It has close ties with existential philosophy, and in concert with existentialism, it provides the theoretical support for the movement in education typified by Summerhill and open-classroom schooling.

Rogers, then, provides the educator with the most available source of explicit psychological assumptions that are implicit in a growing area of educational activity. The educator who has an awareness of these assumptions will find in them a safeguard against allowing these educational movements to degenerate into educational posturing.

On Becoming a Person focuses first upon the nature of a helping relationship and in particular upon the means for facilitating

SOURCE: Carl R. Rogers, *On Becoming a Person: A Therapist's View of Psychotherapy* (Boston: Houghton Mifflin Company, 1970), pp. 39–58, 275–278, 279–296. Copyright © 1961 by Carl R. Rogers. Reprinted by permission of author and publisher.

personal growth. The significant aspect of Rogers' approach to facilitating personal growth is his reversal of the most commonly held methodology. Essentially, Rogers rejects the causal dimension of the method. He no longer sees his own function as a therapist in "treating" or "curing" or even changing a person; therapy is no longer a "doing something to someone." Rather, Rogers seeks to provide, or be the agent for, that kind of relationship which the other person may use as a means for his own growth or cure. Rogers also rejects the entire notion that by giving the individual an intellectual explanation of his behavior he will then be able to alter that behavior. The power to effect a psychological "cure" resides exclusively within the patient himself, not within the therapist. His role is to provide the patient with a relationship that is fully supportive of all attempts the patient may make toward personal growth.

The second focus of Rogers' work is upon the process of "becoming a person." What does it mean for a person to "cure" himself; that is, what kind of change and growth results from a patient's proper use of the therapeutic relationship? The patient finds himself, first of all, with an increasing openness to experience. He no longer needs to restrict his experiencing to fit a preexisting set of expectations. To become a person, the individual also develops a trust in his own organism. Being open to experience, he becomes able to trust his own *processing* of experience, able to accept external and internal states even though they may be in conflict. Still another aspect of becoming a person is manifest in the individual's growing capacity for self-evaluation. He comes to accept himself as the source of all values and to know that values are the result of his choices and that he is solely responsible for them.

Finally, to become a person means the development of the individual's capacity to accept himself as a process, rather than continually seeking to attain some fixed state. He comes to realize that his goals and values are really heuristic devices, guides for action rather than static achievements.

A third focus of Rogers' work is upon the "good life," or what he terms "the fully functioning person." The main thrust of Rogers' position here is to deny that the good life can be equated with fixed states of contentment or happiness. The good life is not to be defined in psychological terms such as tension-reduction, drive-reduction, or homeostasis. For Rogers, the good life is, again, a process rather than a state. It is, as he says, "a direction, not a destination." It is any direction which the individual may choose so long as he is internally or inwardly free to choose any direction. Freedom to choose exists for the individual when he has become open to experience, self-trusting, self-valuing, and accepting of himself as a process.

The fourth area of focus for Rogers is upon the place of research in psychotherapy. The role of research is to provide greater insight and information into what actually transpires during psychotherapy sessions. However, the results of research cannot serve to prescribe what *ought* to take place during such a session. The interpersonal relationships that do and must evolve during the course of therapy require that these relationships be based primarily upon the acceptance by the therapist of the client as a person rather than as an object. The very objective nature of research insists that all elements (including the involved persons) be treated as objects, so that controls can be exercised and confrontations created and manipulated. This objectivity cannot serve a therapeutic relation, however, when the patient is assumed to be without fixed traits and values, because these are ever in flux. Still, Rogers feels that science, especially research, has a clear and valuable role to play in psychotherapy—so long as it is not confused with the therapeutic relationship.

Rogers' fifth focus shifts to the consideration of the broader "implications for living" implicit in his psychoanalytic theory. Of importance to the educator is his discussion of student-centered teaching. Real, significant learning can take place only when the learner is psychologically willing and able to allow it. Therefore it is the student himself who must be in a position to determine the pace and content of his learning activities. The role of the teacher in a student-centered class becomes closely related to that of a therapist. The teacher becomes a facilitator, supportive of any attempt of the student to learn whatever it is he feels the need to learn.

Of equal importance to the educator and to students is Rogers' concern with problems of communication. He feels that all good, that is, open and free, communication is basically therapeutic. The greatest single barrier to good communication is the tendency to evaluate the communication attempts of others. Our tendency is to approve, disapprove, or in some other way judge the statements of others. Can there be any wonder at the lack of good communication in most classrooms?

Education has long espoused the value of creativity while continuing to employ procedures that turn out conformists. Rogers theory of creativity is an attempt to bridge this conflict. He defines creativity as the "emergence in action of a novel relational product, growing out of the uniqueness of the individual on the one hand, and the materials, events, people, or circumstances of his life on the other." Creativity is fostered by encouraging in the individual those qualities of openness to experience, self-trust, and self-valuation that characterize the fully functioning person. In the schools it is the province of free, unfettered, and nonjudgmental communication to encourage the creative mode in each child.

The selections from *On Becoming a Person* included in this volume reflect areas of special interest to the teacher. The first selection describes the characteristics of the "helping relationship," a description of what it means to become a facilitator. Rogers formulates ten questions by which the individual may guide himself toward establishing helping relationships with others. The import of these ten questions may be summarized in four terms: congruence, consistency, warmth, and empathy. Congruence refers to the individual's full awareness of whatever attitude or feeling he may be expressing at any given moment. Consistency in its broadest sense is the understanding by the individual that he cannot help another person grow unless he is also prepared to grow in the same direction—not expecting others to do or become what he is not prepared to do or become. Warmth is his ability to accept the other person in a positive way, finding in himself positive attitudes toward that person. Finally, empathy is his ability to enter fully into the world, values, attitudes of the other person. These are the key ways to develop a healthy relationship and to become a facilitator of learning in the classroom.

The second of these selections introduces the reader to Rogers' most striking thesis, a brief statement containing in itself almost all the bases for current educational procedures out of favor. It may be shocking because he so clearly points out the long way teachers and educators must go to be either willing or able to transform their traditional role of teacher to that of facilitator.

In the final selection, Rogers takes a look at the concept of significant learning. Rogers is convinced that significant learning takes place in psychotherapy. He means, of course, learning that makes a real difference to the individual and does so in a way so as to alter his subsequent behavior. To facilitate this kind of learning in educational settings, the teacher must be seen by the student as "real" and congruent. The teacher must also convey an attitude of acceptance toward the student, and materials must be made available, not forced upon him.

Rogers' thesis is clear: psychology, particularly his form of psychotherapy, has a great deal to say to the educational establishment. If current trends toward more "open" forms of education are to be sustained and advanced, then teachers must be clear about what is really involved in such openness and prepared to grow themselves, to grow personally into Rogers' "fully functioning" individuals. Without that kind of commitment, the change to new forms of educational structures must be ineffectual. Rogers makes the challenge; educators must make the decisions.

THE CHARACTERISTICS OF A HELPING RELATIONSHIP

· · · · ·

My interest in psychotherapy has brought about in me an interest in every kind of helping relationship. By this term I mean a relationship in which at least one of the parties has the intent of promoting the growth, development, maturity, improved functioning, improved coping with life of the other. The other, in this sense, may be one individual or a group. To put it in another way, a helping relationship might be defined as one in which one of the participants intends that there should come about, in one or both parties, more appreciation of, more expression of, more functional use of the latent inner resources of the individual.

Now it is obvious that such a definition covers a wide range of relationships which usually are intended to facilitate growth. It would certainly include the relationship between mother and child, father and child. It would include the relationship between the physician and his patient. The relationship between teacher and pupil would often come under this definition, though some teachers would not have the promotion of growth as their intent. It includes almost all counselor-client relationships, whether we are speaking of educational counseling, vocational counseling, or personal counseling. In this last-mentioned area it would include the wide range of relationships between the psychotherapist and the hospitalized psychotic, the therapist and the troubled or neurotic individual, and the relationship between the therapist and the increasing number of so-called "normal" individuals who enter therapy to improve their own functioning or accelerate their personal growth.

These are largely one-to-one relationships. But we should also think of the large number of individual-group interactions which are intended as helping relationships. Some administrators intend that their relationship to their staff groups shall be of the sort which promotes growth, though other administrators would not have this purpose. The interaction between the group therapy leader and his group belongs here. So does the relationship of the community consultant to a community group. Increasingly the interaction between the industrial consultant and a management group is intended as a helping relationship. Perhaps this listing will point up the fact that a great many of the relationships in which we and others are involved fall within this category of interactions in which there is the purpose of promoting development and more mature and adequate functioning.

THE QUESTION

But what are the characteristics of those relationships which do help, which do facilitate growth? And at the other end of the scale is it possible to discern those characteristics which make a relationship unhelpful, even though it was the sincere intent to promote growth and development? It is to these questions, particularly the first, that I would like to take you with me over some of the paths I have explored, and to tell you where I am, as of now, in my thinking on these issues.

THE ANSWERS GIVEN BY RESEARCH

It is natural to ask first of all whether there is any empirical research which would give us an objective answer to these questions. There has not been a large amount of research in this area as yet, but what there is is stimulating and suggestive. I cannot report all of it but I would like to make a somewhat extensive sampling of the studies which have been done and state very briefly some of the findings. In so doing, oversimplification is necessary, and I am quite aware that I am not doing full justice to the researches I am mentioning, but it may give you the feeling that factual advances are being made and pique your curiosity enough to examine the studies themselves, if you have not already done so.

STUDIES OF ATTITUDES

Most of the studies throw light on the attitudes on the part of the helping person which make a relationship growth-promoting or growth-inhibiting. Let us look at some of these.

A careful study of parent-child relationships made some years ago by Baldwin and others (1) * at the Fels Institute contains interesting evidence. Of the various clusters of parental attitudes toward children, the "acceptant-democratic" seemed most growth-facilitating. Children of these parents with their warm and equalitarian attitudes showed an accelerated intellectual development (an increasing I.Q.), more originality, more emotional security and control, less excitability than children from other types of homes. Though somewhat slow initially in social development, they were, by the time they reached school age, popular, friendly, non-aggressive leaders.

Where parents' attitudes are classed as "actively rejectant" the children show a slightly decelerated intellectual development, relatively poor use of the abilities they do possess, and some lack of originality. They are emotionally unstable, rebellious, aggressive, and quarrelsome. The children of parents with other attitude syndromes tend in various respects to fall in between these extremes.

I am sure that these findings do not surprise us as related to child development. I would like to suggest that they probably apply to other

* [Numbers in parentheses refer to the references at the end of the selection— Eds.]

relationships as well, and that the counselor or physician or administrator who is warmly emotional and expressive, respectful of the individuality of himself and of the other, and who exhibits a non-possessive caring, probably facilitates self-realization much as does a parent with these attitudes.

Let me turn to another careful study in a very different area. White-horn and Betz (2, 27) investigated the degree of success achieved by young resident physicians in working with schizophrenic patients on a psychiatric ward. They chose for special study the seven who had been outstandingly helpful, and seven whose patients had shown the least degree of improvement. Each group had treated about fifty patients. The investigators examined all the available evidence to discover in what ways the A group (the successful group) differed from the B group. Several significant differences were found. The physicians in the A group tended to see the schizophrenic in terms of the personal meaning which various behaviors had to the patient, rather than seeing him as a case history or a descriptive diagnosis. They also tended to work toward goals which were oriented to the personality of the patient, rather than such goals as reducing the symptoms or curing the disease. It was found that the helpful physicians, in their day by day interaction, primarily made use of active personal participation—a person-to-person relationship. They made less use of procedures which could be classed as "passive permissive." They were even less likely to use such procedures as interpretation, instruction or advice, or emphasis upon the practical care of the patient. Finally, they were much more likely than the B group to develop a relationship in which the patient felt trust and confidence in the physician.

Although the authors cautiously emphasize that these findings relate only to the treatment of schizophrenics, I am inclined to disagree. I suspect that similar facts would be found in a research study of almost any class of helping relationship.

Another interesting study focuses upon the way in which the person being helped perceives the relationship. Heine (14) studied individuals who had gone for psychotherapeutic help to psychoanalytic, client-centered, and Adlerian therapists. Regardless of the type of therapy, these clients report similar changes in themselves. But it is their perception of the relationship which is of particular interest to us here. When asked what accounted for the changes which had occurred, they expressed some differing explanations, depending on the orientation of the therapist. But their agreement on the major elements they had found helpful was even more significant. They indicated that these attitudinal elements in the relationship accounted for the changes which had taken place in themselves: the trust they had felt in the therapist; being understood by the therapist; the feeling of independence they had had in making choices and decisions. The therapist procedure which they had found most helpful was that the therapist clarified and openly stated feelings which the client had been approaching hazily and hesitantly.

There was also a high degree of agreement among these clients, regardless of the orientation of their therapists, as to what elements had been unhelpful in the relationship. Such therapist attitudes as lack of interest, remoteness or distance, and an over-degree of sympathy, were perceived as unhelpful. As to procedures, they had found it unhelpful when therapists had given direct specific advice regarding decisions or had emphasized past history rather than present problems. Guiding suggestions mildly given were perceived in an intermediate range—neither clearly helpful nor unhelpful.

Fiedler, in a much quoted study (10), found that expert therapists of differing orientations formed similar relationships with their clients. Less well known are the elements which characterized these relationships, differentiating them from the relationships formed by less expert therapists. These elements are: an ability to understand the client's meanings and feelings; a sensitivity to the client's attitudes; a warm interest without any emotional over-involvement.

A study by Quinn (19) throws light on what is involved in understanding the client's meanings and feelings. His study is surprising in that it shows that "understanding" of the client's meanings is essentially an attitude of *desiring* to understand. Quinn presented his judges only with recorded therapist statements taken from interviews. The raters had no knowledge of what the therapist was responding to or how the client reacted to his response. Yet it was found that the degree of understanding could be judged about as well from this material as from listening to the response in context. This seems rather conclusive evidence that it is an attitude of wanting to understand which is communicated.

As to the emotional quality of the relationship, Seeman (23) found that success in psychotherapy is closely associated with a strong and growing mutual liking and respect between client and therapist.

An interesting study by Dittes (4) indicates how delicate this relationship is. Using a physiological measure, the psychogalvanic reflex, to measure the anxious or threatened or alerted reactions of the client, Dittes correlated the deviations on this measure with judges' ratings of the degree of warm acceptance and permissiveness on the part of the therapist. It was found that whenever the therapist's attitudes changed even slightly in the direction of a lesser degree of acceptance, the number of abrupt GSR deviations significantly increased. Evidently when the relationship is experienced as less acceptant the organism organizes against threat, even at the physiological level.

Without trying fully to integrate the findings from these various studies, it can at least be noted that a few things stand out. One is the fact that it is the attitudes and feelings of the therapist, rather than his theoretical orientation, which is important. His procedures and techniques are less important than his attitudes. It is also worth noting that it is the way in which his attitudes and procedures are *perceived* which makes a difference to the client, and that it is this perception which is crucial.

"MANUFACTURED" RELATIONSHIPS

Let me turn to research of a very different sort, some of which you may find rather abhorrent, but which nevertheless has a bearing upon the nature of a facilitating relationship. These studies have to do with what we might think of as manufactured relationships.

Verplanck (26), Greenspoon (11) and others have shown that operant conditioning of verbal behavior is possible in a relationship. Very briefly, if the experimenter says "Mhm," or "Good," or nods his head after certain types of words or statements, those classes of words tend to increase because of being reinforced. It has been shown that using such procedures one can bring about increases in such diverse verbal categories as plural nouns, hostile words, statements of opinion. The person is completely unaware that he is being influenced in any way by these reinforcers. The implication is that by such selective reinforcement we could bring it about that the other person in the relationship would be using whatever kinds of words and making whatever kinds of statements we had decided to reinforce.

Following still further the principles of operant conditioning as developed by Skinner and his group, Lindsley (17) has shown that a chronic schizophrenic can be placed in a "helping relationship" with a machine. The machine, somewhat like a vending machine, can be set to reward a variety of types of behaviors. Initially it simply rewards—with candy, a cigarette, or the display of a picture—the lever-pressing behavior of the patient. But it is possible to set it so that many pulls on the lever may supply a hungry kitten—visible in a separate enclosure—with a drop of milk. In this case the satisfaction is an altruistic one. Plans are being developed to reward similar social or altruistic behavior directed toward another patient, placed in the next room. The only limit to the kinds of behavior which might be rewarded lies in the degree of mechanical ingenuity of the experimenter.

Lindsley reports that in some patients there has been marked clinical improvement. Personally I cannot help but be impressed by the description of one patient who had gone from a deteriorated chronic state to being given free grounds privileges, this change being quite clearly associated with his interaction with the machine. Then the experimenter decided to study experimental extinction, which, put in more personal terms, means that no matter how many thousands of times the lever was pressed, no reward of any kind was forthcoming. The patient gradually regressed, grew untidy, uncommunicative, and his grounds privilege had to be revoked. This (to me) pathetic incident would seem to indicate that even in a relationship to a machine, trustworthiness is important if the relationship is to be helpful.

Still another interesting study of a manufactured relationship is being carried on by Harlow and his associates (13), this time with monkeys. Infant monkeys, removed from their mothers almost immediately after birth, are, in one phase of the experiment, presented with two objects. One might be termed the "hard mother," a sloping cylinder of wire netting with a nipple from which the baby may feed. The other is a "soft mother," a similar cylinder made of foam rubber and terry cloth. Even when an infant gets all his food from the "hard mother" he clearly and increasingly prefers the "soft mother." Motion pictures show that he definitely "relates" to this object, playing with it, enjoying it, finding security in clinging to it when strange objects are near, and using that security as a home base for venturing into the frightening world. Of the many interesting and challenging implications of this study, one seems reasonably clear. It is that no amount of direct food reward can take the place of certain perceived qualities which the infant appears to need and desire.

TWO RECENT STUDIES

Let me close this wide-ranging—and perhaps perplexing—sampling of research studies with an account of two very recent investigations. The first is an experiment conducted by Ends and Page (5). Working with hardened chronic hospitalized alcoholics who had been committed to a state hospital for sixty days, they tried three different methods of group psychotherapy. The method which they believed would be most effective was therapy based on a two-factor theory of learning; a client-centered approach was expected to be second; a psychoanalytically oriented approach was expected to be least efficient. Their results showed that the therapy based upon a learning theory approach was not only not helpful, but was somewhat deleterious. The outcomes were worse than those in the control group which had no therapy. The analytically oriented therapy produced some positive gain, and the client-centered group therapy was associated with the greatest amount of positive change. Follow-up data, extending over one and one-half years, confirmed the in-hospital findings, with the lasting improvement being greatest in the client-centered approach, next in the analytic, next the control group, and least in those handled by a learning theory approach.

As I have puzzled over this study, unusual in that the approach to which the authors were committed proved *least* effective, I find a clue, I believe, in the description of the therapy based on learning theory (18). Essentially it consisted (*a*) of pointing out and labeling the behaviors which had proved unsatisfying, (*b*) of exploring objectively with the client the reasons behind these behaviors, and (*c*) of establishing through re-education more effective problem-solving habits. But in all of this interaction the aim, as they formulated it, was to be impersonal. The therapist "permits as little of his own personality to intrude as is humanly possible." The "therapist stresses personal anonymity in his activities, i.e., he must studiously avoid impressing the patient with his own (therapist's) individual personality characteristics." To me this seems the most likely clue to the failure of this approach, as I try to interpret the facts in the light of the other research studies. To withhold one's self as a person and to deal with the other person as an object does not have a high probability of being helpful.

The final study I wish to report is one just being completed by Halkides (12). She started from a theoretical formulation of mine regarding the necessary and sufficient conditions for therapeutic change (21). She hypothesized that there would be a significant relationship between the extent of constructive personality change in the client and four counselor variables: (*a*) the degree of empathic understanding of the client manifested by the counselor; (*b*) the degree of positive affective attitude (unconditional positive regard) manifested by the counselor toward the client; (*c*) the extent to which the counselor is genuine, his words matching his own internal feeling; and (*d*) the extent to which the counselor's response matches the client's expression in the intensity of affective expression.

To investigate these hypotheses she first selected, by multiple objective criteria, a group of ten cases which could be classed as "most successful" and a group of ten "least successful" cases. She then took an early and late recorded interview from each of these cases. On a random basis she picked nine client-counselor interaction units—a client statement and a counselor response—from each of these interviews. She thus had nine early interactions and nine later interactions from each case. This gave her several hundred units which were now placed in random order. The units from an early interview of an unsuccessful case might be followed by the units from a late interview of a successful case, etc.

Three judges, who did not know the cases or their degree of success, or the source of any given unit, now listened to this material four different times. They rated each unit on a seven point scale, first as to the degree of empathy, second as to the counselor's positive attitude toward the client, third as to the counselor's congruence or genuineness, and fourth as to the degree to which the counselor's response matched the emotional intensity of the client's expression.

I think all of us who knew of the study regarded it as a very bold venture. Could judges listening to single units of interaction possibly make any reliable rating of such subtle qualities as I have mentioned? And even if suitable reliability could be obtained, could eighteen counselor-client interchanges from each case—a minute sampling of the hundreds or thousands of such interchanges which occurred in each case—possibly bear any relationship to the therapeutic outcome? The chance seemed slim.

The findings are surprising. It proved possible to achieve high reliability between the judges, most of the inter-judge correlations being in the 0.80's or 0.90's, except on the last variable. It was found that a high degree of empathic understanding was significantly associated, at a .001 level, with the more successful cases. A high degree of unconditional positive regard was likewise associated with the more successful cases, at the .001 level. Even the rating of the counselor's genuineness or congruence—the extent to which his words matched his feelings—was associated with the successful outcome of the case, and again at the .001 level of significance. Only in the investigation of the matching intensity of affective expression were the results equivocal.

It is of interest too that high ratings of these variables were not associated more significantly with units from later interviews than with units from early interviews. This means that the counselor's attitudes were quite constant throughout the interviews. If he was highly empathic, he tended to be so from first to last. If he was lacking in genuineness, this tended to be true of both early and late interviews.

As with any study, this investigation has its limitations. It is concerned with a certain type of helping relationship, psychotherapy. It investigated only four variables thought to be significant. Perhaps there are many others. Nevertheless it represents a significant advance in the study of helping relationships. Let me try to state the findings in the simplest possible fashion. It seems to indicate that the quality of the counselor's interaction with a client can be satisfactorily judged on the basis of a very small sampling of his behavior. It also means that if the counselor is congruent or transparent, so that his words are in line with his feelings rather than the two being discrepant; if the counselor likes the client, unconditionally; and if the counselor understands the essential feelings of the client as they seem to the client—then there is a strong probability that this will be an effective helping relationship.

SOME COMMENTS

These then are some of the studies which throw at least a measure of light on the nature of the helping relationship. They have investigated different facets of the problem. They have approached it from very different theoretical contexts. They have used different methods. They are not directly comparable. Yet they seem to me to point to several statements which may be made with some assurance. It seems clear that relationships which are helpful have different characteristics from relationships which are unhelpful. These differential characteristics have to do primarily with the attitudes of the helping person on the one hand and with the perception of the relationship by the "helpee" on the other. It is equally clear that the studies thus far made do not give us any final answers as to what is a helping relationship, nor how it is to be formed.

HOW CAN I CREATE A HELPING RELATIONSHIP?

I believe each of us working in the field of human relationships has a similar problem in knowing how to use such research knowledge. We cannot slavishly follow such findings in a mechanical way or we destroy the personal qualities which these very studies show to be valuable. It seems to me that we have to use these studies, testing them against our own experience and forming new and further personal hypotheses to use and test in our own further personal relationships.

So rather than try to tell you how you should use the findings I have presented I should like to tell you the kind of questions which these studies and my own clinical experience raise for me, and some of the tentative and changing hypotheses which guide my behavior as I enter into what I hope may be helping relationships, whether with students, staff, family, or clients. Let me list a number of these questions and considerations.

1. Can I *be* in some way which will be perceived by the other person as trustworthy, as dependable or consistent in some deep sense? Both research and experience indicate that this is very important, and over the years I have found what I believe are deeper and better ways of answering this question. I used to feel that if I fulfilled all the outer conditions of trustworthiness—keeping appointments, respecting the confidential nature of the interviews, etc.—and if I acted consistently the same during the interviews, then this condition would be fulfilled. But experience drove home the fact that to act consistently acceptant, for example, if in fact I was feeling annoyed or skeptical or some other non-acceptant feeling, was certain in the long run to be perceived as inconsistent or untrustworthy. I have come to recognize that being trustworthy does not demand that I be rigidly consistent but that I be

dependably real. The term "congruent" is one I have used to describe the way I would like to be. By this I mean that whatever feeling or attitude I am experiencing would be matched by my awareness of that attitude. When this is true, then I am a unified or integrated person in that moment, and hence I can *be* whatever I deeply *am*. This is a reality which I find others experience as dependable.

2. A very closely related question is this: Can I be expressive enough as a person that what I am will be communicated unambiguously? I believe that most of my failures to achieve a helping relationship can be traced to unsatisfactory answers to these two questions. When I am experiencing an attitude of annoyance toward another person but am unaware of it, then my communication contains contradictory messages. My words are giving one message, but I am also in subtle ways communicating the annoyance I feel and this confuses the other person and makes him distrustful, though he too may be unaware of what is causing the difficulty. When as a parent or a therapist or a teacher or an administrator I fail to listen to what is going on in me, fail because of my own defensiveness to sense my own feelings, then this kind of failure seems to result. It has made it seem to me that the most basic learning for anyone who hopes to establish any kind of helping relationship is that it is safe to be transparently real. If in a given relationship I am reasonably congruent, if no feelings relevant to the relationship are hidden either to me or the other person, then I can be almost sure that the relationship will be a helpful one.

One way of putting this which may seem strange to you is that if I can form a helping relationship to myself—if I can be sensitively aware of and acceptant toward my own feelings—then the likelihood is great that I can form a helping relationship toward another.

Now, acceptantly to be what I am, in this sense, and to permit this to show through to the other person, is the most difficult task I know and one I never fully achieve. But to realize that this *is* my task has been most rewarding because it has helped me to find what has gone wrong with interpersonal relationships which have become snarled and to put them on a constructive track again. It has meant that if I am to facilitate the personal growth of others in relation to me, then I must grow, and while this is often painful it is also enriching.

3. A third question is: Can I let myself experience positive attitudes toward this other person—attitudes of warmth, caring, liking, interest, respect? It is not easy. I find in myself, and feel that I often see in

others, a certain amount of fear of these feelings. We are afraid that if we let ourselves freely experience these positive feelings toward another we may be trapped by them. They may lead to demands on us or we may be disappointed in our trust, and these outcomes we fear. So as a reaction we tend to build up distance between ourselves and others —aloofness, a "professional" attitude, an impersonal relationship.

I feel quite strongly that one of the important reasons for the professionalization of every field is that it helps to keep this distance. In the clinical areas we develop elaborate diagnostic formulations, seeing the person as an object. In teaching and in administration we develop all kinds of evaluative procedures, so that again the person is perceived as an object. In these ways, I believe, we can keep ourselves from experiencing the caring which would exist if we recognized the relationship as one between two persons. It is a real achievement when we can learn, even in certain relationships or at certain times in those relationships, that it is safe to care, that it is safe to relate to the other as a person for whom we have positive feelings.

4. Another question the importance of which I have learned in my own experience is: Can I be strong enough as a person to be separate from the other? Can I be a sturdy respecter of my own feelings, my own needs, as well as his? Can I own and, if need be, express my own feelings as something belonging to me and separate from his feelings? Am I strong enough in my own separateness that I will not be downcast by his depression, frightened by his fear, nor engulfed by his dependency? Is my inner self hardy enough to realize that I am not destroyed by his anger, taken over by his need for dependence, nor enslaved by his love, but that I exist separate from him with feelings and rights of my own? When I can freely feel this strength of being a separate person, then I find that I can let myself go much more deeply in understanding and accepting him because I am not fearful of losing myself.

5. The next question is closely related. Am I secure enough within myself to permit him his separateness? Can I permit him to be what he is—honest or deceitful, infantile or adult, despairing or over-confident? Can I give him the freedom to be? Or do I feel that he should follow my advice, or remain somewhat dependent on me, or mold himself after me? In this connection I think of the interesting small study by Farson (6) which found that the less well adjusted and less competent counselor tends to induce conformity to himself, to have clients who model themselves after him. On the other hand, the better adjusted

and more competent counselor can interact with a client through many interviews without interfering with the freedom of the client to develop a personality quite separate from that of his therapist. I should prefer to be in this latter class, whether as parent or supervisor or counselor.

6. Another question I ask myself is: Can I let myself enter fully into the world of his feelings and personal meanings and see these as he does? Can I step into his private world so completely that I lose all desire to evaluate or judge it? Can I enter it so sensitively that I can move about in it freely, without trampling on meanings which are precious to him? Can I sense it so accurately that I can catch not only the meanings of his experience which are obvious to him, but those meanings which are only implicit, which he sees only dimly or as confusion? Can I extend this understanding without limit? I think of the client who said, "Whenever I find someone who understands a *part* of me at the time, then it never fails that a point is reached where I know they're *not* understanding me again . . . What I've looked for so hard is for someone to understand."

For myself I find it easier to feel this kind of understanding, and to communicate it, to individual clients than to students in a class or staff members in a group in which I am involved. There is a strong temptation to set students "straight," or to point out to a staff member the errors in his thinking. Yet when I can permit myself to understand in these situations, it is mutually rewarding. And with clients in therapy, I am often impressed with the fact that even a minimal amount of empathic understanding—a bumbling and faulty attempt to catch the confused complexity of the client's meaning—is helpful, though there is no doubt that it is most helpful when I can see and formulate clearly the meanings in his experiencing which for him have been unclear and tangled.

7. Still another issue is whether I can be acceptant of each facet of this other person which he presents to me. Can I receive him as he is? Can I communicate this attitude? Or can I only receive him conditionally, acceptant of some aspects of his feelings and silently or openly disapproving of other aspects? It has been my experience that when my attitude is conditional, then he cannot change or grow in those respects in which I cannot fully receive him. And when—afterward and sometimes too late—I try to discover why I have been unable to accept him in every respect, I usually discover that it is because I have been frightened or threatened in myself by some aspect of his feelings. If I

am to be more helpful, then I must myself grow and accept myself in these respects.

8. A very practical issue is raised by the question: Can I act with sufficient sensitivity in the relationship that my behavior will not be perceived as a threat? The work we are beginning to do in studying the physiological concomitants of psychotherapy confirms the research by Dittes in indicating how easily individuals are threatened at a physiological level. The psychogalvanic reflex—the measure of skin conductance—takes a sharp dip when the therapist responds with some word which is just a little stronger than the client's feelings. And to a phrase such as, "My you *do* look upset," the needle swings almost off the paper. My desire to avoid even such minor threats is not due to a hypersensitivity about my client. It is simply due to the conviction based on experience that if I can free him as completely as possible from external threat, then he can begin to experience and to deal with the internal feelings and conflicts which he finds threatening within himself.

9. A specific aspect of the preceding question but an important one is: Can I free him from the threat of external evaluation? In almost every phase of our lives—at home, at school, at work—we find ourselves under the rewards and punishments of external judgments. "That's good"; "that's naughty." "That's worth an A"; "that's a failure." "That's good counseling"; "that's poor counseling." Such judgments are a part of our lives from infancy to old age. I believe they have a certain social usefulness to institutions and organizations such as schools and professions. Like everyone else I find myself all too often making such evaluations. But, in my experience, they do not make for personal growth and hence I do not believe that they are a part of a helping relationship. Curiously enough a positive evaluation is as threatening in the long run as a negative one, since to inform someone that he is good implies that you also have the right to tell him he is bad. So I have come to feel that the more I can keep a relationship free of judgment and evaluation, the more this will permit the other person to reach the point where he recognizes that the locus of evaluation, the center of responsibility, lies within himself. The meaning and value of his experience is in the last analysis something which is up to him, and no amount of external judgment can alter this. So I should like to work toward a relationship in which I am not, even in my own feelings, evaluating him. This I believe can set him free to be a self-responsible person.

10. One last question: Can I meet this other individual as a person who is in process of *becoming,* or will I be bound by his past and by my past? If, in my encounter with him, I am dealing with him as an immature child, an ignorant student, a neurotic personality, or a psychopath, each of these concepts of mine limits what he can be in the relationship. Martin Buber, the existentialist philosopher of the University of Jerusalem, has a phrase, "confirming the other," which has had meaning for me. He says "Confirming means . . . accepting the whole potentiality of the other. . . . I can recognize in him, know in him, the person he has been . . . *created* to become. . . . I confirm him in myself, and then in him, in relation to this potentiality that . . . can now be developed, can evolve" (3). If I accept the other person as something fixed, already diagnosed and classified, already shaped by his past, then I am doing my part to confirm this limited hypothesis. If I accept him as a process of becoming, then I am doing what I can to confirm or make real his potentialities.

It is at this point that I see Verplanck, Lindsley, and Skinner, working in operant conditioning, coming together with Buber, the philosopher or mystic. At least they come together in principle, in an odd way. If I see a relationship as only an opportunity to reinforce certain types of words or opinions in the other, then I tend to confirm him as an object—a basically mechanical, manipulable object. And if I see this as his potentiality, he tends to act in ways which support this hypothesis. If, on the other hand, I see a relationship as an opportunity to "reinforce" *all* that he is, the person that he is with all his existent potentialities, then he tends to act in ways which support *this* hypothesis. I have then—to use Buber's term—confirmed him as a living person, capable of creative inner development. Personally I prefer this second type of hypothesis.

CONCLUSION

In the early portion of this paper I reviewed some of the contributions which research is making to our knowledge *about* relationships. Endeavoring to keep that knowledge in mind I then took up the kind of questions which arise from an inner and subjective point of view as I enter, as a person, into relationships. If I could, in myself, answer all the questions I have raised in the affirmative, then I believe that any relationships in which I was involved would be helping relationships, would involve growth. But I cannot give a positive answer to most of these questions. I can only work in the direction of the positive answer.

This has raised in my mind the strong suspicion that the optimal helping relationship is the kind of relationship created by a person who is psychologically mature. Or to put it in another way, the degree to which I can create relationships which facilitate the growth of others as separate persons is a measure of the growth I have achieved in myself. In some respects this is a disturbing thought, but it is also a promising or challenging one. It would indicate that if I am interested in creating helping relationships I have a fascinating lifetime job ahead of me, stretching and developing my potentialities in the direction of growth.

I am left with the uncomfortable thought that what I have been working out for myself in this paper may have little relationship to your interests and your work. If so, I regret it. But I am at least partially comforted by the fact that all of us who are working in the field of human relationships and trying to understand the basic orderliness of that field are engaged in the most crucial enterprise in today's world. If we are thoughtfully trying to understand our tasks as administrators, teachers, educational counselors, vocational counselors, therapists, then we are working on the problem which will determine the future of this planet. For it is not upon the physical sciences that the future will depend. It is upon us who are trying to understand and deal with the interactions between human beings— who are trying to create helping relationships. So I hope that the questions I ask of myself will be of some use to you in gaining understanding and perspective as you endeavor, in your way, to facilitate growth in your relationships.

· · · · ·

PERSONAL THOUGHTS ON TEACHING AND LEARNING

· · · · ·

I wish to present some very brief remarks, in the hope that if they bring forth any reaction from you, I may get some new light on my own ideas.

I find it a very troubling thing to *think,* particularly when I think about my own experiences and try to extract from those experiences the meaning that seems genuinely inherent in them. At first such thinking is very satisfying, because it seems to discover sense and pattern in a whole host of discrete events. But then it very often becomes dismaying, because I realize how ridiculous these thoughts, which have much value to me, would seem to most people. My impression is that if I try to find the meaning of my own experience it leads me, nearly always, in directions regarded as absurd.

So in the next three or four minutes, I will try to digest some of the meanings which have come to me from my classroom experience and the experience I have had in individual and group therapy. They are in no way intended as conclusions for some one else, or a guide to what others should do or be. They are the very tentative meanings, as of April 1952, which my experience has had for me, and some of the bothersome questions which their absurdity raises. I will put each idea or meaning in a separate lettered paragraph, not because they are in any particular logical order, but because each meaning is separately important to me.

a. I may as well start with this one in view of the purposes of this conference. *My experience has been that I cannot teach another person how to teach.* To attempt it is for me, in the long run, futile.

b. *It seems to me that anything that can be taught to another is relatively inconsequential, and has little or no significant influence on behavior.* That sounds so ridiculous I can't help but question it at the same time that I present it.

c. *I realize increasingly that I am only interested in learnings which significantly influence behavior.* Quite possibly this is simply a personal idiosyncrasy.

d. *I have come to feel that the only learning which significantly influences behavior is self-discovered, self-appropriated learning.*

e. *Such self-discovered learning, truth that has been personally appropriated and assimilated in experience, cannot be directly communicated to another.* As soon as an individual tries to communicate such experience directly, often with a quite natural enthusiasm, it becomes teaching, and its results are inconsequential. It was some relief recently to discover that Søren Kierkegaard, the Danish philosopher, had found this too, in his own experience, and stated it very clearly a century ago. It made it seem less absurd.

f. As a consequence of the above, *I realize that I have lost interest in being a teacher.*

g. When I try to teach, as I do sometimes, I am appalled by the results, which seem a little more than inconsequential, because sometimes the teaching appears to succeed. When this happens I find that the results are damaging. It seems to cause the individual to distrust his own experience, and to stifle significant learning. *Hence I have come to feel that the outcomes of teaching are either unimportant or hurtful.*

h. When I look back at the results of my past teaching, the real results seem the same—either damage was done, or nothing significant occurred. This is frankly troubling.

i. As a consequence, *I realize that I am only interested in being a learner, preferably learning things that matter, that have some significant influence on my own behavior.*

j. *I find it very rewarding to learn,* in groups, in relationships with one person as in therapy, or by myself.

k. *I find that one of the best, but most difficult ways for me to learn is to drop my own defensiveness, at least temporarily, and to try to understand the way in which his experience seems and feels to the other person.*

l. *I find that another way of learning for me is to state my own uncertainties, to try to clarify my puzzlements, and thus get closer to the meaning that my experience actually seems to have.*

m. This whole train of experiencing, and the meanings that I have thus far discovered in it, seem to have launched me on a process which is both fascinating and at times a little frightening. *It seems to mean letting my experience carry me on, in a direction which appears to be forward, toward goals that I can but dimly define, as I try to understand at least the current meaning of that experience.* The sensation is that of floating with a complex stream of experience, with the fascinating possibility of trying to comprehend its ever changing complexity.

I am almost afraid I may seem to have gotten away from any discussion of learning, as well as teaching. Let me again introduce a practical note by saying that by themselves these interpretations of my own experience may sound queer and aberrant, but not particularly shocking. It is when I realize the *implications* that I shudder a bit at the distance I have come from the commonsense world that everyone knows is right. I can best illustrate that by saying that if the experiences of others had been the same as mine, and if they had discovered similar meanings in it, many consequences would be implied.

a. Such experience would imply that we would do away with teaching. People would get together if they wished to learn.

b. We would do away with examinations. They measure only the inconsequential type of learning.

c. The implication would be that we would do away with grades and credits for the same reason.

d. We would do away with degrees as a measure of competence partly for the same reason. Another reason is that a degree marks an end or a conclusion of something, and a learner is only interested in the continuing process of learning.

e. It would imply doing away with the exposition of conclusions, for we would realize that no one learns significantly from conclusions.

I think I had better stop there. I do not want to become too fantastic. I want to know primarily whether anything in my inward thinking as I have tried to describe it, speaks to anything in your experience of the classroom as you have lived it, and if so, what the meanings are that exist for you in *your* experience.

SIGNIFICANT LEARNING: IN THERAPY AND IN EDUCATION

. . . . .

Presented here is a thesis, a point of view, regarding the implications which psychotherapy has for education. It is a stand which I take tentatively, and with some hesitation. I have many unanswered questions about this thesis. But it has, I think, some clarity in it, and hence it may provide a starting point from which clear differences can emerge.

SIGNIFICANT LEARNING IN PSYCHOTHERAPY

Let me begin by saying that my long experience as a therapist convinces me that significant learning is facilitated in psychotherapy, and occurs in that relationship. By significant learning I mean learning which is more than an accumulation of facts. It is learning which makes a difference—in the individual's behavior, in the course of action he chooses in the future, in his attitudes and in his personality. It is a pervasive learning which is not just an accretion of knowledge, but which interpenetrates with every portion of his existence.

Now it is not only my subjective feeling that such learning takes place. This feeling is substantiated by research. In client-centered therapy, the orientation with which I am most familiar, and in which the most research has been done, we know that exposure to such therapy produces learnings, or changes, of these sorts:

> The person comes to see himself differently.
> He accepts himself and his feelings more fully.
> He becomes more self-confident and self-directing.
> He becomes more the person he would like to be.
> He becomes more flexible, less rigid, in his perceptions.
> He adopts more realistic goals for himself.
> He behaves in a more mature fashion.
> He changes his maladjustive behaviors, even such a long-established one as chronic alcoholism.
> He becomes more acceptant of others.
> He becomes more open to the evidence, both to what is going on outside of himself, and to what is going on inside of himself.
> He changes in his basic personality characteristics, in constructive ways.*

* For evidence supporting these statements see references (20) and (22).

I think perhaps this is sufficient to indicate that these are learnings which are significant, which do make a difference.

SIGNIFICANT LEARNING IN EDUCATION

I believe I am accurate in saying that educators too are interested in learnings which make a difference. Simple knowledge of facts has its value. To know who won the battle of Poltava, or when the umpteenth opus of Mozart was first performed, may win $64,000 or some other sum for the possessor of this information, but I believe educators in general are a little embarrassed by the assumption that the acquisition of such knowledge constitutes education. Speaking of this reminds me of a forceful statement made by a professor of agronomy in my freshman year in college. Whatever knowledge I gained in his course has departed completely, but I remember how, with World War I as his background, he was comparing factual knowledge with ammunition. He wound up his little discourse with the exhortation, "Don't be a damned ammunition wagon; be a rifle!" I believe most educators would share this sentiment that knowledge exists primarily for use.

To the extent then that educators are interested in learnings which are functional, which make a difference, which pervade the person and his actions, then they might well look to the field of psychotherapy for leads or ideas. Some adaptation for education of the learning process which takes place in psychotherapy seems like a promising possibility.

THE CONDITIONS OF LEARNING IN PSYCHOTHERAPY

Let us then see what is involved, essentially, in making possible the learning which occurs in therapy. I would like to spell out, as clearly as I can, the conditions which seem to be present when this phenomenon occurs.

FACING A PROBLEM

The client is, first of all, up against a situation which he perceives as a serious and meaningful problem. It may be that he finds himself behaving in ways in which he cannot control, or he is overwhelmed by confusions and conflicts, or his marriage is going on the rocks, or he finds himself unhappy in his work. He is, in short, faced with a problem with which he has tried to cope, and found himself unsuccessful. He is therefore eager to learn, even though at the same time he is frightened that what he discovers in himself may be disturbing. Thus one of the conditions nearly always present is an uncertain and ambivalent desire to learn or to change, growing out of a perceived difficulty in meeting life.

What are the conditions which this individual meets when he comes to a therapist? I have recently formulated a theoretical picture of the necessary and sufficient conditions which the therapist provides, if constructive change or significant learning is to occur (21). This theory is currently being tested in several of its aspects by empirical research, but it must still be regarded as theory based upon clinical experience rather than proven fact. Let me describe briefly the conditions which it seems essential that the therapist should provide.

CONGRUENCE

If therapy is to occur, it seems necessary that the therapist be, in the relationship, a unified, or integrated, or congruent person. What I mean is that within the relationship he is exactly what he *is*—not a façade, or a role, or a pretense. I have used the term "congruence" to refer to this accurate matching of experience with awareness. It is when the therapist is fully and accurately aware of what he is experiencing at this moment in the relationship, that he is fully congruent. Unless this congruence is present to a considerable degree it is unlikely that significant learning can occur.

Though this concept of congruence is actually a complex one, I believe all of us recognize it in an intuitive and commonsense way in individuals with whom we deal. With one individual we recognize that he not only means exactly what he says, but that his deepest feelings also match what he is expressing. Thus whether he is angry or affectionate or ashamed or enthusiastic, we sense that he is the same at all levels—in what he is experiencing at an organismic level, in his awareness at the conscious level, and in his words and communications. We furthermore recognize that he is acceptant of his immediate feelings. We say of such a person that we know "exactly where he stands." We tend to feel comfortable and secure in such a relationship. With another person we recognize that what he is saying is almost certainly a front or a façade. We wonder what he *really* feels, what he is really experiencing, behind this façade. We may also wonder if *he* knows what he really feels, recognizing that he may be quite unaware of the feelings he is actually experiencing. With such a person we tend to be cautious and wary. It is not the kind of relationship in which defenses can be dropped or in which significant learning and change can occur.

Thus this second condition for therapy is that the therapist is characterized by a considerable degree of congruence in the relationship.

He is freely, deeply, and acceptantly himself, with his actual experience of his feelings and reactions matched by an accurate awareness of these feelings and reactions as they occur and as they change.

UNCONDITIONAL POSITIVE REGARD

A third condition is that the therapist experiences a warm caring for the client—a caring which is not possessive, which demands no personal gratification. It is an atmosphere which simply demonstrates "I care"; not "I care for you *if* you behave thus and so." Standal (25) has termed this attitude "unconditional positive regard," since it has no conditions of worth attached to it. I have often used the term "acceptance" to describe this aspect of the therapeutic climate. It involves as much feeling of acceptance for the client's expression of negative, "bad," painful, fearful, and abnormal feelings as for his expression of "good," positive, mature, confident and social feelings. It involves an acceptance of and a caring for the client as a *separate* person, with permission for him to have his own feelings and experiences, and to find his own meanings in them. To the degree that the therapist can provide this safety-creating climate of unconditional positive regard, significant learning is likely to take place.

AN EMPATHIC UNDERSTANDING

The fourth condition for therapy is that the therapist is experiencing an accurate, empathic understanding of the client's world as seen from the inside. To sense the client's private world as if it were your own, but without ever losing the "as if" quality—this is empathy, and this seems essential to therapy. To sense the client's anger, fear, or confusion as if it were your own, yet without your own anger, fear, or confusion getting bound up in it, is the condition we are endeavoring to describe. When the client's world is this clear to the therapist, and he moves about in it freely, then he can both communicate his understanding of what is clearly known to the client and can also voice meanings in the client's experience of which the client is scarcely aware. That such penetrating empathy is important for therapy is indicated by Fiedler's research in which items such as the following placed high in the description of relationships created by experienced therapists:

The therapist is well able to understand the patient's feelings.

The therapist is never in any doubt about what the patient means.

The therapist's remarks fit in just right with the patient's mood and content.

The therapist's tone of voice conveys the complete ability to share the patient's feelings. (9)

FIFTH CONDITION

A fifth condition for significant learning in therapy is that the client should experience or perceive something of the therapist's congruence, acceptance, and empathy. It is not enough that these conditions exist in the therapist. They must, to some degree, have been successfully communicated to the client.

THE PROCESS OF LEARNING IN THERAPY

It has been our experience that when these five conditions exist, a process of change inevitably occurs. The client's rigid perceptions of himself and of others loosen and become open to reality. The rigid ways in which he has construed the meaning of his experience are looked at, and he finds himself questioning many of the "facts" of his life, discovering that they are only "facts" because he has regarded them so. He discovers feelings of which he has been unaware, and experiences them, often vividly, in the therapeutic relationship. Thus he learns to be more open to all of his experience —the evidence within himself as well as the evidence without. He learns to *be* more of his experience—to be the feelings of which he has been frightened as well as the feelings he has regarded as more acceptable. He becomes a more fluid, changing, learning person.

THE MAINSPRING OF CHANGE

In this process it is not necessary for the therapist to "motivate" the client or to supply the energy which brings about the change. Nor, in some sense, is the motivation supplied by the client, at least in any conscious way. Let us say rather that the motivation for learning and change springs from the self-actualizing tendency of life itself, the tendency for the organism to flow into all the differentiated channels of potential development, insofar as these are experienced as enhancing.

I could go on at very considerable length on this, but it is not my purpose to focus on the process of therapy and the learnings which take place, nor on the motivation for these learnings, but rather on the conditions which make them possible. So I will simply conclude this description of therapy by saying that it is a type of significant learning which takes place when five conditions are met:

When the client perceives himself as faced by a serious and meaningful problem;

When the therapist is a congruent person in the relationship, able to *be* the person he *is;*

When the therapist feels an unconditional positive regard for the client;

When the therapist experiences an accurate empathic understanding of the client's private world, and communicates this;

When the client to some degree experiences the therapist's congruence, acceptance, and empathy.

IMPLICATIONS FOR EDUCATION

What do these conditions mean if applied to education? Undoubtedly the teacher will be able to give a better answer than I out of his own experience, but I will at least suggest some of the implications.

CONTACT WITH PROBLEMS

In the first place it means that significant learning occurs more readily in relation to situations perceived as problems. I believe I have observed evidence to support this. In my own varying attempts to conduct courses and groups in ways consistent with my therapeutic experience, I have found such an approach more effective, I believe, in workshops than in regular courses, in extension courses than in campus courses. Individuals who come to workshops or extension courses are those who are in contact with problems which they recognize as problems. The student in the regular university course, and particularly in the required course, is apt to view the course as an experience in which he expects to remain passive or resentful or both, an experience which he certainly does not often see as relevant to his own problems.

Yet it has also been my experience that when a regular university class does perceive the course as an experience they can use to resolve problems which *are* of concern to them, the sense of release, and the thrust of forward movement is astonishing. And this is true of courses as diverse as Mathematics and Personality.

I believe the current situation in Russian education also supplies evidence on this point. When a whole nation perceives itself as being faced with the urgent problem of being behind—in agriculture, in industrial production, in scientific development, in weapons development—then an astonishing amount of significant learning takes place, of which the Sputniks are but one observable example.

So the first implication for education might well be that we permit the student, at any level, to be in real contact with the relevant problems of his existence, so that he perceives problems and issues which he wishes to resolve. I am quite aware that this implication, like the others I shall mention, runs sharply contrary to the current trends in our culture, but I shall comment on that later.

I believe it would be quite clear from my description of therapy that an overall implication for education would be that the task of the teacher is to create a facilitating classroom climate in which significant learning can take place. This general implication can be broken down into several sub-sections.

THE TEACHER'S REAL-NESS

Learning will be facilitated, it would seem, if the teacher is congruent. This involves the teacher's being the person that he is, and being openly aware of the attitudes he holds. It means that he feels acceptant toward his own real feelings. Thus he becomes a real person in the relationship with his students. He can be enthusiastic about subjects he likes, and bored by topics he does not like. He can be angry, but he can also be sensitive or sympathetic. Because he accepts his feelings as *his* feelings, he has no need to impose them on his students, or to insist that they feel the same way. He is a *person*, not a faceless embodiment of a curricular requirement, or a sterile pipe through which knowledge is passed from one generation to the next.

I can suggest only one bit of evidence which might support this view. As I think back over a number of teachers who have facilitated my own learning, it seems to me each one has this quality of being a real person. I wonder if your memory is the same. If so, perhaps it is less important that a teacher cover the allotted amount of the curriculum, or use the most approved audio-visual devices, than that he be congruent, real, in his relation to his students.

ACCEPTANCE AND UNDERSTANDING

Another implication for the teacher is that significant learning may take place if the teacher can accept the student as he is, and can understand the feelings he possesses. Taking the third and fourth conditions of therapy as specified above, the teacher who can warmly accept, who can provide an unconditional positive regard, and who can empathize with the feelings of fear, anticipation, and discouragement which are involved in meeting new material, will have done a great deal toward setting the conditions for learning. Clark Moustakas, in his book, *The Teacher and the Child,* has given many excellent examples of individual and group situations from kindergarten to high school, in which the teacher has worked toward just this type of goal. It will perhaps disturb some that when the teacher holds such attitudes, when he is willing to be acceptant of feelings, it is not only attitudes toward school work itself which are expressed, but feelings about parents, feelings of hatred for brother or sister, feelings of concern about self—the whole gamut of attitudes. Do such feelings have a right to exist openly in a school setting? It is my thesis that they do. They are related to the person's becoming, to his effective learning and effective functioning, and to deal understandingly and acceptantly with such feelings has a definite relationship to the learning of long division or the geography of Pakistan.

PROVISION OF RESOURCES

This brings me to another implication which therapy holds for education. In therapy the resources for learning one's self lie within. There is very little data which the therapist can supply which will be of help since the data to be dealt with exist within the person. In education this is not true. There are many resources of knowledge, of techniques, of theory, which constitute raw material for use. It seems to me that what I have said about therapy suggests that these materials, these resources, be made available to the students, not forced upon them. Here a wide range of ingenuity and sensitivity is an asset.

I do not need to list the usual resources which come to mind—

books, maps, workbooks, materials, recordings, work-space, tools, and the like. Let me focus for a moment on the way the teacher uses himself and his knowledge and experience as a resource. If the teacher holds the point of view I have been expressing then he would probably want to make himself available to his class in at least the following ways:

He would want to let them know of special experience and knowledge he has in the field, and to let them know they could call on this knowledge. Yet he would not want them to feel that they must use him in this way.

He would want them to know that his own way of thinking about the field, and of organizing it, was available to them, even in lecture form, if they wished. Yet again he would want this to be perceived as an offer, which could as readily be refused as accepted.

He would want to make himself known as a resource-finder. Whatever might be seriously wanted by an individual or by the whole group to promote their learning, he would be very willing to consider the possibilities of obtaining such a resource.

He would want the quality of his relationship to the group to be such that his feelings could be freely available to them, without being imposed on them or becoming a restrictive influence on them. He thus could share the excitements and enthusiasms of his own learnings, without insisting that the students follow in his footsteps; the feelings of disinterest, satisfaction, bafflement, or pleasure which he feels toward individual or group activities, without this becoming either a carrot or a stick for the student. His hope would be that he could say, simply for himself, "I don't like that," and that the student with equal freedom could say, "But I do."

Thus whatever the resource he supplies—a book, space to work, a new tool, an opportunity for observation of an industrial process, a lecture based on his own study, a picture, graph or map, his own emotional reactions—he would feel that these were, and would hope they would be perceived as, offerings to be used if they were useful to the student. He would not feel them to be guides, or expectations, or commands, or impositions or requirements. He would offer himself, and all the other resources he could discover, for use.

THE BASIC MOTIVE

It should be clear from this that his basic reliance would be upon the self-actualizing tendency in his students. The hypothesis upon which he would build is that students who are in real contact with life problems wish to learn, want to grow, seek to find out, hope to master, desire to create. He would see his function as that of developing such a personal relationship with his students, and such a climate in his classroom, that these natural tendencies could come to their fruition.

SOME OMISSIONS

These I see as some of the things which are implied by a therapeutic viewpoint for the educational process. To make them a bit sharper, let me point out some of the things which are not implied.

I have not included lectures, talks, or expositions of subject matter which are imposed on the students. All of these procedures might be a part of the experience if they were desired, explicitly or implicitly, by the students. Yet even here, a teacher whose work was following through a hypothesis based on therapy would be quick to sense a shift in that desire. He might have been requested to lecture to the group (and to give a *requested* lecture is *very* different from the usual classroom experience), but if he detected a growing disinterest and boredom, he would respond to that, trying to understand the feeling which had arisen in the group, since his response to their feelings and attitudes would take precedence over his interest in expounding material.

I have not included any program of evaluation of the student's learnings in terms of external criteria. I have not, in other words, included examinations. I believe that the testing of the student's achievements in order to see if he meets some criterion held by the teacher, is directly contrary to the implications of therapy for significant learning. In therapy, the examinations are set by *life*. The client meets them, sometimes passing, sometimes failing. He finds that he can use the resources of the therapeutic relationship and his experience in it to organize himself so that he can meet life's tests more satisfyingly next time. I see this as the paradigm for education also. Let me try to spell out a fantasy of what it would mean.

In such an education, the requirements for many life situations would be a part of the resources the teacher provides. The student would have available the knowledge that he cannot enter engineering school without so much math; that he cannot get a job in X corporation unless he has a college diploma; that he cannot become a psychologist without doing an independent doctoral research; that he cannot be a doctor without knowledge of chemistry; that he cannot even drive a car without passing an examination on rules of the road. These are requirements set, not by the teacher, but by life. The teacher is there to provide the resources which the student can use to learn so as to be able to meet these tests.

There would be other in-school evaluations of similar sort. The student might well be faced with the fact that he cannot join the Math Club until he makes a certain score on a standardized mathematics test; that he cannot develop his camera film until he has shown an adequate knowledge of chemistry and lab techniques; that he cannot join the special literature section until he has shown evidence of both wide reading and creative writing. The natural place of evaluation in life is as a ticket of entrance, not as a club over the recalcitrant. Our experience in therapy would suggest that it should be the same way in the school. It would leave the student as a self-respecting, self-motivated person, free to choose whether he wished to put forth the effort to gain these tickets of entrance. It would thus refrain from forcing him into conformity, from sacrificing his creativity, and from causing him to live his life in terms of the standards of others.

I am quite aware that the two elements of which I have just been speaking—the lectures and expositions imposed by the teacher on the group, and the evaluation of the individual by the teacher, constitute the two major ingredients of current education. So when I say that experience in psychotherapy would suggest that they both be omitted, it should be quite clear that the implications of psychotherapy for education are startling indeed.

PROBABLE OUTCOMES

If we are to consider such drastic changes as I have outlined, what would be the results which would justify them? There have been some research investigations of the outcomes of a student-centered type of teaching (7, 8, 15), though these studies are far from adequate. For one thing, the situations studied vary greatly in the extent to which they meet the conditions I have described. Most of them have extended only over a period of a few months, though one recent study with lower class children extended over a full year (15). Some involve the use of adequate controls, some do not.

I think we may say that these studies indicate that in classroom situations which at least attempt to approximate the climate I have described, the findings are as follows: Factual and curricular learning is roughly equal to the learning in conventional classes. Some studies report slightly more, some slightly less. The student-centered group shows gains significantly greater than the conventional class in personal adjustment, in self-initiated extra-curricular learning, in creativity, in self-responsibility.

I have come to realize, as I have considered these studies, and puzzled over the design of better studies which should be more informative and conclusive, that findings from such research will never answer our questions. For all such findings must be evaluated in terms of the goals we have for education. If we value primarily the learning of knowledge, then we may discard the conditions I have described as useless, since there is no evidence that they lead to a greater rate or amount of factual knowledge. We may then favor such measures as the one which I understand is advocated by a number of members of Congress—the setting up of a training school for scientists, modeled upon the military academies. But if we value creativity, if we deplore the fact that all of our germinal ideas in atomic physics, in psychology, and in other sciences have been borrowed from Europe, then we may wish to give a trial to ways of facilitating learning which give more promise of freeing the mind. If we value independence, if we are disturbed by the growing conformity of knowledge, of values, of attitudes, which our present system induces, then we may wish to set up conditions of learning which make for uniqueness, for self-direction, and for self-initiated learning.

SOME CONCLUDING ISSUES

I have tried to sketch the kind of education which would be implied by what we have learned in the field of psychotherapy. I have endeavored to suggest very briefly what it would mean if the central focus of the teacher's effort were to develop a relationship, an atmosphere, which was conducive to self-motivated, self-actualizing, significant learning. But this is a direction which leads sharply away from current educational practices and educational trends. Let me mention a few of the very diverse issues and questions which need to be faced if we are to think constructively about such an approach.

In the first place, how do we conceive the goals of education? The approach I have outlined has, I believe, advantages for achieving certain goals, but not for achieving others. We need to be clear as to the way we see the purposes of education.

What are the actual outcomes of the kind of education I have described? We need a great deal more of rigorous, hard-headed research to know the actual results of this kind of education as compared with conventional education. Then we can choose on the basis of the facts.

Even if we were to try such an approach to the facilitation of learning, there are many difficult issues. Could we possibly permit students to come in contact with real issues? Our whole culture— through custom, through the law, through the efforts of labor unions and management, through the attitudes of parents and teachers— is deeply committed to keeping young people away from any touch with real problems. They are not to work, they should not carry responsibility, they have no business in civic or political problems, they have no place in international concerns, they simply should be guarded from any direct contact with the real problems of individual and group living. They are not expected to help about the home, to earn a living, to contribute to science, to deal with moral issues. This is a deep seated trend which has lasted for more than a generation. Could it possibly be reversed?

Another issue is whether we could permit knowledge to be organized in and by the individual, or whether it is to be organized *for* the individual. Here teachers and educators line up with parents and national leaders to insist that the pupil must be guided. He must be inducted into knowledge we have organized for him. He cannot be trusted to organize knowledge in functional terms for himself. As Herbert Hoover says of high school students, "You simply cannot expect kids of those ages to determine the sort of education they need unless they have some guidance." * This seems so obvious to most people that even to question it is to seem somewhat unbalanced. Even a chancellor of a university questions whether freedom is really necessary in education, saying that perhaps we have overestimated its value. He says the Russians have advanced mightily in science without it, and implies that we should learn from them.

* *Time,* December 2, 1957.

Still another issue is whether we would wish to oppose the strong current trend toward education as drill in factual knowledge. All must learn the same facts in the same way. Admiral Rickover states it as his belief that "in some fashion we must devise a way to introduce uniform standards into American education. . . . For the first time, parents would have a real yardstick to measure their schools. If the local school continued to teach such pleasant subjects as 'life adjustment' . . . instead of French and physics, its diploma would be, for all the world to see, inferior." † This is a statement of a very prevalent view. Even such a friend of forward-looking views in education as Max Lerner says at one point, "All that a school can ever hope to do is to equip the student with tools which he can later use to become an educated man" (16, p. 741). It is quite clear that he despairs of significant learning taking place in our school system, and feels that it must take place outside. All the school can do is to pound in the tools.

One of the most painless ways of inculcating such factual tool knowledge is the "teaching machine" being devised by B. F. Skinner and his associates (24). This group is demonstrating that the teacher is an outmoded and ineffective instrument for teaching arithmetic, trigonometry, French, literary appreciation, geography, or other factual subjects. There is simply no doubt in my mind that these teaching machines, providing immediate rewards for "right" answers, will be further developed, and will come into wide use. Here is a new contribution from the field of the behavioral sciences with which we must come to terms. Does it take the place of the approach I have described, or is it supplemental to it? Here is one of the problems we must consider as we face toward the future.

I hope that by posing these issues, I have made it clear that the double-barreled question of what constitutes significant learning, and how it is to be achieved, poses deep and serious problems for all of us. It is not a time when timid answers will suffice. I have tried to give a definition of significant learning as it appears in psychotherapy, and a description of the conditions which facilitate such learning. I have tried to indicate some implications of these conditions for education. I have, in other words, proposed one answer to these questions. Perhaps we can use what I have said, against the twin

† *Ibid.*

backdrops of current public opinion and current knowledge in the behavioral sciences, as a start for discovering some fresh answers of our own.

REFERENCES

1. Baldwin, A. L., J. Kalhorn, and F. H. Breese. Patterns of parent behavior. *Psychol. Monogr.*, 1945, *58*, No. 268, 1–75.
2. Betz, B. J., and J. C. Whitehorn. The relationship of the therapist to the outcome of therapy in schizophrenia. *Psychiat. Research Reports #5. Research techniques in schizophrenia*. Washington, D.C.: American Psychiatric Association, 1956, 89–117.
3. Buber, M., and C. Rogers. Transcription of dialogue held April 18, 1957, Ann Arbor, Mich. Unpublished manuscript.
4. Dittes, J. E. Galvanic skin response as a measure of patient's reaction to therapist's permissiveness. *J. Abnorm. & Soc. Psychol.*, 1957, *55*, 295–303.
5. Ends, E. J., and C. W. Page. A study of three types of group psychotherapy with hospitalized male inebriates. *Quar. J. Stud. Alcohol*, 1957, *18*, 263–277.
6. Farson, R. E. Introjection in the psychotherapeutic relationship. Unpublished doctoral dissertation, University of Chicago, 1955.
7. Faw, Volney. A psychotherapeutic method of teaching psychology. *Amer. Psychol. 4:* 104–109, 1949.
8. Faw, Volney. "Evaluation of student-centered teaching." Unpublished manuscript, 1954.
9. Fiedler, F. E. A comparison of therapeutic relationships in psychoanalytic, non-directive and Adlerian therapy. *J. Consult. Psychol.*, 1950, *14*, 436–445.
10. Fiedler, F. E. Quantitative studies on the role of therapists' feelings toward their patients. In Mowrer, O. H. (Ed.), *Psychotherapy: Theory and Research*. New York: Ronald Press, 1953, Chap. 12.
11. Greenspoon, J. The reinforcing effect of two spoken sounds on the frequency of two responses. *Amer. J. Psychol.*, 1955, *68*, 409–416.
12. Halkides, G. An experimental study of four conditions necessary for therapeutic change. Unpublished doctoral dissertation, University of Chicago, 1958.
13. Harlow, H. F. The nature of love. *Amer. Psychol.*, 1958, *13*, 673–685.
14. Heine, R. W. A comparison of patients' reports on psychotherapeutic experience with psychoanalytic, nondirective, and Adlerian therapists. Unpublished doctoral dissertation, University of Chicago, 1950.
15. Jackson, John H. The relationship between psychological climate and

the quality of learning outcomes among lower-status pupils. Unpublished Ph.D. thesis, University of Chicago, 1957.

16. Lerner, Max. *America as a Civilization.* New York: Simon & Schuster, 1957.

17. Lindsley, O. R. Operant conditioning methods applied to research in chronic schizophrenia. *Psychiat. Research Reports #5. Research techniques in schizophrenia.* Washington, D.C.: American Psychiatric Association, 1956, 118–153.

18. Page, C. W., and E. J. Ends. A review and synthesis of the literature suggesting a psychotherapeutic technique based on two-factor learning theory. Unpublished manuscript, loaned to the writer.

19. Quinn, R. D. Psychotherapists' expressions as an index to the quality of early therapeutic relationships. Unpublished doctoral dissertation, University of Chicago, 1950.

20. Rogers, C. R. *Client-Centered Therapy.* Boston: Houghton Mifflin Co., 1951.

21. Rogers, C. R. The necessary and sufficient conditions of therapeutic personality change. *J. Consult. Psychol.,* 1957, *21,* 95–103.

22. Rogers, C. R., and R. Dymond (Eds.). *Psychotherapy and Personality Change.* Chicago: University of Chicago Press, 1954.

23. Seeman, J. Counselor judgments of therapeutic process and outcome. In Rogers, C. R., and R. F. Dymond (Eds.). *Psychotherapy and Personality Change.* Chicago: University of Chicago Press, 1954, Chap. 7.

24. Skinner, B. F. The science of learning and the art of teaching. *Harvard Educational Review,* 1954, *24,* 86–97.

25. Standal, Stanley. The need for positive regard: A contribution to client-centered theory. Unpublished Ph.D. thesis, University of Chicago, 1954.

26. Verplanck, W. S. The control of the content of conversation: reinforcement of statements of opinion. *J. Abnorm. & Soc. Psychol.,* 1955, *51,* 668–676.

27. Whitehorn, J. C., and B. J. Betz. A study of psychotherapeutic relationships between physicians and schizophrenic patients. *Amer. J. Psychiat.,* 1954, *111,* 321–331.

The process of education

JEROME S. BRUNER

Jerome Bruner's *The Process of Education* represents his attempt to bring together the highlights and the principal themes that emerged from the ten-day conference held at Woods Hole, Massachusetts, in September 1959. The excitement generated by the launching of Russia's Sputnik I in 1957 sent scientists and mathematicians scurrying to find means of improving and accelerating education in the math-science area. Projects were soon undertaken to design and develop new high school courses in physics, biology, chemistry, and mathematics. The Woods Hole Conference brought together those scientists and mathematicians involved in the various projects with psychologists concerned with learning, intelligence, and motivation. The conference was also attended by teachers, historians, and media technicians.

In retrospect it is clear that there was at least one positive outcome of this conference—Bruner's *The Process of Education*. This short, ninety-three-page book not only succinctly states the emergent conference themes; it is also a major position paper of educational theory. *The Process of Education* has become a landmark in the literature of American education. When the various curriculum projects that lie behind Bruner's work become modified or supplanted, this little book will continue to have its impact on American educational thought and, either directly or indirectly, influence the educational system for decades to come.

SOURCE: Jerome S. Bruner, *The Process of Education* (New York: Vintage Books, 1963), pp. 1, 3–10, 11–12, 17–32. Copyright © 1960 by the President and Fellows of Harvard College. Excerpted by permission of the author and the publishers.

After an introductory chapter, Bruner proceeds to develop the four themes which emerged from the discussions and papers of the Woods Hole Conference. These themes are structure, learning readiness, intuitive and analytic thinking, and motives for learning. Bruner concludes his book with a brief discussion of some of the aids to learning or "devices for vicarious experiences."

Learning how things are related is, for Bruner, what it means to learn structure. Too much instructional time is spent in teaching specific items or discrete bits of knowledge. While the gifted student will learn to discern the relationships between such bits of knowledge, the less able student is left with only "specifics," which may or may not find an application outside the classroom. To emphasize the structure of a particular subject matter is to emphasize that aspect of it which is most practical. The student who comes to grasp how bits of information within a subject area are related is able to continually and independently relate additional information to this field. Moreover, this student is able to transfer his understanding of structure to other areas of interest— he seeks structure (relationships) within all fields of his experience. Given the limited time for schooling and the amount of information and data available to be learned, clearly the most practical way of proceeding is to focus teaching upon the structure of the various disciplines. Equipped with structural insight, the student will be able to efficiently and effectively utilize whatever specific information is at hand.

Learning readiness is Bruner's second theme. It is in connection with this theme that Bruner's now famous hypothesis occurs; namely, that any subject can be taught in some intellectually honest form to any child at any age. This hypothesis is derived from the realization that the basic concepts of science and mathematics, as well as the basic themes reflected in literature, are "as simple as they are powerful." Our previous notions of difficulty must be altered. What is required is that the structure of a subject be translated into the child's view of things; it is only subject matter presented in its fully developed, logically and linguistically organized form that renders the learning of it difficult. The basic concepts and themes are available to all individuals in a form or structure suitable to the individual's stage of intellectual development.

Bruner sees the act of learning as consisting of three almost simultaneous processes: acquisition, transformation, and evaluation. "Acquisition" is, of course, the grasping of new information. Such information may be "new" in the sense of a novel addition to one's store of data; it may also replace previously acquired information, or it may merely refine or further qualify previous information. "Transformation" refers to the individual's capacity to process new information in such a way as to be able to transcend or go beyond it. Means for processing such information are extrapolation, interpolation, or translation into another form. "Evaluation" refers to the determination of whether or not our information has been processed in a way which renders it appropriate for dealing with a particular task or problem. What is educationally critical is that for each educational task the teacher must determine the appropriate emphasis to be given each of these processes, for it must be appropriate to the task and to the student's stage of development. But all three processes must be present for learning to take place.

Intuitive and analytic thinking constitute Bruner's third theme. Intuitive thinking involves the "training of hunches." It is that aspect of intellectual activity which allows the individual to formulate a hypothesis directly without going through the various analytic procedures. However, intuitive and analytic thinking are complementary; that is, intuitive thinking must ultimately base its claim to correctness upon analytic procedures. The student must be given those supportive conditions or situations in which intuitive thinking can be developed, but at the same time the student must be held responsible to confirm or disprove the value or correctness of his intuitive assumptions. Analytic procedures are his means to do so, for they are not steps leading to discovery, but the means to establish the validity of discoveries.

The educator is presented with real difficulty when he decides to allow for intuitive thinking within the curriculum and within teaching methods. There exists very little psychological data on how intuitive thinking really functions. Neither is there much known about how intuitive thinking can be promoted and developed as an educational outcome. Recent curricular innovations try to incorporate within their framework a place for discovery which, ideally, should precede analysis. At any rate, intuitive thinking and its role in the classroom is a problem that psychologists and educators must face for its desired enhancement of the educational process.

Bruner's fourth and final theme deals with the motives for learning. The problem here, as Bruner sees it, is the problem of arriving at a middle ground between "frenzied activity" and "apathy." What is the ideal level where each student is attentive and at the same time has the freedom for reflection and evaluation? And what is the advantage of short-term versus long-term interest arousal? Bruner's position is that learning motivation—whatever that may prove to be—should not become passive. The motivation must be based upon the development of real interest and not upon external reward, which may lead the student to succumb to that form of wasteful competition Bruner calls "meritocracy." Advanced planning with regard to educational aims can allow for more careful selection of the motives for learning behavior, and it affords both teacher and psychologist the opportunity to study, design, and develop combinations of motivating techniques that will complement educational aims.

Bruner makes some final comments on the development of aids to teaching. Here again, Bruner warns of the need for careful planning in order to fully integrate new teaching aids into a preplanned curriculum. The mere existence of film projectors, television, and the like does not mean better teaching. The wide variety of devices now available *can* enhance the teacher's role of communicator and model. Devices can serve to expand the experiences of the classroom; they can make it more personal, provide vicarious experience where first-hand ones are not possible. But devices may also be used as a substitute for education, providing the means by which the child escapes the real and personal task at hand.

"The Importance of Structure," included in this selection of readings, is the most significant of the four themes developed by Bruner. It is not only the dominant theme of Bruner's work, it is also the theme around which much curricular development has taken place in the last decade. Bruner's discussion of structure establishes this work as a contribution to educational theory.

The basic assumption that underlies the essay on the importance of structure in the teaching of a subject area is that learning some "thing" should be the end of learning, but that this learning should contribute to subsequent learning. It is structure that provides the basis for this kind of specific transfer of learning. But it is structure, too, that provides for the nonspecific transfer of principles and attitudes. Mastery of fundamentals includes not only mastery of general principles, but also the acquisition of a whole range of attitudes: attitudes toward learning, inquiry, orderliness of nature, and so on. More specifically, Bruner makes four claims for teaching the basic structure of a subject. First, acquisition of a truly fundamental aspect of the basic structure of a single subject area makes the subject itself more understandable. Second, the ability to learn and to recall later some bit of information is directly related to the learner's having a structural pattern into which that information can fit. Third, the occurrence of transfer of learning is much more frequent when that learning is of a basic, general nature. Fourth, by insisting upon structure as the basis for curriculum design, we ensure some continuity between elementary knowledge in a subject and its later advanced form.

Bruner's thesis is that the process of education will be vastly improved when the entire curriculum reflects a strong commitment to the fundamental structure of the various subject areas. The focus of teaching, too, should be upon the mastery of the structural relationships within a field of study. Yet, in this brief book of Bruner's, he has succeeded more in clearly stating a central educational issue than in resolving one, but for this alone we are indebted to him. In Bruner's continuing efforts to develop curriculum and materials to achieve his aims, the task itself—altering the process of education—is still far from realized.

INTRODUCTION

Each generation gives new form to the aspirations that shape education in its time. What may be emerging as a mark of our own generation is a widespread renewal of concern for the quality and intellectual aims of education—but without abandonment of the ideal that education should serve as a means of training well-balanced citizens for a democracy. Rather, we have reached a level of public education in America where a considerable portion of our population has become interested in a question that until recently was the concern of specialists: "What shall we teach and to what end?" The new spirit perhaps reflects the profound scientific revolution of our times as well. The trend is accentuated by what is almost certain to be a long-range crisis in national security, a crisis whose resolution will depend upon a well-educated citizenry.

• • • • •

An additional word of background is needed to appreciate the significance of present curricular efforts in the changing educational scene. The past half century has witnessed the rise of the American university graduate school with its strong emphasis upon advanced study and research. One consequence of this development has been the growing separation of first-rank scholars and scientists from the task of presenting their own subjects in primary and secondary schools—indeed even in elementary courses for undergraduates. The chief contact between those on the frontiers of scholarship and students in schools was through the occasional textbooks for high schools prepared by such distinguished scientists as Millikan or by historians of the stature of Beard or Commager. For the most part, however, the scholars at the forefront of their disciplines, those who might be able to make the greatest contribution to the substantive reorganization of their fields, were not involved in the development of curricula for the elementary and secondary schools. In consequence, school programs have often dealt inadequately or incorrectly with contemporary knowledge, and we have not reaped the benefits that might have come from a joining of the efforts of eminent scholars, wise and skillful teachers, and those trained in the fields related to teaching and learning. Now there appears to be a reversal of this trend. It consists in the renewed involvement of many of America's most distinguished scientists in the planning of school study programs in their field, in the preparation of textbooks and laboratory demonstrations, in the construction of films and television programs.

This same half century saw American psychology move away from its earlier concern with the nature of learning as it occurs in school. The psychology of learning tended to become involved with the precise details of learning in highly simplified short-term situations and thereby lost much of its contact with the long-term educational effects of learning. For their part, educational psychologists turned their attention with great effect to the study of aptitude and achievement and to social and motivational aspects of education, but did not concern themselves directly with the intellectual structure of class activities.

Other considerations led to a neglect of curriculum problems by psychologists. The ever-changing pattern of American educational philosophy played a part in the matter as well. There has always been a dualism in our educational ideal, a striving for a balance between what Benjamin Franklin referred to as the "useful" and the "ornamental." As he put it, in the mid-eighteenth century: "It would be well if they could be taught everything that is useful and everything that is ornamental: but art is long and their time is short. It is therefore proposed that they learn those things that are likely to be most useful and most ornamental." The concept of the useful in Franklin and in the American educational ideal afterwards was twofold: it involved, on the one hand, *skills* of a specific kind and, on the other, *general understanding,* to enable one better to deal with the affairs of life. Skills were matters of direct concern to one's profession. As early as the 1750's we find Ben Franklin urging that future merchants be taught French, German, and Spanish, and that pupils be taught agriculture, supplemented by farm visits and the like. General understanding was to be achieved through a knowledge of history plus the discipline produced by the diligent study of mathematics and logic, and by training in careful observation of the natural world around one; it required a well-disciplined, well-stocked mind.

The American secondary school has tried to strike a balance between the two concepts of usefulness—and most often with some regard for the ornamental as well. But as the proportion of the population registered in secondary schools increased, and as the proportion of new Americans in the school population went up, the balance between instruction in the useful skills and in disciplined understanding was harder to maintain. Dr. Conant's recent plea for the comprehensive high school is addressed to the problem of that balance.

It is interesting that around the turn of the last century the conception of the learning process as depicted by psychology gradually shifted away from an emphasis upon the production of general understanding to an emphasis on the acquisition of specific skills. The study of "transfer" provides the type case—the problem of the gain in mastery of other activities that one achieves from having mastered a particular learning task. Whereas the earlier emphasis had led to research studies on the transfer of formal discipline—the value obtained from the training of such "faculties" as analysis, judgment, memory, and so forth—later work tended to explore the transfer of identical elements or specific skills. In consequence, there was relatively little work by American psychologists during the first four decades of this century on the manner in which the student could be trained to grasp the underlying structure or significance of complex knowledge. Virtually all of the evidence of the last two decades on the nature of learning and transfer has indicated that, while the original theory of formal discipline was poorly stated in terms of the training of faculties, it is indeed a fact that massive general transfer can be achieved by appropriate learning, even to the degree that learning properly under optimum conditions leads one to "learn how to learn." These studies have stimulated a renewed interest in complex learning of a kind that one finds in schools, learning designed to produce general understanding of the structure of a subject matter. Interest in curricular problems at large has, in consequence, been rekindled among psychologists concerned with the learning process.

A word is needed at this point to explain in fuller detail what is meant by the *structure* of a subject, for we shall have occasion to return to this idea often in later pages. Three simple examples—from biology, from mathematics, and from the learning of language—help to make the idea clearer. Take first a set of observations on an inchworm crossing a sheet of graph paper mounted on a board. The board is horizontal; the animal moves in a straight line. We tilt the board so that the inclined plane or upward grade is 30°. We observe that the animal does not go straight up, but travels at an angle of 45° from the line of maximum climb. We now tilt the board to 60°. At what angle does the animal travel with respect to the line of maximum climb? Now, say, he travels along a line 75° off the straight-up line. From these two measures, we may infer that inchworms "prefer" to travel uphill, if uphill they must go, along an incline of 15°. We have discovered a tropism, as it is called, indeed a geotropism. It is not an isolated fact. We can go on to show that among simple organisms, such phenomena—regulation of locomotion according to a fixed or built-in standard—are the rule. There is a preferred level of illumination toward which lower organisms orient, a preferred level of salinity, of temperature, and so on. Once a student grasps this basic relation between external stimulation and locomotor action, he is well on his way toward being able to handle a good deal of seemingly new but, in fact, highly related information. The swarming of locusts where temperature determines the swarm density in which locusts are forced to travel, the species maintenance of insects at different altitudes on the side of a mountain where cross-breeding is prevented by the tendency of each species to travel in its preferred oxygen zone, and many other phenomena in biology can be understood in the light of tropisms. Grasping the structure of a subject is understanding it in a way that permits many other things to be related to it meaningfully. To learn structure, in short, is to learn how things are related.

Much more briefly, to take an example from mathematics, algebra is a way of arranging knowns and unknowns in equations so that the unknowns are made knowable. The three fundamentals involved in working with these equations are commutation, distribution, and association. Once a student grasps the ideas embodied by these three fundamentals, he is in a position to recognize wherein "new" equations to be solved are not new at all, but variants on a familiar theme. Whether the student knows the formal names of these operations is less important for transfer than whether he is able to use them.

The often unconscious nature of learning structures is perhaps best illustrated in learning one's native language. Having grasped the subtle structure of a sentence, the child very rapidly learns to generate many other sentences based on this model though different in content from the original sentence learned. And having mastered the rules for transforming sentences without altering their meaning—"The dog bit the man" and "The man was bitten by the dog"—the child is able to vary his sentences much more widely. Yet, while young children are able to *use* the structural rules of English, they are certainly not able to say what the rules are.

The scientists constructing curricula in physics and mathematics have been highly mindful of the problem of teaching the structure of their subjects, and it may be that their early successes have been due to this emphasis. Their emphasis upon structure has stimulated students of the learning process. The reader will find the emphasis reflected many times in the pages that follow.

Clearly there are general questions to be faced before one can look at specific problems of courses, sequences, and the like. The moment one begins to ask questions about the value of specific courses, one is asking about the objectives of education. The construction of curricula proceeds in a world where changing social, cultural, and political conditions continually alter the surroundings and the goals of schools and their students. We are concerned with curricula designed for Americans, for their ways and their needs in a complex world. Americans are a changing people; their geographical mobility makes imperative some degree of uniformity among high schools and primary schools. Yet the diversity of American communities and of American life in general makes equally imperative some degree of variety in curricula. And whatever the limits placed on education by the demands of diversity and uniformity, there are also requirements for productivity to be met: are we producing enough scholars, scientists, poets, lawmakers, to meet the demands of our times? Moreover, schools must also contribute to the social and emotional development of the child if they are to fulfill their function of education for life in a democratic community and for fruitful family life. If the emphasis in what follows is principally on the intellectual side of education, it is not that the other objectives of education are less important.

We may take as perhaps the most general objective of education that it cultivate excellence; but it should be clear in what sense this phrase is used. It here refers not only to schooling the better student but also to helping each student achieve his optimum intellectual development. Good teaching that emphasizes the structure of a subject is probably even more valuable for the less able student than for the gifted one, for it is the former rather than the latter who is most easily thrown off the track by poor teaching. This is not to say that the pace or the content of courses need be identical for all students—though, as one member of the Conference put it, "When you teach well, it always seems as if seventy-five per cent of the students are above the median." Careful investigation and research can tell us wherein differences must be introduced. One thing seems clear: if all students are helped to the full utilization of their intellectual powers, we will have a better chance of surviving as a democracy in an age of enormous technological and social complexity.

• • • • •

. . . The first [theme] has already been introduced: the role of structure in learning and how it may be made central in teaching. The approach taken is a practical one. Students, perforce, have a limited exposure to the materials they are to learn. How can this exposure be made to count in their thinking for the rest of their lives? The dominant view among men who have been engaged in preparing and teaching new curricula is that the answer to this question lies in giving students an understanding of the fundamental structure of whatever subjects we choose to teach. This is a minimum requirement for using knowledge, for bringing it to bear on problems and events one encounters outside a classroom—or in classrooms one enters later in one's training. The teaching and learning of structure, rather than simply the mastery of facts and techniques, is at the center of the classic problem of transfer. There are many things that go into learning of this kind, not the least of which are supporting habits and skills that make possible the active use of the materials one has come to understand. If earlier learning is to render later learning easier, it must do so by providing a general picture in terms of which the relations between things encountered earlier and later are made as clear as possible.

Given the importance of this theme, much too little is known about how to teach fundamental structure effectively or how to provide learning conditions that foster it. Much of the discussion in the chapter devoted to this topic has to do with ways and means of achieving such teaching and learning and with the kinds of research needed to help in preparing curricula with emphasis on structure.

· · · · ·

THE IMPORTANCE OF STRUCTURE

The first object of any act of learning, over and beyond the pleasure it may give, is that it should serve us in the future. Learning should not only take us somewhere; it should allow us later to go further more easily. There are two ways in which learning serves the future. One is through its specific applicability to tasks that are highly similar to those we originally learned to perform. Psychologists refer to this phenomenon as specific transfer of training; perhaps it should be called the extension of habits or associations. Its utility appears to be limited in the main to what we usually speak of as skills. Having learned how to hammer nails, we are better able later to learn how to hammer tacks or chip wood. Learning in school undoubtedly creates skills of a kind that transfers to activities encountered later, either in school or after. A second way in which earlier learning renders later performance more efficient is through what is conveniently called nonspecific transfer or, more accurately, the transfer of principles and attitudes. In essence, it consists of learning initially not a skill but a general idea, which can then be used as a basis for recognizing subsequent problems as special cases of the idea originally mastered. This type of transfer is at the heart of the educational process—the continual broadening and deepening of knowledge in terms of basic and general ideas.

The continuity of learning that is produced by the second type of transfer, transfer of principles, is dependent upon mastery of the structure of the subject matter, as structure was described in the preceding chapter. That is to say, in order for a person to be able to recognize the applicability or inapplicability of an idea to a new situation and to broaden his learning thereby, he must have clearly in mind the general nature of the phenomenon with which he is dealing. The more fundamental or basic is the idea he has learned, almost by definition, the greater will be its breadth of applicability to new problems. Indeed, this is almost a tautology, for what is meant by "fundamental" in this sense is precisely that an idea has wide as well as powerful applicability. It is simple enough to proclaim, of course, that school curricula and methods of teaching should be geared to the teaching of fundamental ideas in whatever subject is being taught. But as soon as one makes such a statement a host of problems arise, many of which can be solved only with the aid of considerably more research. We turn to some of these now.

The first and most obvious problem is how to construct curricula that can be taught by ordinary teachers to ordinary students and that at the same time reflect clearly the basic or underlying principles of various fields of inquiry. The problem is twofold: first, how to have the basic subjects rewritten and their teaching materials revamped in such a way that the pervading and powerful ideas and attitudes relating to them are given a central role; second, how to match the levels of these materials to the capacities of students of different abilities at different grades in school.

The experience of the past several years has taught at least one important lesson about the design of a curriculum that is true to the underlying structure of its subject matter. It is that the best minds in any particular discipline must be put to work on the task. The decision as to what should be taught in American history to elementary school children or what should be taught in arithmetic is a decision that can best be reached with the aid of those with a high degree of vision and competence in each of these fields. To decide that the elementary ideas of algebra depend upon the fundamentals of the commutative, distributive, and associative laws, one must be a mathematician in a position to appreciate and understand the fundamentals of mathematics. Whether schoolchildren require an understanding of Frederick Jackson Turner's ideas about the role of the frontier in American history before they can sort out the facts and trends of American history—this again is a decision that requires the help of the scholar who has a deep understanding of the American past. Only by the use of our best minds in devising curricula will we bring the fruits of scholarship and wisdom to the student just beginning his studies.

The question will be raised, "How enlist the aid of our most able scholars and scientists in designing curricula for primary and secondary schools?" The answer has already been given, at least in part. The School Mathematics Study Group, the University of Illinois mathematics projects, the Physical Science Study Committee, and the Biological Sciences Curriculum Study have indeed been enlisting the aid of eminent men in their various fields, doing so by means of summer projects, supplemented in part by year-long leaves of absence for certain key people involved. They have been aided in these projects by outstanding elementary and secondary school teachers and, for special purposes, by professional writers, film makers, designers, and others required in such a complex enterprise.

There is at least one major matter that is left unsettled even by a large-scale revision of curricula in the direction indicated. Mastery of the fundamental ideas of a field involves not only the grasping of general principles, but also the development of an attitude toward learning and inquiry, toward guessing and hunches, toward the possibility of solving problems on one's own. Just as a physicist has certain attitudes about the ultimate orderliness of nature and a conviction that order can be discovered, so a young physics student needs some working version of these attitudes if he is to organize his learning in such a way as to make what he learns usable and meaningful in his thinking. To instill such attitudes by teaching requires something more than the mere presentation of fundamental ideas. Just what it takes to bring off such teaching is something on which a great deal of research is needed, but it would seem that an important ingredient is a sense of excitement about discovery—discovery of regularities of previously unrecognized relations and similarities between ideas, with a resulting sense of self-confidence in one's abilities. Various people who have worked on curricula in science and mathematics have urged that it is possible to present the fundamental structure of a discipline in such a way as to preserve some of the exciting sequences that lead a student to discover for himself.

It is particularly the Committee on School Mathematics and the Arithmetic Project of the University of Illinois that have emphasized the importance of discovery as an aid to teaching. They have been active in devising methods that permit a student to discover for himself the generalization that lies behind a particular mathematical operation, and they contrast this approach with the "method of assertion and proof" in which the generalization is first stated by the teacher and the class asked to proceed through the proof. It has also been pointed out by the Illinois group that the method of discovery would be too time-consuming for presenting all of what a student must cover in mathematics. The proper balance between the two is anything but plain, and research is in progress to elucidate the matter, though more is needed. Is the inductive approach a better technique for teaching principles? Does it have a desirable effect on attitudes?

That the method of discovery need not be limited to such highly formalized subjects as mathematics and physics is illustrated by some experimentation on social studies carried out by the Harvard Cognition Project. A sixth-grade class, having been through a conventional unit on the social and economic geography of the Southeastern states, was introduced to the North Central region by being asked to locate the major cities of the area on a map containing physical features and natural resources, but no place names. The resulting class discussion very rapidly produced a variety of plausible theories concerning the requirements of a city—a water transportation theory that placed Chicago at the junction of the three lakes, a mineral resources theory that placed it near the Mesabi range, a food-supply theory that put a great city on the rich soil of Iowa, and so on. The level of interest as well as the level of conceptual sophistication was far above that of control classes. Most striking, however, was the attitude of children to whom, for the first time, the location of a city appeared as a problem, and one to which an answer could be discovered by taking thought. Not only was there pleasure and excitement in the pursuit of a question, but in the end the discovery was worth making, at least for urban children for whom the phenomenon of the city was something that had before been taken for granted.

How do we tailor fundamental knowledge to the interests and capacities of children? This is a theme we shall return to later, and only a word need be said about it here. It requires a combination of deep understanding and patient honesty to present physical or any other phenomena in a way that is simultaneously exciting, correct, and rewardingly comprehensible. In examining certain teaching materials in physics, for example, we have found much patient honesty in presentation that has come to naught because the authors did not have a deep enough understanding of the subject they were presenting.

A good case in point is to be found in the usual attempt to explain the nature of tides. Ask the majority of high school students to explain tides and they will speak of the gravitational pull of the moon on the surface of the earth and how it pulls the water on the moon's side into a bulge. Ask them now why there is also a bulge of less magnitude on the side of the earth opposite to the moon, and they will almost always be without a satisfactory answer. Or ask them where the maximum bulge of the incoming tide is with respect to the relative position of the earth and moon, and the answer will usually be that it is at the point on the earth's surface nearest to the moon. If the student knows there is a lag in the tidal crest, he will usually not know why. The failure in both cases comes from an inadequate picture of how gravity acts upon a free-moving elastic body, and a failure to connect the idea of inertia with the idea of gravitational action. In short, the tides are explained without a share of the excitement that can come from understanding Newton's great discovery of universal gravitation and its mode of action. Correct and illuminating explanations are no more difficult and often easier to grasp than ones that are partly correct and therefore too complicated and too restricted.

It is the consensus of virtually all the men and women who have been working on curriculum projects that making material interesting is in no way incompatible with presenting it soundly; indeed, a correct general explanation is often the most interesting of all. Inherent in the preceding discussions are at least four general claims that can be made for teaching the fundamental structure of a subject, claims in need of detailed study.

The first is that understanding fundamentals makes a subject more comprehensible. This is true not only in physics and mathematics, where we have principally illustrated the point, but equally in the social studies and literature. Once one has grasped the fundamental idea that a nation must trade in order to live, then such a presumably special phenomenon as the Triangular Trade of the American colonies becomes altogether simpler to understand as something more than commerce in molasses, sugar cane, rum, and slaves in an atmosphere of violation of British trade regulations. The high school student reading *Moby Dick* can only understand more deeply if he can be led to understand that Melville's novel is, among other things, a study of the theme of evil and the plight of those pursuing this "killing whale." And if the student is led further to understand that there are a relatively limited number of human plights about which novels are written, he understands literature the better for it.

The second point relates to human memory. Perhaps the most basic thing that can be said about human memory, after a century of intensive research, is that unless detail is placed into a structured pattern, it is rapidly forgotten. Detailed material is conserved in memory by the use of simplified ways of representing it. These simplified representations have what may be called a "regenerative" character. A good example of this regenerative property of long-term memory can be found in science. A scientist does not try to remember the distances traversed by falling bodies in different gravitational fields over different periods of time. What he carries in memory instead is a formula that permits him with varying degrees of accuracy to regenerate the details on which the more easily remembered formula is based. So he commits to memory the formula $s = \frac{1}{2}gt^2$ and not a handbook of distances, times, and gravitational constants. Similarly, one does not remember exactly what Marlow, the commentator in *Lord Jim,* said about the chief protagonist's plight, but, rather, simply that he was the dispassionate onlooker, the man who tried to understand without judging what had led Lord Jim into the straits in which he found himself. We remember a formula, a vivid detail that carries the meaning of an event, an average that stands for a range of events, a caricature or picture that preserves an essence—all of them techniques of condensation and representation. What learning general or fundamental principles does is to ensure that memory loss will not mean total loss, that what remains will permit us to reconstruct the details when needed. A good theory is the vehicle not only for understanding a phenomenon now but also for remembering it tomorrow.

Third, an understanding of fundamental principles and ideas, as noted earlier, appears to be the main road to adequate "transfer of training." To understand something as a specific instance of a more general case—which is what understanding a more fundamental principle or structure means—is to have learned not only a specific thing but also a model for understanding other things like it that one may encounter. If a student could grasp in its most human sense the weariness of Europe at the close of the Hundred Years' War and how it created the conditions for a workable but not ideologically absolute Treaty of Westphalia, he might be better able to think about the ideological struggle of East and West—though the parallel is anything but exact. A carefully wrought understanding should also permit him to recognize the limits of the generalization as well. The idea of "principles" and "concepts" as a basis for transfer is hardly new. It is much in need of more research of a specific kind that would provide detailed knowledge of how best to proceed in the teaching of different subjects in different grades.

The fourth claim for emphasis on structure and principles in teaching is that by constantly reexamining material taught in elementary and secondary schools for its fundamental character, one is able to narrow the gap between "advanced" knowledge and "elementary" knowledge. Part of the difficulty now found in the progression from primary school through high school to college is that material learned earlier is either out of date or misleading by virtue of its lagging too far behind developments in a field. This gap can be reduced by the kind of emphasis set forth in the preceding discussion.

Consider now some specific problems that received considerable discussion at Woods Hole. One of them has to do with the troubled topic of "general science." There are certain recurrent ideas that appear in virtually all branches of science. If in one subject one has learned them well and generally, that achievement should make the task of learning them again in different form elsewhere in science much easier. Various teachers and scientists have raised the question whether these basic ideas should not be "isolated," so to speak, and taught more explicitly in ₊a manner that frees them from specific areas of science. The type of idea can be easily illustrated: categorization and its uses, the unit of measure and its development, the indirectness of information in science and the need for operational definition of ideas, and so forth. With respect to the last, for example, we do not *see* pressure or the chemical bond directly but infer it indirectly from a set of measures. So too body temperature. So too sadness in another person. Can these and similar ideas be presented effectively and with a variety of concrete illustrations in the early grades in order to give the child a better basis for understanding their specific representation in various special disciplines later? Is it wise to teach such "general science" as an introduction to disciplinary sciences in the later grades? How should they be taught and what could we reasonably expect by way of easier learning later? Much research is needed on this promising topic—research not only on the usefulness of such an approach, but also on the kinds of general scientific ideas that might be taught.

Indeed, it may well be that there are certain general attitudes or approaches toward science or literature that can be taught in the earlier grades that would have considerable relevance for later learning. The attitude that things are connected and not isolated is a case in point. One can indeed imagine kindergarten games designed to make children more actively alert to how things affect or are connected with each other—a kind of introduction to the idea of multiple determination of events in the physical and the social world. Any working scientist is usually able to say something about the ways of thinking or attitudes that are a part of his craft. Historians have written rather extensively on this subject as far as their field is concerned. Literary men have even evolved a genre of writing about the forms of sensibility that make for literary taste and vigor. In mathematics, this subject has a formal name, "heuristic," to describe the approach one takes to solving problems. One may well argue, as it was argued at Woods Hole by men in widely differing disciplines, that it might be wise to assess what attitudes or heuristic devices are most pervasive and useful, and that an effort should be made to teach children a rudimentary version of them that might be further refined as they progress through school. Again, the reader will sense that the argument for such an approach is premised on the assumption that there is a continuity between what a scholar does on the forefront of his discipline and what a child does in approaching it for the first time. This is not to say that the task is a simple one, only that it is worthy of careful consideration and research.

Perhaps the chief arguments put forward in opposition to the idea of such efforts at teaching general principles and general attitudes are, first, that it is better to approach the general through the specific and, second, that working attitudes should be kept implicit rather than being made explicit. For example, one of the principal organizing concepts in biology is the persistent question, "What function does this thing serve?"—a question premised on the assumption that everything one finds in an organism serves some function or it probably would not have survived. Other general ideas are related to this question. The student who makes progress in biology learns to ask the question more and more subtly, to relate more and more things to it. At the next step he asks what function a particular structure or process serves in the light of what is required in the total functioning of an organism. Measuring and categorizing are carried out in the service of the general idea of function. Then beyond that he may organize his knowledge in terms of a still more comprehensive notion of function, turning to cellular structure or to phylogenetic comparison. It may well be that the style of thought of a particular discipline is necessary as a background for learning the working meaning of general concepts, in which case a general introduction to the meaning of "function" might be less effective than teaching it in the context of biology.

As for "attitude" teaching or even the teaching of heuristic in mathematics, the argument runs that if the learner becomes too aware of his own attitudes or approach, he may become mechanical or trick-oriented in his work. No evidence exists on the point, and research is needed before any effort is made to teach in this way. Work is now going on at Illinois on training children to be more effective in asking questions about physical phenomena, but much more information is needed before the issue is clear.

One hears often the distinction between "doing" and "understanding." It is a distinction applied to the case, for example, of a student who presumably understands a mathematical idea but does not know how to use it in computation. While the distinction is probably a false one—since how can one know what a student understands save by seeing what he does—it points to an interesting difference in emphasis in teaching and in learning. Thus one finds in some of the classic books on the psychology of problem solving (such as Max Wertheimer's *Productive Thinking*) a sharp line drawn between "rote drill" and "understanding." In point of fact, drill need not be rote and, alas, emphasis on understanding may lead the student to a certain verbal glibness. It has been the experience of members of the School Mathematics Study Group that computational practice may be a necessary step toward understanding conceptual ideas in mathematics. Similarly one may try to give the high school student a sense of styles by having him read contrasting authors, yet final insight into style may come only when the student himself tries his hand at writing in different styles. Indeed, it is the underlying premise of laboratory exercises that doing something helps one understand it. There is a certain wisdom in the quip made by a psychologist at Woods Hole: "How do I know what I think until I feel what I do?" In any case, the distinction is not a very helpful one. What is more to the point is to ask what methods of exercise in any given field are most likely to give the student a sense of intelligent mastery over the material. What are the most fruitful computational exercises that one can use in various branches of mathematics? Does the effort to write in the style of Henry James gives one an especially good insight into that author's style? Perhaps a good start toward understanding such matters would be to study the methods used by successful teachers. It would be surprising if the information compiled failed to suggest a host of worthwhile laboratory studies on techniques of teaching —or, indeed, on techniques of imparting complex information generally.

A word is needed, finally, on examinations. It is obvious that an examination can be bad in the sense of emphasizing trivial aspects of a subject. Such examinations can encourage teaching in a disconnected fashion and learning by rote. What is often overlooked, however, is that examinations can also be allies in the battle to improve curricula and teaching. Whether an examination is of the "objective" type involving multiple choices or of the essay type, it can be devised so as to emphasize an understanding of the broad principles of a subject. Indeed, even when one examines on detailed knowledge, it can be done in such a way as to require an understanding by the student of the connectedness between specific facts. There is a concerted effort now under way among national testing organizations like the Educational Testing Service to construct examinations that will emphasize an understanding of fundamental principles. Such efforts can be of great help. Additional help might be given to local school systems by making available to them manuals that describe the variety of ways in which examinations can be constructed. The searching examination is not easy to make, and a thoughtful manual on the subject would be welcome.

To recapitulate, the main theme of this chapter has been that the curriculum of a subject should be determined by the most fundamental understanding that can be achieved of the underlying principles that give structure to that subject. Teaching specific topics or skills without making clear their context in the broader fundamental structure of a field of knowledge is uneconomical in several deep senses. In the first place, such teaching makes it exceedingly difficult for the student to generalize from what he has learned to what he will encounter later. In the second place, learning that has fallen short of a grasp of general principles has little reward in terms of intellectual excitement. The best way to create interest in a subject is to render it worth knowing, which means to make the knowledge gained usable in one's thinking beyond the situation in which the learning has occurred. Third, knowledge one has acquired without sufficient structure to tie it together is knowledge that is likely to be forgotten. An unconnected set of facts has a pitiably short half-life in memory. Organizing facts in terms of principles and ideas from which they may be inferred is the only known way of reducing the quick rate of loss of human memory.

Designing curricula in a way that reflects the basic structure of a field of knowledge requires the most fundamental understanding of that field. It is a task that cannot be carried out without the active participation of the ablest scholars and scientists. The experience of the past several years has shown that such scholars and scientists, working in conjunction with experienced teachers and students of child development, can prepare curricula of the sort we have been considering. Much more effort in the actual preparation of curriculum materials, in teacher training, and in supporting research will be necessary if improvements in our educational practices are to be of an order that will meet the challenges of the scientific and social revolution through which we are now living.

There are many problems of how to teach general principles in a way that will be both effective and interesting, and several of the key issues have been passed in review. What is abundantly clear is that much work remains to be done by way of examining currently effective practices, fashioning curricula that may be tried out on an experimental basis, and carrying out the kinds of research that can give support and guidance to the general effort at improving teaching.

Crisis in the classroom

CHARLES E. SILBERMAN

It is appropriate that this analysis of contemporary education be brought to a close with a selection from Charles Silberman's *Crisis in the Classroom*. Silberman does not claim membership in the group of more radical writers on the contemporary educational scene, writers such as Paul Goodman and John Holt; yet he fully accepts the proposition that our present society is in a state of crisis and that this crisis is clearly manifest in our schools. He deviates from the radical group in his belief that the required educational changes can be attained within the American educational system. He calls for sweeping reforms—but reforms within the system.

The value of Silberman's book is that it represents a putting together of most of the criticisms of public education that have poured forth during the past few years. The book constitutes the report of the Director of the Carnegie Study of the Education of Educators—a study that extended over a three-year period. It is divided into four parts, and it is noteworthy that only one of the parts is exclusively devoted to "how the schools should be changed." The major portion of the work is devoted to a description of the nature and extent of the "crisis" facing our schools.

In Part One, "The Educating Society," Silberman first poses the question, "Education for what?" He insists that public schools can be organized in such a way as to enhance the joy in learning. They can also be organized to develop esthetic qualities and character in the individual student. It is our "mindlessness," Silberman asserts, that prevents us from seriously concerning ourselves with

SOURCE: Charles E. Silberman, *Crisis in the Classroom* (New York: Vintage Books, 1970), pp. 135–156. Copyright © 1970 by Charles E. Silberman. Reprinted by permission of Random House, Inc.

educational purpose and from questioning current educational practices. Our schools must become pervaded with a sense of purpose, and this sense of purpose must be subject to continual reexamination.

The next question posed is whether American education is a success or failure. Silberman answers with a citation from the autobiography of John Stuart Mill:

> Suppose that all your objects in life were realized: that all the changes in institutions and opinions which you are looking forward to could be completely effected at this very instant: would this be a great joy and happiness to you? And an irrepressible self-consciousness answered, "No!" At this my heart sank within me: the whole foundation on which my life was constructed fell down.

The "failure" of our schools lies in their unrealized potential and in the resistance they offer to attempts to move them in positive directions. The current obsession with this failure of the schools obscures the facts which attest to the incredible progress and success of American public education during the past twenty years. The percentage of population attending the schools, the length of time in school, the degree of integration, and other factors indicate a level of public education undreamed of twenty years ago. However, most educational changes during the past two decades have been of a quantitative nature. The present "crisis" has been caused by the failure of public education to provide for the qualitative development of the individual. In short, while more and more of our youth are acquiring higher and higher levels of learning, this learning is having less and less meaning for them. The relationship between knowledge, degrees, and the "good life" is no longer accepted as obvious by growing numbers of the youth. The expectancies implicit in current notions of the good life far exceed the capacity of most schools to provide for, much less guarantee. However, Silberman maintains that there are changes (albeit radical ones) possible within our present schools that will restore some degree of meaning to the educating process. Part Three of his work provides examples of such changes.

Before turning to these examples, some comment should be

made regarding Part Two, "What's Wrong With the Schools." This part represents the most important contribution of Silberman's work. Here he synthesizes and clearly articulates all the major criticisms of public education that have been presented during the past decade. These criticisms are categorized under three headings: Education and Equality, Education for Docility, and The Failures of Educational Reform.

Under the heading "Education and Equality," Silberman demonstrates the relatively poor job the schools are doing toward facilitating a just and humane society. Silberman amply illustrates how schools help to perpetuate minority group differences in socioeconomic and cultural status. His contention is that the public schools are geared to a middle-class value system and that this system has shown little ability to adapt itself to the basic educational needs of the lower classes, especially to the needs of ethnic minorities. Those members of ethnic minorities who have succeeded in achieving middle-class status often have done so at a tremendous personal and psychological cost. Still, it is what Silberman calls "mindlessness" that accounts for this failure on the part of the schools, rather than any "maliciousness." It is a mindlessness that perpetuates the self-fulfilling prophecy asserted by so many teachers, either implicitly or explicitly, that children from some low socio-economic backgrounds or from certain ethnic families or communities cannot be expected to do well in school. The very attitude of these teachers ensures that the children will not do well, even before the children enter the school.

Turning from the somewhat specialized criticisms (that is, criticisms of the schools' failure to deal adequately with children of minority groups or with children from nonmiddle-class backgrounds), Silberman summarizes the criticisms that can be made against schools in general. "Education for Docility" is the heading he provides for this set of criticisms. It is from this section of his book that the selection presented is taken, because it is here that Silberman presents his most severe indictment of the schools. In general, Silberman finds the schools to be "grim," "repressive," and "joyless." The student is denied both the right to live fully and naturally as a child and the right to an adequate preparation for adult life. Silberman makes his point so eloquently in the selection given that we will leave it in his own words and move on to the final topic of Part Two.

Silberman places the final set of criticisms under the heading of "The Failures of Educational Reform." He catalogs the various reforms begun in the 1950's, reforms begun with the greatest expectancies, and all of which have resulted in little or no impact on the schools. He looks, too, at the current educational revolution fostered by the present technological revolution and finds it just as mindless as those which failed before. It is mindlessness that accounts for the failures; a mindlessness that keeps the educator and teacher from raising the basic questions "Education for what?" and "What knowledge is of most worth?" Without answers to these and other fundamental questions, educational reforms cannot hope to succeed.

Part Three of *Crisis in the Classroom* raises the question of how the schools should be changed. Silberman presents the reader with the case of the "new" English primary schools, schools which were transformed as the result of the report of the Plowden Committee. The transformation was from a formal atmosphere to an informal one. This informality is related to the ideas of John Dewey and to those of the psychologist Jean Piaget. However, Silberman is careful to distinguish this informality from the more radical forms developed in the American progressive education movement. For Silberman, the teacher will always retain a guiding role, but a role which allows for and encourages individual growth of the child as well as his spontaneity. He believes that this informalization of the schools can and should happen here in the United States. We should abolish the authoritarian and rigid atmosphere of our classrooms and institute in its stead the spontaneous and joyful enthusiasm for learning that cannot be attained in an atmosphere of formality.

While most of Silberman's examples and comments are directed toward the elementary school, he takes the opportunity at the end of this part to direct his remarks toward the American high school. Here he finds even greater repression and authoritarianism. The symptoms of conformity and docility are everywhere in evidence. Again, it is informality, an informality based upon trust and respect, that Silberman recommends. He rejects any freedom based upon sentimentality, but advocates a freedom coupled with responsibility.

In the final part of Silberman's work, he addresses himself to the education of educators. If we are to humanize our schools, then we must recognize that those qualities that are essential to the job are the sole possession of people. Only by means of a humanized teacher can a classroom become a humane place in which pupils can themselves become truly human. Teachers today are not prepared to think seriously about what they are doing and why. Our present teacher-training programs produce teachers who perpetuate the mindlessness of our school system. The resistance of our schools to change is attributable to the inability of teachers to think deeply about the aims, purposes, and goals of education—or even to think about what they are doing in the classroom. Thus, first and foremost, teachers must be liberally and humanely educated, trained to think seriously about fundamental human questions. But this is not all. Teachers also require professional training. About this there is little argument; the real question is about what kind of training this should be. Here, Silberman mentions such prospects as sensitivity training and T-group experiences. Such experiences may serve to make the teacher less defensive and hence less in need of assuming an authoritarian role.

All in all, Silberman provides most convincing argument and data in support of his contention that our classrooms are in a state of crisis. Furthermore, he brilliantly illuminates the nature of the crisis itself. Still, his suggestions as to how to change and what kind of change ought to occur are far less compelling. The force of argument and data are far weaker here. Even so, the real contribution of *Crisis in the Classroom* is not diminished, for in this work we are provided with an invaluable summation of the educational criticisms of our time. We are also afforded considerable insight into a social crisis, as well as an educational one.

EDUCATION FOR DOCILITY

· · · · ·

. . . Schools discourage students from developing the capacity to learn by and for themselves; they make it impossible for a youngster to take responsibility for his own education, for they are structured in such a way as to make students totally dependent upon the teachers. Whatever rhetoric they may subscribe to, most schools in practice define education as something teachers do to or for students, not something students do to and for themselves, with a teacher's assistance. "Seated at his desk, the teacher is in a position to do something," Jackson reports. *"It is the teacher's job to declare what that something shall be."* [Emphasis added] "It is the teacher who decides who will speak and in what order," and it is the teacher who decides who will have access to the materials of learning.

ITEM: From *Up the Down Staircase.*

> There is a premium on conformity, and on silence. Enthusiasm is frowned upon, since it is likely to be noisy. The Admiral [the administrative assistant] had caught a few kids who came to school before class, eager to practice on the typewriters. He issued a manifesto forbidding any students in the building before 8:20 or after 3:00—outside of school hours, students are "unauthorized." They are not allowed to remain in a classroom unsupervised by a teacher. They are not allowed to linger in the corridors. They are not allowed to speak without raising a hand. They are not allowed to feel too strongly or to laugh too loudly.

The result is to destroy students' curiosity along with their ability—more serious, their desire—to think or act for themselves.

ITEM: A large suburban high school informs its juniors that they will be able, the following year, to pursue a course of independent study on a topic of their own choosing, under faculty guidance, in lieu of a conventional course. In a class of eight or nine hundred, half of whom will be going to college, and in a year in which "relevance" has become an almost universal student catchword and demand, only three students bother to apply. The school has done its job well!

The vignette is not an isolated instance. "Schools that experiment with independent study," J. Lloyd Trump and Dorsey Baynham of the National Education Association reported in 1961, "find it difficult to stimulate even the most able students to do truly creative, independent work. They are accustomed to doing only what the teacher assigns and little more. Teachers' assignments have left little room in many cases for the exercise of initiative." Even when teachers, principals, and curriculum designers seriously try to give students room "for the exercise of initiative," they cannot drop the habit of looking over the students' shoulders. . . . In many of the schools Trump and Baynham examined, for example, "what was supposed to be independent study looked quite similar to the homework that usually occurs." [1]

It is understandable that that be so, for Trump himself, in one of the "supporting papers" he sends schoolmen interested in participating in the N.E.A.'s National Association of Secondary School Principals' "Model Schools Project," defines independent study "simply as what pupils do when their teachers stop talking. It is sometimes done individually," he goes on to explain, "more often in various sized groups. Pupils read, view, listen, write, think, and do both what their teachers require and what is described as working in greater depth or being creative." Indeed, one of the purposes of regular classroom meetings, Trump explains, is to give the teacher an opportunity to make "assignments so that each pupil may engage successfully in independent study." [2]

The reluctance to turn children free—to let them follow their own curiosity—is understandable in the context of the way schools operate. "Truly creative, independent work can be messy, expensive, and time-consuming," as Anthony G. Oettinger observes. "Schools are organized for neatness, low budgets and time compression." Hence most of the great experiments in "individualized instruction" define individualization in the narrowest terms; as Oettinger describes it, "each pupil is free to go more or less rapidly where he's told to go."

At the heart of the schoolmen's inability to turn responsibility over to the students is the fact that the teacher-student relationship in its conventional form is, as Willard Waller states, "a form of institutionalized dominance and subordination. Teacher and pupil confront each other in the school with an original conflict of desires, and however much that conflict may be reduced in amount, or however much it may be hidden, it still remains. The teacher represents the adult group, ever the enemy

---

[1] J. Lloyd Trump and Dorsey Baynham, *Guide to Better Schools*, Chicago: Rand McNally, 1961.

[2] J. Lloyd Trump, "Needed Changes for Further Improvement of Secondary Education in the United States," and "How Excellent Are Teaching and Learning in Your School," National Association of Secondary School Principals, mimeographed.

of the spontaneous life of groups of children. The teacher represents the formal curriculum, and his interest is in imposing that curriculum upon the children in the form of tasks; pupils are much more interested in life in their own world than in the desiccated bits of adult life which teachers have to offer. The teacher represents the established social order in the school, and his interest is in maintaining that order, whereas pupils have only a negative interest in that feudal super-structure. Teacher and pupil confront each other with attitudes from which the underlying hostility can never be altogether removed." There is a kernel of truth, in short, as well as a large element of self-pity in the young rebels' fondness for the metaphor of the "student as nigger."

A major source of the underlying hostility is the preoccupation with grades. "Tests are as indigenous to the school environment as are text-books or pieces of chalk," Jackson observes. "But tests, though they are the classic form of educational evaluation, are not all there is to the process." Indeed, the use of tests "is insufficient to explain the dis-tinctively evaluative atmosphere that pervades the classroom from the earliest grades onward," for almost anything and everything the student does is likely to be evaluated and graded.

The teacher, of course, is the chief source of evaluation. "He is called upon continuously to make judgments of students' work and behavior and to communicate that judgment to the students in question and to others. No one who has observed an elementary classroom for any length of time can have failed to be impressed by the vast number of times the teacher performs this function. Typically, in most class-rooms students come to know when things are right or wrong, good or bad, pretty or ugly, largely as a result of what the teacher tells them."

Evaluation per se is not the problem. . . . Evaluation is an important and indeed intrinsic part of education—essential if teachers are to judge the effectiveness of their teaching, and if students are to judge what they know and what they are having trouble learning. The pur-pose should be diagnostic: to indicate where teachers and students have gone wrong and how they might improve their performance. And since students will have to judge their own performance, they need experience in self-evaluation.

But schools rarely evaluate in this way. They make it clear that the purpose of evaluation is rating: to produce grades that enable ad-ministrators to rate and sort children, to categorize them so rigidly that they can rarely escape. "Each teacher," Professor Benjamin S. Bloom of the University of Chicago writes, "begins a new term (or course) with the expectation that about a third of his students will adequately learn what he has to teach. He expects about a third of his students to fail or to just 'get by.' Finally, he expects another third to learn a good deal of what he has to teach, but not enough to be regarded as 'good students.' This set of expectations, supported by school policies and practices in grading, becomes transmitted to the students through the grading procedures and through the methods and materials of instruction. The system creates a self-fulfilling prophecy such that the final sorting of students through the grading process becomes approximately equal to the original expectations. This set of expectations, which fixes the academic goals of teachers and students," Bloom adds, "is the most wasteful and destructive aspect of the present educational system," reducing students' motivation to learn and systematically destroying the ego and sense of self of large numbers of students.[3]

The assault on the student's self-esteem and sense of self is frequently overt, with teachers virtually demanding failure from some children.

I T E M : A fourth-grade math teacher writes a half-dozen problems on the board for the class to do. "I think I can pick at least four children who can't do them," she tells the class, and proceeds to call four youngsters to the board to demonstrate, for all to see, how correct the teacher's judgment is. Needless to say, the children fulfill the prophecy.

I T E M : An elementary school in a wealthy Northeastern suburb whose name is almost synonymous with concern for education. Three children are in a special class for children with perceptual problems. The teacher insists on talking with the visitor about the children in their presence, as though congenital deafness were part of their difficulty. "Now, watch, I'm giving them papers to see if they can spot the ovals, but you'll see that this one"—he nods in the direction of a little boy—"isn't going to be able to do it." A few seconds later, he says triumphantly, "See, I told you he couldn't. He never gets that one right. Now I'll put something on the overhead projector, and this one"—this time, a nod toward

[3] Benjamin S. Bloom, "Learning for Mastery," in *Evaluation Comment,* Vol. 1, No. 2, May 1968, published by the UCLA Center for the Study of Evaluation of Instructional Programs.

a little girl—"won't stay with it for more than a line." Five seconds later, with evident disappointment: "Well, that's the first time she ever did *that*. But keep watching. By the next line, she'll have flubbed it." The child gets the next one right, too, and the teacher's disappointment mounts. "This *is* unusual, but just stick around . . ." Sure enough, the child goofs at line five. "See, I told you so!"

The problem is compounded by the misuse of IQ and other standardized tests. "Although the validity and reliability of all standardized tests is far from perfect," David A. Goslin of the Russell Sage Foundation writes, "a precise numerical score frequently takes on a kind of absolute validity when it appears on a child's record card. Teachers and administrators alike, when confronted with a child's IQ score or his percentile rank on an achievement test like the Iowa Test of Basic Skills, often tend to disregard the considerable degree of imprecision that is inherent in such measures." The result, Goslin adds, "is that in a variety of ways we are tending to put individuals into cubby holes." [4]

A corollary of teacher dominance is the teacher's role in doling out privileges from which status flows. "In elementary classrooms, it is usually the teacher who assigns coveted duties, such as serving on the safety patrol, or running the movie projector, or clapping erasers, or handing out supplies," Jackson observes. "Although the delegation of these duties may not take up much of the teacher's time, it does help to give structure to the activities of the room and to fashion the quality of the total experience for many of the participants."

The phenomenon is not limited to elementary schools. "The concept of privilege is important at Milgrim," Edgar Z. Friedenberg observes of one of the representative high schools he describes in *Coming of Age in America*. "Teachers go to the head of the chow line at lunch; whenever I would attempt quietly to stand in line the teacher on hall duty would remonstrate with me. He was right, probably; I was fouling up an entire informal social system by my ostentation. Students on hall patrol also, when relieved from duty, were privileged to come bouncing up to the head of the line; so did seniors. Much of the behavior Milgrim depends on to keep it going is motivated by the reward of getting a government-surplus peanut butter or tuna fish sandwich without standing in line for it."

[4] David A. Goslin, *The School in Contemporary Society*, Glenview, Ill.: Scott, Foresman, 1965.

Still another by-product of teacher dominance, one that has profound consequences for children's attitudes toward learning, is the sharp but wholly artificial dichotomy between work and play which schools create and maintain. Young children make no such distinction. They learn through play, and until they have been taught to make the distinction ("Let's stop playing now, children; it's time to start our work"), they regard all activities in the same light. But the dichotomy grows out of the assumption that nothing can happen unless the teacher makes it happen. "Work entails becoming engaged in a purposeful activity that has been prescribed for us by someone else, an activity in which we would not at that moment be engaged if it were not for some system of authority relationships," Jackson explains. "The teacher, with his prescriptive dicta and his surveillance over the student's attention, provides the missing ingredient that makes work real. The teacher, although he may disclaim the title, is the student's first 'Boss.' "

Why are schools so bad?

To read some of the more important and influential contemporary critics of education—men like Edgar Friedenberg, Paul Goodman, John Holt, Jonathan Kozol—one might think that the schools are staffed by sadists and clods who are drawn into teaching by the lure of upward mobility and the opportunity to take out their anger—Friedenberg prefers the sociological term *ressentiment,* or "a kind of free floating ill-temper"—on the students.[5] This impression is conveyed less by explicit statement than by nuance and tone—a kind of "aristocratic insouciance," as David Riesman calls it, which these writers affect, in turn reflecting the general snobbery of the educated upper middle class toward the white collar, lower-middle-class world of teachers, social workers, civil servants, and policemen. In recent years this snobbery has become a nasty and sometimes spiteful form of bigotry on the part of many self-made intellectuals, who seem to feel the need to demonstrate their moral and cultural superiority to the lower middle class from which they escaped. A number of critics of American culture, moreover, such as Friedenberg, who is a conscious elitist, Paul Goodman, Norman Mailer, and Leslie Fiedler seem to be particularly attracted by the virility and violence of lower-class life, which they tend to romanticize. They seem unable to show empathy for the problems

[5] Edgar Z. Friedenberg, "The Gifted Student and His Enemies," in Friedenberg, *The Dignity of Youth & Other Atavisms,* Boston: Beacon Press, 1965.

of the lower-middle-class teacher, whose passivity and fear of violence they deride as effeminate and whose humanity they seem, at times, almost to deny.[6]

But teachers *are* human. To be sure, teaching—like the ministry, law, medicine, business, and government—has its share of angry, hostile, and incompetent people. Most teachers, however, are decent, honest, well-intentioned people who do their best under the most trying circumstances. If they appear otherwise, it is because the institution in which they are engulfed demands it of them. . . . Transforming the school transforms teacher as well as student behavior. If placed in an atmosphere of freedom and trust, if treated as professionals and as people of worth, teachers behave like the caring, concerned people they would like to be. They, no less than their students, are victimized by the way in which schools are currently organized and run.

Certainly nothing in the way most schools are built or run suggests respect for teachers as teachers, or as human beings. After visiting some 260 classrooms in 100 elementary schools in thirteen states, for example, John Goodlad, dean of the UCLA Graduate School of Education, concluded that the schools are "anything but the 'palaces' of an affluent society." On the contrary, he writes, they look "more like the artifacts of a society that did not really care about its schools, a society that expressed its disregard by creating schools less suited to human habitation than its prisons." [7] Goodlad and his colleagues had hoped to conduct long interviews with the teachers they observed, but few schools had either quiet or attractive places in which to meet; they held their interviews on the run, therefore, unless they were able to meet the teachers for breakfast or dinner. Nor was Goodlad's experience atypical. Teachers rarely have offices of their own, and if there is a teachers' lounge, more often than not it is a shabbily furnished room designed to permit no more than a fast smoke.

The shabbiness of the teachers' physical environment is exceeded only by the churlishness of their social environment, a fact that educational critics and reformers tend to ignore or to acknowledge only in passing. "Reform literature," as Dean Robert J. Schaeffer of Teachers College has written, "has failed to examine the total educational experi-

---

[6] Cf. David Riesman, Introduction to the Grosset Universal Library edition of Reuel Denney's *The Astonished Muse.*

[7] John Goodlad, "The Schools vs. Education," *Saturday Review,* April 19, 1969.

ence of teachers, and has narrowly concentrated upon preservice preparation to the neglect of the educative or the debilitating effects of
the job itself." And the job *is* debilitating. In a section on "What
Teaching Does to Teachers" in *The Sociology of Teaching,* Willard
Waller talks about "that peculiar blight which affects the teacher
mind, which creeps over it gradually, and possessing it bit by bit, de-
vours its creative resources."

This "peculiar blight" is a product of a number of forces. There is
the low regard in which teachers are held by the rest of the community,
reflected not only in the salaries and physical plants teachers are provided, but also in the unflattering stereotypes of teachers with which
American literature (and films and TV programs) are filled.[8] There is
the atmosphere of meanness and distrust in which teachers work; they
punch time clocks like factory workers or clerks and are rarely if ever
consulted about things that concern them most, such as the content of
the curriculum or the selection of textbooks. And there are the conditions of work themselves: teaching loads that provide no time for reflection or for privacy, and menial tasks such as "patrol duty" in the
halls or cafeteria that demean or deny professional status. "Whatever
becomes of our method, the conditions stand fast—six hours, and thirty,
fifty, or a hundred and fifty pupils," Ralph Waldo Emerson observed
more than a century ago. "Something must be done and done speedily,
and in this distress the wisest are tempted to adopt violent means, to
proclaim martial law, corporal punishment, mechanical arrangements,
bribes, spies, wrath, main strength and ignorance. . . . And the gentle
teacher, who wishes to be a Providence to youth, is grown a martinet,
sore with suspicions . . . and his love of learning is lost in the routine
of grammar and books of elements."

Despite the continuous contact with children, moreover, teaching is

___

[8] In a study of occupational prestige conducted by the National Opinion Research Center, teaching ranked thirty-fifth from the top—just below the building
contractor and just above the railroad engineer. Cf. W. W. Charters, Jr., "The
Social Background of Teaching," in N. L. Gage, ed., *Handbook of Research on
Teaching,* Chicago: Rand McNally, 1963. The status problem mainly affects male
teachers, the great majority of whom teach in secondary schools. For women,
teaching is a highly prestigious occupation; indeed, teaching is a low-status and
low-paying occupation for men in large part because it traditionally has been
dominated by women and so is regarded as a female occupation. Cf. Dan C.
Lortie, "The Balance of Control and Autonomy in Elementary School Teaching,"
in Amitai Etzioni, ed., *The Semi-Professions and Their Organization,* New York:
Free Press, 1969.

a lonely profession. Teachers rarely get a chance to discuss their problems or their successes with their colleagues, nor do they, as a rule, receive any kind of meaningful help from their supervisors, not even in the first year of teaching. "When we first started working in the schools," members of the Yale University's Psycho-Educational Clinic report, "we were asked in several instances in the early weeks not to go into several classrooms *because* the teachers were new." [9] (Emphasis in the original.)

If teachers are obsessed with silence and lack of movement, therefore, it is in large part because it is the chief means by which their competence is judged. A teacher will rarely, if ever, be called on the carpet or denied tenure because his students have not learned anything; he most certainly will be rebuked if his students are talking or moving about the classroom, or—even worse—found outside the room, and he may earn the censure of his colleagues as well. Nor will teachers receive suggestions from their supervisors as to how to improve their teaching methods and materials; they will receive suggestions for improving "discipline." Thus, the vows of silence and stillness are often imposed on teachers who might prefer a more open, lively classroom.

ITEM: From *Up the Down Staircase.*

> There was one heady moment when I was able to excite the class by an idea: I had put on the blackboard Browning's "A man's reach should exceed his grasp, or what's a heaven for?" and we got involved in a spirited discussion of aspiration vs. reality. Is it wise, I asked, to aim higher than one's capacity? Does it not doom one to failure? No, no, some said, that's ambition and progress! No, no, others cried, that's frustration and defeat! What about hope? What about despair?—You've got to be practical!—You've got to have a dream! They said this in their own words, you understand, startled into discovery. To the young, clichés seem freshly minted. Hitch your wagon to a star! Shoemaker, stick to your last! And when the dismissal bell rang, they paid me the highest compliment: they groaned! They crowded in the doorway, chirping like agitated sparrows, pecking at the seeds I

[9] Seymour B. Sarason, Murray Levine, I. Ira Goldenberg, Dennis L. Cherlin, and Edward M. Bennett, *Psychology in Community Settings: Clinical, Educational, Vocational, Social Aspects,* New York: John Wiley, 1966.

had strewn—when who should appear but [the administrative assistant to the principal].

"What is the meaning of this noise?"

"It's the sound of thinking, Mr. McHabe," I said.

In my letter box that afternoon was a note from him, with copies to my principal and chairman (and—who knows?— perhaps a sealed indictment dispatched to the Board?) which read:

> "I have observed that in your class the class entering your room is held up because the pupils exiting from your room are exiting in a disorganized fashion, blocking the doorway unnecessarily and *talking*. An orderly flow of traffic is the responsibility of the teacher whose class is exiting from the room."

The cardinal sin, strange as it may seem in an institution of learning, is talking.

I T E M : A sixth-grade science teacher in a highly regarded suburban school, learning that one of his pupils is the son of a local butcher, obtains the heart and lungs of a cow. Next day, elbow-deep in tissue and blood, he shows the class how the respiratory system operates. When he returns from lunch, he finds a note from the Superintendent, who had looked in on the class that morning: "Teachers are not supposed to remove their jackets in class. If the jacket must be removed, the shirt-sleeves certainly should not be rolled up."

If schools are repressive, then, it is not the teachers' fault, certainly not their fault alone. Nearly two-thirds of the high school students' parents surveyed in early 1969 for *Life* by Louis Harris, for example, believe that "maintaining discipline is more important than student self-inquiry"; the comparable figure among teachers is only 27 percent. The United States, in short, has the kinds of schools its citizens have thus far demanded. The role of taskmaster is thrust upon the teachers, some of whom accept it willingly, some reluctantly; all are affected by it. "The teacher-pupil relationship," Waller writes, "is a special form of dominance and subordination, a very unstable relationship and in quivering equilibrium. . . . It is an unfortunate role, that of Simon Legree, and has corrupted the best of men."

What schools do to both students and teachers can be understood best if one realizes that in a number of respects, schools resemble "total institutions" like hospitals, armed services, and even prisons. In all of these, as Philip Jackson puts it, "one sub-group of their clientele (the students) are involuntarily committed to the institution, whereas another sub-group (the staff) has greater freedom of movement and, most important, has the ultimate freedom to leave the institution entirely. Under these circumstances it is common for the more privileged group to guard the exits, either figuratively or literally." Even when teachers operate "democratic" classrooms, Jackson insists, "their responsibilities bear some resemblance to those of prison guards. In 'progressive' prisons, as in most classrooms, the inhabitants are allowed certain freedoms, but there are real limits. In both institutions the inmates might be allowed to plan a Christmas party, but in neither place are they allowed to plan a 'break.' " [10]

To survive in school, as in other "total institutions," the students, like the teachers, are forced to develop a variety of adaptive strategies and attitudes. And survival—getting through and compiling a good record or avoiding a bad record—does become the goal. It is inevitable that this be so, given the obsession with routine and given also the frequency with which students are evaluated, the arbitrariness and mysteriousness (at least to the students) of the criteria by which they are judged, and the importance attached to these evaluations by parents, teachers, colleges, graduate and professional schools, and prospective employers.

I T E M : A high school student talking: "School is just like roulette or something. You can't just ask: 'Well, what's the point of it?' . . . The point of it is to do it, to get through and get into college. But you have to figure the system or you can't win, because the odds are all on the house's side." [11]

Unfortunately, survival has little to do with learning in the sense of cognitive development. "For children," as John Holt documents in some

---

[10] Cf. Willard Waller, *The Sociology of Teaching,* especially Chapters 2 and 14; and Gertrude H. S. McPherson, *The Role-Set of the Elementary School Teacher: A Case Study,* unpublished Ph.D. dissertation, Columbia University Library.

[11] Quoted in Kathryn Johnston Noyes and Gordon L. McAndrew, "Is This What Schools Are For?" *Saturday Review,* December 21, 1968.

detail, "the central business of school is not learning, whatever this vague word means; it is getting those daily tasks done, or at least out of the way, with a minimum of effort and unpleasantness. Each task is an end in itself." [12] This is so, as Mary Alice White of Teachers College has explained with great sensitivity, because "the view from the pupil's desk" bears little resemblance to the view from the teacher's or the curriculum designer's desk. "What the pupil is going to learn is to him far away in time and entirely mysterious," Professor White writes. "All he knows is what he *has* been taught, and he only remembers part of that, often in an isolated fashion. Why he is made to learn this and not that, or this before that, is another mystery to him; nor does he know what the alternative choices might be. Since little of what he is asked to learn makes much sense to him, except perhaps the more visible skills of reading, writing, and computation, he rarely asks why he has been asked to learn them. He also senses that he is going to be taught whatever the teacher has decided she is going to teach, so the question is useless." [13]

In any case, the student has no cognitive map to guide him through the labyrinth of knowledge he is asked to master. He is guided instead, Professor White suggests, by his map of school experience. Thus, elementary school students almost invariably regard mathematics as the most important subject in the curriculum—not because of its structure or its elegance, but because math has the most homework, because the homework is corrected the most promptly, and because tests are given more frequently than in any other subject. The youngsters regard spelling as the next most important subject, because of the frequency of spelling tests. "To a pupil," Professor White explains, "the workload and evaluation demands obviously must reflect what the teacher thinks is important to learn."

It is not simply the students' ignorance of the purposes of what they are asked to learn that makes them subordinate learning to survival. Almost from the first day, students learn that the game is not to acquire knowledge but to discover what answer the teacher wants, and in what form she wants it; there are few classroom scenes more familiar than that of the teacher brushing aside or penalizing correct answers

[12] John Holt, *How Children Fail,* New York: Pitman, 1964.

[13] Mary Alice White, "The View from the Pupil's Desk," *The Urban Review,* Vol. II, No. 5, April 1968.

that don't happen to be the ones she had in mind. "It is soon clear to students what types of responses are likely to be successful at playing the school game," a group of dissident Maryland students write in a biting critique of their county's schools. "And so, before long, a student's approach to questions and problems undergoes a basic change. It quickly becomes clear that approaching a question on a test by saying 'What is my own response to this question?' is risky indeed, and totally unwise if one covets the highest grade possible (and the school system teaches the student that he should). Rather, the real question is clear to any student who knows anything about how schools work: 'What is the answer the teacher wants me to give? What can I write that will please the teacher?' " [14]

These tendencies are almost built into the way most classrooms operate. "In training a child to activity of thought," Alfred North Whitehead wrote, "above all things we must beware of what I will call 'inert ideas'—that is to say, ideas that are merely received into the mind without being utilised, or tested, or thrown into fresh combinations." [15] In most classrooms, however, the teacher sits or stands at the front of the room, dispensing "inert ideas" to his passive students, as if they were so many empty vessels to be filled.

I T E M : "A high-school teacher displays the following sales pitch on his bulletin board: 'FREE. Every Monday through Friday. Knowledge. Bring your own containers.' " (From *Reader's Digest,* October 1969.)

Without realizing it, moreover (few have been exposed to any other way of teaching), most teachers dominate the classroom, giving students no option except that of passivity. Exhaustive studies of classroom language in almost every part of the country, and in almost every kind of school, reveal a pattern that is striking in its uniformity: teachers do almost all the talking, accounting, on average, for two-thirds to three-quarters of all classroom communication. There are differences, of

[14] Montgomery County Student Alliance, "Wanted: A Humane Education: An Urgent Call for Reconciliation Between Rhetoric and Reality," Bethesda, Md.: Montgomery County Student Alliance, 1969 (mimeographed), reprinted in Ronald and Beatrice Gross, eds., *Radical School Reform,* New York: Simon and Schuster, 1969.

[15] Alfred North Whitehead, *The Aims of Education,* New York: New American Library Mentor Books, 1949.

course, from teacher to teacher, but the differences are surprisingly small. In the most child-centered classroom in a private school known for its child-centeredness, for example, Philip Jackson found that the teacher initiated 55.2 percent of the conversation; in the most teacher-dominated room, the ratio was 80.7 percent. Equally significant, analyses of the nature of student and teacher conversation indicates that the student's role is passive, being confined, for the most part, to responses to teacher questions or statements. In almost all the systems of "interaction analysis" that have been devised to analyze the different kinds of classroom communication—there are now several dozen—three-quarters or so of the "talk" categories refer to teachers.[16]

Small wonder, then, that students seem unable to take responsibility for their learning; the following description of a Massachusetts school system could apply to almost any other in the United States.

> Watertown's young people do not find school an intellectually exciting place. Although the Study Staff observed some good schools staffed in part by able, hard-working, creative teachers, instructing youngsters who were happy, vibrant, and actively engaged in the learning process, these bright spots are overshadowed by evidence that too often Watertown's students look without enthusiasm upon their schools and the learning required in them. In many of the classes observed by

[16] Herbert M. Kliebard, "The Observation of Classroom Behavior," in *The Way Teaching Is,* Washington, D.C.: Association for Supervision and Curriculum Development and National Education Association, 1966; Arno Bellack, Herbert M. Kliebard, Ronald T. Hyman, and Frank L. Smith Jr., *The Language of the Classroom,* New York: Teachers College Press, 1966; Donald M. Medley and Harold F. Mitzel, "Measuring Classroom Behavior by Systematic Observation," in N. L. Gage, ed., *Handbook of Research in Teaching,* Rand McNally, 1963; Ned A. Flanders, "Interaction Analysis: A Technique for Quantifying Teacher Influence," paper delivered at American Educational Research Association, Chicago, February 1962; Edmund J. Amidon and Ned A. Flanders, "The Role of the Teacher in the Classroom: A Manual for Understanding and Improving Teachers' Classroom Behavior," Minneapolis, Minn.: Paul S. Amidon & Associates, 1963; John B. Hough, "Training in the Control of Verbal Teaching Behavior—Theory and Implications," paper read at A.E.R.A. Convention, New York City, 1967; Philip M. Jackson, "Teacher-Pupil Communication: An Observational Study," paper read at A.E.R.A. Convention, February 1965; Marie N. Hughes, "The Utah Study of the Assessment of Teaching," in A. A. Bellack, ed., *Theory and Research in Teaching,* Teachers College Press, 1963; Cf. *Interaction Analysis Newsletter* for complete bibliography of past and new studies.

the Study Staff, students remained passive and uninvolved in their own education.

Watertown's schools do not give the student many opportunities to assume responsibility for his own learning. The student is not encouraged to explore, to stretch his thinking, to pursue an independent line of inquiry. The program of studies is defined by the school, and the student is expected to learn what the school decides he should learn. Rarely does the student in Watertown have the chance to make meaningful decisions; rarely does he have a chance to discover for himself what learning is all about.

The pervasive method of instruction consists of lectures and teacher-dominated activities. The teacher talks; the students are expected to listen or recite in response to the teacher's cues. The emphasis is on the acquisition of factual information untempered by reflective thought. Textbooks determine course content and organization, and many courses are untouched by current thought in curriculum development. In Watertown, the student succeeds by being quiet, by following directions, and by memorizing the information which the teacher doles out. The teacher succeeds by following textbook instructions.[17]

The phenomenon is not limited to elementary and secondary schools. Because college students' academic relationship to faculty and administration is also one of subjection, Howard S. Becker, Blanche Geer, and Everett C. Hughes argue, "students seek only the information faculty wants, and direct their efforts toward producing whatever impression is required to get a good grade," and "learning for its own sake flies out the window." In medical school, too, the goal is to get through.[18]

One of the ways of getting through is by cheating. "Learning how to

[17] *Watertown: The Education of Its Children,* Harvard Graduate School of Education Center for Field Studies, 1967.

[18] Howard S. Becker, Blanche Geer, and Everett C. Hughes, *Making the Grade: The Academic Side of College Life,* New York: John Wiley, 1968; Howard S. Becker, Blanche Geer, Everett C. Hughes, and Anselm Strauss, *Boys in White: Student Culture in Medical School,* University of Chicago Press, 1961. For a somewhat different view of medical school, see Robert K. Merton, George C. Reader, and Patricia L. Kendall, eds., *The Student Physician: Introductory Studies in the Sociology of Medical Education,* Harvard University Press, 1957.

make it in school," as Jackson observes, "involves, in part, learning how to falsify our behavior." Some of the forms of falsification involve little more than the petty dissembling common to adult social discourse, e.g., feigning interest in what another is saying. Some involve outright cheating, e.g., copying on a test. In their classic studies of character education of forty years ago, Hartshorne and May discovered that children's tendency to cheat depended on the risk of detection and the effort required rather than on intrinsic notions of morality; noncheaters were more cautious than the cheaters, but not more honest.[19]

These findings, which have been confirmed by a number of subsequent studies, reflect the primitive morality which the culture of the school actively cultivates. "While most elementary school children are aware of, and concerned about, the harm done others by acts of aggression or theft," Professor Lawrence Kohlberg of Harvard, the leading contemporary student of moral education, writes, "their only reason for not cheating is their fear of being caught and punished. Even at older ages, teachers give children few moral or mature reasons to think cheating is bad. Sixth-grade children tell us their teachers tell them not to cheat because they will get punished"—the most primitive level of moral judgment—"or because 'the person you copied from might have it wrong and so it won't do you any good,'" a level of judgment only one step up on Kohlberg's hierarchy. Teachers are always and unavoidably moralizing to children about rules, values, and behavior, but they rarely think about the values they are communicating. "Many teachers would be most mortified and surprised to know what their students perceive to be their moral values and concerns," Kohlberg observes.

Getting through school also involves learning how to suppress one's feelings and emotions and to subordinate one's own interests and desires to those of the teachers. Up to a point, this, too, is useful—a necessary aspect of learning to live in society. But schools tend to turn what could be a virtue into a fault by in effect excluding the child's interests altogether. The result, Peter Marin, a former high school principal suggests, is to create "a cultural schizophrenia in which the

---

[19] H. Hartshorne and M. A. May, *Studies in the Nature of Character,* quoted in Lawrence Kohlberg, "Moral Education in the Schools: A Developmental View," *The School Review,* Vol. 74, No. 1, Spring 1966; Lawrence Kohlberg, *The Development of Children's Orientations to a Moral Order,* New York: Holt, Rinehart and Winston, Inc., expected to be published late 1971.

student is forced to choose between his own relation to reality and the one demanded by the institution." Children frequently respond by learning to live in two worlds. "Children acquire great dexterity in exhibiting in conventional and expected ways the *form* of attention to school work," John Dewey observed, "while reserving the inner play of their own thoughts, images, and emotions for subjects that are more important to them, but quite irrelevant."

Some students, however, survive by withdrawing into apathy, whether feigned or real; in the constantly evaluative atmosphere of the school, one way for them to avoid the pain of failure is to persuade themselves that they do not care. But those who do care, and who do do well on tests, are not free from pain, either; they may bear the marks of caring for the rest of their lives, particularly if they go on to college and graduate or professional school. One of the first discoveries that Sigmund Freud made when he began studying the significance of dreams was the near-universality, among people with advanced degrees, of what he called the "examination dream." In it, the dreamer imagines himself back at school and about to take an examination for which he is hopelessly unprepared and almost certain to fail. The dream—still common among university graduates—is marked by acute anxiety; the dreamer often awakens in a cold sweat.

The most important strategy for survival is docility and conformity. "Most students soon learn that rewards are granted to those who lead a good life. And in school the good life consists, principally, of doing what the teacher says," Jackson observes. "Every school child quickly learns what makes teachers angry. He learns that in most classrooms the behavior that triggers the teacher's ire has little to do with wrong answers or other indicators of scholastic failure. Rather, it is violations of institutional expectations that really get under the teacher's skin"; for example, "coming into the room late, or making too much noise, or not listening to directions, or pushing while in line. Occasionally, teachers do become publicly vexed by their students' academic shortcomings, but to really send them off on a tirade of invective, the young student soon discovers, nothing works better than a partially suppressed giggle during arithmetic period."

The encouragement of docility may explain why girls tend to be more successful in school than boys: passivity and docility are more in keeping with the behavior the culture expects of girls outside of school than the behavior it expects of boys. The phenomenon is cumulative and self-reinforcing: the behavior demanded in school is more feminine than masculine; girls adapt better, therefore school, and an interest in school affairs, tends to be defined as feminine, particularly among ethnic and social groups that place a high premium on masculinity. Perhaps as a result—or perhaps also because boys develop at a different rate than girls, a fact that the schools ignore—boys tend to do less well in school than girls, and are vastly more susceptible to learning and emotional problems. Thus, boys account for three-quarters of all referrals to reading clinics; more than two-thirds of the children who are "retained" (left back) in a grade for one or more years are boys; between three and four times as many boys as girls are stutterers.[20]

Docility is not only encouraged but frequently demanded, for teachers and administrators seem unable to distinguish between authority and power. "The generalization that the schools have a despotic political structure," Waller writes, "seems to hold true for nearly all types of schools, and for all about equally, without very much difference in fact to correspond to radical differences in theory."

I T E M : The director of physical education for girls in a well-regarded suburban school system insists that a thirteen-year-old girl change into gym shorts and sit on the sidelines each time her class has gym, despite the fact that the girl has been excused for medical reasons. "There's no reason you can't watch, or keep score if the other girls are playing a game," the director tells the child, whose cancerous right leg has just been amputated at the hip, and who cannot yet be fitted with an artificial limb. Not until her mother carries the appeal to the superintendent of schools is the youngster spared this thrice-weekly humiliation.

I T E M : A boy, being put on detention, protests his innocence, politely but insistently presenting his version of what happened. (The incident in question had involved another teacher.) The teacher giving the punishment responds each time by telling the boy how important it is to respect his elders, insisting that he should go on detention first and then tell the teacher involved why he thought the punishment was unfair. "You have to prove you're a man and can take orders." The boy

---

[20] Frances Bentzen, "Sex Ratios in Learning and Behavior Disorders," *The National Elementary Principal*, Vol. XLVI, No. 2, November 1966; M. L. Kellmer Pringle, N. R. Butler, R. Davie, *11,000 Seven-Year-Olds*, London: Longmans, Green, 1966; Patricia Sexton, *The Feminized Male*, New York: Random House, 1969.

finally agrees to go to detention, "but under protest." The scene ends with the teacher smirking as the boy walks away.[21]

Docility is demanded outside the school as well as inside; students learn fairly rapidly that their participation in civic affairs is not welcome, except for one ceremonial day a year when they are allowed to play at being superintendent of schools, principal, or teacher for the photographers from the local newspaper.

I T E M : A high school senior—eighth in a class of 779, active in a host of extracurricular activities (student marshalls, General Organization, Key Club, after-school tutoring program, president of the Debate Society, among others), and described on the school's record as "intelligent, highly motivated and mature" with "excellent leadership and academic potentials"—is barred from the school's chapter of the National Honor Society on the grounds of poor character. At an open meeting of school board candidates the preceding spring, he had politely asked a question that implied some criticism of the high school. In the opinion of eight of the Honor Society's fifteen faculty advisers, none of whom had been present at the meeting in question and none of whom knew the boy, criticism of the high school is equivalent to disloyalty, and disloyalty constitutes bad character. The seven faculty advisers who know the youngster fight for his admission but are overruled.

I T E M : Memorandum to teachers from the principal of a high school in a Washington, D.C., suburb: "If you see any copies of the *Washington Free Press* [a local student "underground" newspaper] in the possession of a student, confiscate it immediately. Any questions from the student regarding this confiscation should be referred to the administration. If you see a student selling or distributing this paper, refer them [*sic*] to an administrator and they will be suspended." [22]

I T E M : The principal of a Queens, N.Y., high school went further: every student *"seen reading or carrying—or even suspected of pos-*

---

[21] From the film *High School,* produced by Frederick Wiseman.

[22] Montgomery County Student Alliance, "Wanted: A Humane Education: An Urgent Call for Reconciliation Between Rhetoric and Reality," Bethesda, Md.: Montgomery County Student Alliance, 1969, in R. and B. Gross, eds., *Radical School Reform.*

sessing—copies" of *The High School Free Press,* a New York underground paper, was suspended.[23] (Emphasis added.)

The tragedy is that the great majority of students do not rebel; they accept the stultifying rules, the lack of privacy, the authoritarianism, the abuse of power—indeed, virtually every aspect of school life—as The Way Things Are. "All weakness tends to corrupt, and impotence corrupts absolutely," Edgar Friedenberg sardonically observes. Hence students "accept the school as the way life is and close their minds against the anxiety of perceiving alternatives. Many students like high school; others loathe and fear it. But even these do not object to it on principle; the school effectively obstructs their learning of the principles on which objection might be based. . . ."

I T E M : A high school student talking. "The main thing is not to take it personal, to understand that it's just a system and it treats you the same way it treats everybody else, like an engine or a machine or something mechanical. Our names get fed into it—*we* get fed into it —when we're five years old, and if we catch on and watch our step, it spits us out when we're 17 or 18. . . ." [24]

The sociologist Buford Rhea, who set out to study high school students' alienation, discovered that most students are not alienated and do not want power because they feel they would not know what to do with it if they had it. They have remarkable faith in the high schools' paternalism and so see no need to question what their teachers are doing or why. "It is the teacher's job to know what to tell the student to do, and it is therefore the teacher's responsibility to know *why the* student should do it," Rhea reports. Indeed, academically ambitious students quite literally will themselves into believing in their teachers' ability. "Unable to withdraw or rebel (this route leads to failure), these ambitious students seem eager to detect, and perhaps even to fantasy, competence and concern among the staff." [25]

23 Nicholas Pileggi, "Revolutionaries Who Have to Be Home by 7:30," *Phi Delta Kappan,* June 1969.

24 From Noyes and McAndrew, "Is This What Schools Are For?", *Saturday Review,* December 21, 1968.

25 Buford Rhea, "Institutional Paternalism in High School," *The Urban Review,* February 1968.

As a result, schools are able to manipulate students into doing much of the dirty work of control under the guise of self-government. As Waller pointed out nearly forty years ago, "Self-government is rarely real. Usually it is but a mask for the rule of the teacher oligarchy," or "in its most liberal form the rule of a student oligarchy carefully selected and supervised by the faculty."

About the authors

Jerome S. Bruner (1915–   ). An eminent psychologist, Bruner was born in New York City. He took his undergraduate degree at Duke University in 1937 and received his doctorate in psychology from Harvard University in 1941. He is currently Professor of Psychology at Harvard, where he has taught since 1945, and director of the university's Center for Cognitive Studies. In addition to *The Process of Education,* he has published several other works, including *On Knowing, A Study of Thinking,* and *Toward a Theory of Instruction.*

James Bryant Conant (1893–   ). This scientist, scholar, statesman, and educator was born in Dorchester, Massachusetts, and educated at Harvard, completing his undergraduate work in 1913 and his doctorate in 1916. He was given an appointment at Harvard in 1916 and became Professor of Organic Chemistry in 1927. He became president of Harvard in 1933. Later he served as chairman of the National Defense Research Committee, as a senior advisor to the National Science Foundation and the Atomic Energy Commission, as United States High Commissioner for Germany, and as ambassador to Germany. His works that have distinguished him among educators include *Education and Liberty, The Education of American Teachers,* and *Shaping Educational Policy.*

John Dewey (1859–1952). Born in Vermont, this most famous American philosopher and educator graduated from the University of Vermont, taught briefly in Pennsylvania, and then went to Johns Hopkins University as a doctoral student in 1882. In 1884 he accepted an instructorship in philosophy at the University of Michigan. Subsequently, he taught at the universities of Minnesota and Chicago and Columbia University, retiring from

Columbia in 1930. Of his voluminous writings, spanning seventy years, those most influential for education have been *Democracy and Education, How We Think,* "My Pedagogic Creed," *Experience and Education,* and *Art as Experience.*

Erik H. Erikson (1902–   ). This famous psychologist was born in Germany. He received an honorary M.A. from Harvard in 1960 and an honorary LL.D. from the University of California in 1968. He has served as Professor of Psychology at the University of California from 1950 to 1951, at the School of Medicine in Pittsburgh from 1951 to 1960, and is currently Professor of Human Development at Harvard. His works that have made him of importance to educators include *Identity, Youth and Crisis* and *Childhood and Society.*

Paul Goodman (1911–1972). Born in New York, this writer-reformer received his undergraduate degree from the City College of New York and a doctorate in humanities from the University of Chicago. He taught and lectured at numerous universities, and was associated with the University Seminar at Columbia University, as well as the New York and Cleveland institutes for Gestalt Therapy. He was also a Fellow of the City Institute for Policy Studies in Washington, D.C. He wrote for many journals and published fiction and verse. Among his social commentaries, *Growing Up Absurd* has had by far the greatest impact upon educators.

John Holt (1923–   ). An educator and critic, Holt was born in New York City. He is a graduate of Yale University and has been observing schools and teaching for more than seventeen years. He has taught fifth grade (all subjects), experimental mathematics at all elementary grades, beginning reading, and English, French, and mathematics at the high-school level. He has lectured on education at Harvard's Graduate School of Education and has taught composition to prospective teachers at the University of California at Berkeley. Currently, he is a consultant with the Fayerweather Street School in Cambridge, Massachusetts. His major works are *How Children Fail, How Children Learn,* and *The Underachieving School.*

Carl R. Rogers (1902–   ). Born in Illinois, this noted psychologist did his undergraduate work in clinical psychology at the University of Wisconsin, obtaining his B.A. in 1924. He went on to earn the M.A. from Columbia University in 1928 and a doctorate in education and clinical psychology from that university in 1931. He served as Professor of Psychology at the University of Wisconsin from 1957 to 1963. Since 1964, Rogers has been a Fellow of the Western Behavioral Science Institute in La Jolla, California. His major work is *On Becoming a Person;* more recently he has published *Freedom to Learn.*

Charles E. Silberman (1925–   ). This scholar-journalist was born in Iowa. He received his education in the New York public schools and at Columbia College and the Graduate Faculty of Political Science at Columbia University. A previous work, *Crisis in Black and White,* became a national best seller. *Crisis in the Classroom* was named one of the twelve best books of the year by *The New York Times Book Review.* From 1953 to 1971, Silberman was on the editorial staff of *Fortune Magazine* and is currently a Field Foundation Fellow.

Alfred North Whitehead (1861–1947). This outstanding philosopher and metaphysician was born in England. He studied mathematics at Cambridge University and became a Fellow at Trinity College, where he began teaching mathematics in 1885. He was elected to the Royal Society in 1903. *Principia Mathematica,* produced after ten years of collaboration with Bertrand Russell, became an intellectual cornerstone of twentieth-century philosophical thought. His interest in education grew out of subsequent teaching in various London educational institutions. At sixty-three Whitehead joined the Harvard philosophy faculty, where he developed his unique organismic philosophy. His major works of importance to education are the *Aims of Education, Modes of Thought,* and *Science and Philosophy.*